SHELTER

Also by Lawrence Jackson

*Hold It Real Still: Clint Eastwood, Race, and
the Cinema of the American West*

Chester B. Himes: A Biography

My Father's Name: A Black Virginia Family After the Civil War

*The Indignant Generation: A Narrative History of African
American Writers and Critics, 1934–1960*

Ralph Ellison: Emergence of Genius

SHELTER

A Black Tale of Homeland, Baltimore

Lawrence Jackson

Graywolf Press

Copyright © 2022 by Lawrence Jackson

"Epiphany: Sunday Boys" appeared in different form under the title "Letter from Baltimore" in the *Paris Review*.

This publication is made possible, in part, by the voters of Minnesota through a Minnesota State Arts Board Operating Support grant, thanks to a legislative appropriation from the arts and cultural heritage fund. Significant support has also been provided by the McKnight Foundation, the Lannan Foundation, the Amazon Literary Partnership, and other generous contributions from foundations, corporations, and individuals. To these organizations and individuals we offer our heartfelt thanks.

MINNESOTA STATE ARTS BOARD

CLEAN WATER LAND & LEGACY AMENDMENT

Published by Graywolf Press
212 Third Avenue North, Suite 485
Minneapolis, Minnesota 55401

All rights reserved.

www.graywolfpress.org

Published in the United States of America

ISBN 978-1-64445-083-3

2 4 6 8 9 7 5 3 1
First Graywolf Printing, 2022

Library of Congress Control Number: 2021940585

Cover design: Kimberly Glyder Design

Cover photo: Courtesy of the author

To

Mitchell

Katani

and

Nathaniel

We learned early that to own the roof which gave us shelter was one of our first duties and to become a contributor to the expenses of our community by being a tax payer was an obligation which every citizen owes to the government which protects him and provides conveniences to his comfort and well-being.

—Harry S. Cummings, Baltimore City Council (1910–1913)

Contents

SHELTER

John of Rampayne, an excellent juggler and minstrel, undertook to effect the escape of one Audulf de Bracy, by presenting himself in disguise . . . and succeeded in imposing himself on the king, as an Ethiopian minstrel. He effected, by stratagem, the escape of the prisoner. Negroes, therefore, must have been known in England in the dark ages.

—Walter Scott, *Ivanhoe* (1819)

Just think of a man surrounded by color storms rising almost to a hurricane.

—J. V. L. McMahon to D. M. Perine, January 16, 1865

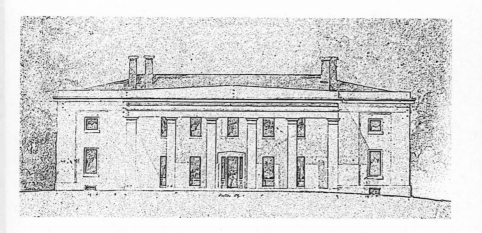

Advent: Color Storms Rising
Almost to a Hurricane

I plotted my return the day after the heaviest snowfall in a decade, a bright January afternoon. I was in Baltimore with my sons, who were sitting for entrance examinations at a local boys' country day school. While they speed-penciled the bubbles, I would look at neighborhoods for our new home. I had grown up with two people who held real estate licenses in Maryland, but I didn't quite think of them. I would be looking in another part of town.

Although, relative to rank and compensation, the offer I had been made outlined an executive job, I wasn't billeted in a waterfront hotel downtown. The boys and I had taken a cab from the airport to my mother's rowhouse in the Northwest, the part of the city where I had been raised. The night we arrived, three feet of snow blanketed the land. I awoke in a panic at 5:00 a.m. and headed outdoors to shovel my mother's car out of the drift. I thought it was ungenerous to pitch the snow into the street or build an impassable igloo on the sidewalk, so I baled the heavy frozen cotton onto the neighbor's yard. I shoveled steadily for two hours. When I looked in the mirror later that day I thought I was coming down with pink eye: my wintertime labor had burst a blood vessel.

The administrator of the college I would be joining had recommended a realtor. Earlier in our negotiations she had asked my preference for neighborhood, and I answered with an instinctive gaffe. "Homewood, maybe Homeland?" I responded genially. "I've forgotten the difference." I had not been on the inside of a home in either neighborhood, whose names sounded enough alike to me to be indistinguishable. I was also translating an instinctive response in one tongue to another language altogether. But my imprecision was promptly addressed. "Oh, they're not the same at all," the administrator, a city native whose family had migrated to the suburbs, replied with cheery obduracy. To Baltimoreans of another sort, people who were accustomed to understand or benefit from the exactness of the law, precisely accounting these neighborhoods meant something else entirely. Homewood and Homeland are somewhat contiguous through other signature tracts, Guilford and Roland Park, but one signifies the Johns Hopkins campus, and the other a residential world beyond it. I had grown up in Baltimore without ever once imagining the antebellum histories of either neighborhood, and the way that those pasts would necessarily collide with my own.

I took the clarification easily. Working to appear mild-mannered and hiding petulance are my gifts to the world.

I dropped the lads and my mother off at the preparatory school to endure what is only a preliminary regimen of assessment that will continue over the next few months in Atlanta. Although both children have been exceptional students their entire lives, they have attended public schools in Georgia and need to be measured against the nation's nine- and eleven-year-olds from the "independent" schools. The colors of the school signal the ancient unification, the blue and the gray. Neither child will be offered admission.

A mile away I found the realtor, a trim, energetic, dark-haired Tab drinker. She drove an upgraded model SUV, freshly detailed despite the snow and salt, and when I climbed in she handed off a folder with a dozen listings. The realtor had not grown up in the city, and her words twanged with eastern water's edge. Her son had recently graduated from my old Jesuit high school and she was easily familiar with me in a way that emphasized her presumption that with only slightly different decisions she could be the executive recruit and I the local factor working on commission. I was reluctant to concede this, not simply because it was so readily true, but because the more clear-eyed fact was that she was my better. As soon as I told her where my mother lived she would know the sort of visa I required to visit her part of the world. How long would it take or in what manner would the company have to be mixed before my own country idiom began to show?

The gulf between us was temporary. I had no way of imagining in such short time exactly how much I would rely on the agent's efficient professionalism. I lived in Georgia and she would be the person selecting the home inspector and attending the home inspection. Her mouth would chip down the price when the inspector's report came back. Her hands would deliver the tidy sums and promises of more. I would have to trust her, although she had fundamentally divided loyalties since her profit came from my paying more, not less, for the house. The commission from the sale would be in the range of $15,000 and the agent would be entitled to half of that. All I could do was pay.

We begin the outing in Homewood, near the campus stadium, peering into elegantly appointed, English-style rowhouses on University Parkway, followed by a couple of duplexes as we climb the hill. The first residence of the "Home" neighborhoods is to me a place of ethnographic wonder. The opened doors reveal the organs of a species akin to but akimbo from the tribes where my own life debuted. The interiors of these lodges are guarded by identical fireplace sentinels: framed city maps from the Early National period. The mouths of these charts open at the basin of the Patapsco River, then are mounted by neighborhood cheeks called Fells Point, Jonestown, and Baltimore Town. Strewn about the living and dining rooms are the same wing back Windsor and Queen Anne chairs, highboys and credenzas, the Persian rugs never differing by texture, the Pikesville and Sagamore Rye whiskeys brushing shoulders on a sideboard not far away.

It is difficult to control my initial impression of a contented bonanza, this invitation to a crown molding affair. Years of browsing antiques, purchasing an occasional curiosity at a museum gift shop, scouring the libraries for maps of Pittsylvania County, and making furniture by hand have led me here. I found a satisfying charm and a longed for but achingly unfamiliar residue of pedigree. Four miles to the west, where I was born, seemed like another land.

The most opulent houses within the same price range as my two-story Craftsman in Atlanta—a sharply more competitive market, but, thanks to 1864, with little history and even more draconian, sweeping, habitational logics—are at the edge of Guilford, one block from York Road on broad one-way streets. The streets that only allowed car traffic to push east are designed to limit the access to the workers in the rowhouses just beyond. The exiled are people whom I knew quite well. My grandmother's sister, a dandelion-wine maker, had lived on Ivanhoe, a lonely, hilly, intersecting road on the other side of the divide during my first thirty years. Rusted iron gates at the top of the street gesture to the old separation between Aunt Daisy's neighborhood and the rundown mansions of Guilford. They are filled with bowed parquet floors and lime-painted foyers, chipped gilded hallway mirrors, heavy cast-iron plumbing, and brittle asbestos-insulated ungrounded electric lines. I am all fixer-upper—the true source of any economic boon, undervaluation—but the houses aspiring to opulence mildly offend my Shaker tastes. They are also a quarter mile on the other side of the catchment zone for the noteworthy public grade school. The courts had not yet decided whether my sons would live with me or their mother, and I do not yet know if we will win admission to private schools. Access to quality public education is essential to where I might choose to live. And considering what I don't already have in my corner, if I ever hope to resell the house, I will need every advantage.

In a sense, the pièce de résistance of the tour, of any tour in the family-style portion of the city really, is Roland Park. The exclusivity of the neighborhood is palpable, a tangible force to city natives. Historically, the genteelness was owed to legally restrictive covenants. Today, the city can't sustain enough high-paying jobs to break new blood onto the half-acre wooded lots among the preppies with lacrosse goals in their front yards.

On Upland Avenue on Roland Park's East Side, a realtor lounges with such convincing nonchalance that I almost think him in his own home in his pajamas. He conducts his part of the tour from a sprawled perch on the window seat, and although he wears Birkenstock clogs and looks the part of a yoga instructor from Hamburg, an unctuous feline confidence and self-approval trailed his every gesture. I already doubted that I would ever live in one of Roland Park's three-story cedar shingle cottages. How did they heat those wooden hulks in winter? It seemed possible that even the single fireplace huts with dirt floors of the ancient rural poor might be warmer.

But in the years to come, I would understand that Roland Park's East Side, sometimes parceled into little siblings called "Evergreen" and "Wyndhurst," was actually more happily similar than I had first thought to Candler Park, my old neighborhood in Atlanta. I had enjoyed living there. Candler Park is horseshoed around ample recreational fields and a public golf course and hosts cheery annual music festivals. It took ten years, more or less, to get to Candler Park, and the wrench I had used had broken apart my life. Nonetheless, the ordinary act of walking beside my son Nathaniel as he rode his kindergartener's bicycle to Mary Lin Elementary School, an easygoing, competent primary, remains the crowning achievement of my adult life. My son only needed to walk ten minutes away from his bedroom Thomas the Train table to reach his classroom cubby and put away his lunch. He lived in the same house with his mother and father and his older sister and younger brother. His sister was an A student and an athlete and we had attended church as a family. We had eaten good home-cooked meals together. The idyll lasted for barely twenty-four months. It was not idyll at the end.

Those morning bike rides are what the oblivious would describe as an example of my "privilege," as if it were a birthright, not what it was, a beachhead under fire. The labor and stinting sacrifice, as well as the wrench, are opaque. The benefice in Candler Park was the result of more than ten years of sometimes precarious economic climbing, ten years during which it had required my salary to more than double to limp over the line into the new place. I lived there three years renting before I was able to purchase a house, and by then the odyssey had also included divorce, a financial and spiritual ordeal, like eighteen years of bankruptcy seasoned by clipped ligaments and tendons and plague.

Few Candler Park residents had been born in Atlanta. Rootless among the unrooted, I could live in the neighborhood like a tourist, without any of the obligations made by the past. I could be as chatty or as distant as I chose in the amiable, walkable place, with its typically quiet, mildly used park. I knew I lived in the Deep South, and it was unremarkable to see Confederate flags or pistols on the bed at an Open House, but I didn't have to know, on a daily basis, about the more vivid examples of life structured by strong violence. I could consider the fat possums skedaddling along the fence posts or the deadly gun battle at the sneaker boutique for the latest Lebron James shoe, the flock of sheep eating down the weeds, or the public pool closure because the children who lived beyond the railroad tracks relieved themselves of solid waste in the water, all with a similar aloof dismay. As it turned out, the public amenities had obliterated a block of African American homes, the day before segregation under the law ended. For more than a quarter of a mile, from McLendon to Euclid, in 1946 the city excavated away the very ground upon which the houses had stood, scooping out a stadium-size bowl. Not so different from today, power and influence find more value in golf than black citizens retaining property that increases in value.

Candler Park sits on the south side of Ponce de Leon, and across the street is the opulent neighborhood Druid Hills, anchored by its large private country club. Baltimore's Roland Park, or certainly the half of it west of Roland Avenue, is also buttoned to a private club, the Baltimore Country Club. To play tennis there today, club rules require white athletic clothes, an assertion of their steady commitment to the propriety and legacy of the past. Roland Park is Baltimore's highest-rent district, house for house. The villagers there pay the largest share of the property tax of any residential neighborhood in the city, and their houses are, as a group, appraised the highest. Founded by the Roland Park Company in 1911, they sometimes claim to be America's oldest suburb. The Olmsted urban green space planning firm, then headed by the son of Frederick Law Olmsted, the designer who created Manhattan's Central Park, drew the plans for both neighborhoods in Atlanta and Baltimore. Americans of affluence and pedigreed educations tend to be drawn to cities with Olmsted parkscapes, and neighborhoods complete with Craftsmen homes finished with old-world touches.

Although it actually has seven sides, Baltimore is shaped

mainly like baseball's home plate, only that the vertex of its bottom tacks to the right and a chunk of that bowel of land is bitten off by the salty Patapsco River. After the Benin and the Biafra, we have roosted on the Bight of the Patapsco. Charles Street is the city's spine (although it must give way to Hanover Street to cross the river), climbing the hill and separating the city into west and east sides. North Avenue splits the city again into northern and southern halves, though the main geographical distinction is "west" or "east" of Charles. The Homewood, Roland Park, and Homeland neighborhoods are bunched around Charles Street, the name an ancient echo of the English civil war and of Maryland's founders' House of Stuart Jacobite leanings. Beyond the Johns Hopkins University Homewood campus, west of York Road and east of the Jones Falls, lies the Royalist residential part of the city. With the agent I surge up Roland Avenue, parallel to Charles Street and just slightly west, encountering the college assistant dean, who represents the university in my contractual negotiations, on a perilous morning jog among the snowbanks. We pass the grocer who fields a doorman and adds a one-dollar surcharge to every item, beyond the country school where my sons are submitting to high-stakes tests.

At the four-lane Northern Parkway, we turn east. In high school I used to catch the no. 44 bus on my way home from school when we had a half day. Back then, I would walk into Towson and get the no. 8, or, less frequently, go down the hill to UMBC to the no. 11. One afternoon, my friends and I outflanked a yellow boy with green eyes; one of the spheres was a little slow and because we were in a group we teased him with the catcall "Dead Eye." He went to Northern High but lived over on the west side where we did, or got the Rogers Avenue subway. Sometimes when I was by myself and saw him, he would stare back. He was a good size and I was not.

Northern Parkway is near the border of Baltimore County's

genuine suburbia. The agent and I cantilever our way back from the snowbanked boulevard onto a street filled with meticulous, retiring, brick or stone colonial-style cottages. One house, right off the corner from the Methodist church, offered a fetching price, but the overwrought flower beds suffocating the walkway between the rear door and the garage, and the cloisonné and djibouterie stacked high on every shelf and cabinet let me know that it is an unlikely option. The owner had devoted herself to the task of membership in her class with so much intensity that she would never discard a darling fawn, like the person who sucks up the entire kitty playing Hearts. We didn't see the world the same way. The negotiations would break down over an improperly cherished memento by the boy who had once ridden by her house on the no. 44.

Unable to chain myself to flower beds and curios, we work over to another street and dip south. In the cabs of motley pickup trucks outfitted with plows and hoppers spilling salt I see more men with three-day stubble wearing John Deere billed caps and spitting tobacco juice into worn paper cups than ever before. Maryland has notable destinations near the Appalachian range to the west and between the Chesapeake and the Atlantic to the east, farming country, that is the province of such men. But my experience has not beheld this group in the city.

The realtor pulls up alongside a house but is reluctant to knock at the front door. No sign is in the yard. The house on Albion Road in Homeland has gone into the system only a couple of hours earlier, and the family is at home.

In the city of Decatur or Atlanta, if you were looking in an attractive neighborhood with a high-performing public school and didn't make an offer before the premises were on the market, there was no hope of success. Both times I bought a house, I had endlessly reconnoitered on foot and by car the neighborhoods I desired, looking for the little sign to sprout or marking evidence of imminent absconding, before moving as rapidly as

I could to plunk down the earnest money, the first tulip of the down payment.

Somewhat reluctantly the agent telephoned the new sellers and asked if they could offer a hasty tour for an out-of-town money-bags. The owners are a South Asian man from the Northeast and his wife, a Scottish immigrant. Both are medical professionals, and they are parents to a toddler and an infant. From my point of view as a city native, the youth and wealth of the second- and first-generation immigrant couple astound me. They sprinkle their casual conversation with Latin phrases familiar to attorneys and physicians and which I wonder if they presume I know. The surgeon has rewired the complete hull of his dwelling, priming it for moments of abundant light and sound. Full of reams of chatty information about the house and the neighborhood, he also clarifies the meaning of dimmers and cable wires that run alongside the furnace and HVAC unit. He has a double-jointed manner and I find him impossible to understand. My mind is also elsewhere, searching for wrinkles in the ceilings and warping on the deck of the floor. I grasp that the doctors are anxious to leave the city for more space and lower taxes. It seems that they have seasoned financially in the Northeast or the West, and the booster rockets are still firing their middle-class flight of upward mobility.

Two weeks later when I accept the job I realize I will need to sell the Atlanta house and make arrangements for myself and, hopefully, for my children, in Baltimore. I make an instinctive decision to put in an offer on the Albion Road house. I can only vaguely remember it as a cairn piled in the snow, similar to the others, and close to work. I recall nothing specific about its location in the neighborhood, although it had seemed shielded from the areas of heavier automobile traffic. I have never before made a decision of such magnitude with such haste, though this condition of perilous unease will become increasingly more familiar. Ordinary values and standards of taste—sifting out the bruised vegetables at the market—are losing their sway. Better now to gather tidbits swiftly, pay, and discard junk later. Hoard precious emotion for attachments to people. I was making a spreadsheet sort of a decision, devoid of human nature, devoid of tradition and upbringing, just a raw tangle with the market. A swift-made contract for staggering debt (which even I had enough sense to know I wanted as much of as I could get) sold in bundles to remote financial entities the day of their execution, impenetrable legal documents explained by paraprofessional finessers, and all of it with the sense that the institutions behind these deals themselves are nebulous amoebas: invisible, spineless, acquisitive, encompassing, ammoniac. People got in and out of marriage, or took care of their biological children using the same techniques.

The personal sense of unease in the high-stakes world of American domicile adulthood only deepens with experience. To buy my Candler Park fiberboard two-story in Atlanta, which the contractors in that Zion of southern building code deregulation had assembled without as much as a scrap of felt under the roofing shingles, I had had to sell my first residence during the Great Recession. My single-story rancher, with the basement that had to have a French drain cut into it to win final buyer's approval, languished on the market, staged or unstaged, with renters and without, until I finally cut my own throat and sold it for 75 percent of what I had paid for it ten years earlier. During my divorce proceedings, which, undercapitalized, I attended unattorneyed, renting that house out for a fraction of its mortgage, insurance, and taxes, became the crown jewel of my financial empire. At that time the trumpets were blaring that property was the safest, surest investment since the crucifixion, just like they had about the technology stocks. My move from one story to two story, from engineered plank to stone, is unlikely to keep the wolves at bay. I don't think I'll live long enough for another increment and, if I do, three flights of stairs and an acre of grounds to maintain will be my physical undoing.

Pulling the trigger involved a more crucial decision than putting my life's savings into the earnest money deposit. I would take on yet another thirty-year mortgage, but this time in my late forties. What I knew gave me pause. My dad passed away at fifty-six; his father had lived to be eighty; my grandfather's father seems to have lived to almost ninety. That man had been born in slavery in 1855. My mother's family had borne the wiles of the Old South by taking advantage of life on either side of the color line. Her self-emancipated great-grandfather remarried for the third time at the age of fifty-four and I don't know when he left the earth; her grandfather passed away in the country at sixty-five; her father passed on in the city at sixty-seven, broken; her brother took his own life at twenty-eight. I can grasp a trend line. The known causes and the known cures lead to the same ends: the medicine—which would be home-distilled whiskey—despondency, cortisol surges, divorce and rumors of divorce, the joys of joining a new workforce, a new school, a new neighborhood, all of it wrapped up in making their way in business where whites signed the checks. Obviously the longest lived of those men never even approached owning a house, just satisfied himself with shack chic.

Once upon a time we lived in the country on an old tobacco farm. Before slavery ended and after the Civil War, both of my parents' had great-grandparents who bought land. After the Great War, the grandchildren moved to the city. In 1940 my mother's parents bought a rowhouse in Baltimore for $1,500. In 1965 my parents bought a rowhouse with a yard in Baltimore for $11,250. In 2003 in Dekalb County, Georgia, I bought a rancher on a one-third-acre lot for $227,000. Ten years later I bought a wooden two-story in Atlanta for $475,000. In 2016 I bought a house in Baltimore for a bit more. Perhaps the banks that create loan programs with heavy upfront fees to wedge borrowers into restructured downstream deals then relabeled and resold before the inevitable bankruptcy are doing everybody the favor they claim they are doing. In a way, it is perfect. You pay for the house, then die before your retirement gets used up. Where does that escrowed projection eventually wind up? My mother got a pay-out from the YMCA, where my dad worked in the late 1970s, a full twenty-seven years after his funeral. If she had received the money when it was due her, or even twenty years ago, she might have been able to have made electrical and plumbing repairs to her own house that seemed like impossible luxuries. The Christian life of leveraged debt beyond the mortal world might be our downfall.

I decided to finance the gem through my retirement broker, a move that I would be soundly chastised for on Interstate 85, the same day I sold my house in Atlanta. Gummed up in the afternoon traffic impasse on the south side of Charlotte, North Carolina, the new snaggle on the north–south express between Queens and Fort Lauderdale, I fielded a call from the neophyte loan officer to heave some notarized form to him before the end of business. Without my signature and Social Security number on this new duplicate form, the federal government's maximal insurable amount would not make its way electronically to the holding company within the required ninety-six hours. In Atlanta I had just sent the proceeds from the financial transaction at my own house ahead to Baltimore. I pulled off the road for this iPhone Hail Mary, fuming at the intemperate expectation of the millennials and their world of electronic screens and broadband.

I'm neither a veteran negotiator nor a passable accountant. But I do have a tendency. I try to handle my business like the unflinchingly honest crack shot from a Western. My James Arness from television (my childhood ideal of tough male probity) doesn't make any sense to people. Besides, I also have a huge personality flaw in any negotiation: I can't bear stating the obvious, for fear of seeming pedantic. Zebulon Macahan I may be in my mind's eye, but, even though I coached kindergarten basketball at the Decatur YMCA, I am most reluctant to launch into a philippic over a prominent imperfection. But this would have to be done. The house had its original eighty-year-old slate roof, now brittle and starting to shed into sections as fine as a fish's scale. I had, by then, replaced two roofs and did not wish to mend the skull of yet another house, so I relayed through the agent that the seller had to come down from the asking price. Improbably, we hammered out a compromise, just as if they had sold houses to debt-eligible black Christians every day. I sent flowers to the people involved in the deal. Three of my new neighbors gave me welcome baskets filled with the local goodies. One week after the closing, I was still too new to ownership to object when the doctor, on an errand from his spouse, came to unscrew the vanity shelf in the basement loo.

The three-bay-wide, two-story, stone colonial cottage, with Doric columns upholding a pediment portico, bespoke unimpeachable middle-class standing. The garage is impressive enough that my people think it is a detached bungalow on the property. Unlike the skins of the Atlanta houses—the cream-painted brick rancher in Clairmont Heights and the Candler Park barn made of engineered wood dust—the eighteen-inch-thick walls of the Homeland manor indicate permanence. My Albion Road house comes to me in default mode: black painted shutters and doors and all of the wooden trim in plain white, attired like a Puritan going to meeting, the costume of many, many homes in the United States. Although I am uninspired by the paint, the place makes me feel noble. The lot is the standard American quarter acre, precisely 74 feet by 138 feet. There are only two houses on our western side of the block; while my yard has not grown, my privacy is nearly immaculate. My view alternates from woodland to moderately trimmed greens to stone gables. What is more, the five ponds for trysting, the Olmsted-like feature that conveys the aura to the neighborhood of a well-tended stately village, are a mere furlong away. I grew up on a city block with ten households and a public bus line, the elevated subway in sight and the carwash, gas station, and liquor store down the street. Albion Road seems the epitome of the pastoral.

Inside, a center hall stairway, flanked by a large living room and a dining room and small remodeled kitchen, leads to three upstairs bedrooms. The interior is spare and modest, pronouncing the simple beauty of the flat-grained, white oak, two-and-a-quarter-inch flooring. But a cavernous wound opens in me as I rapidly unpack boxes: I lack shelves for the small matter, like CDs. Two unopened crates ache and scrape me into obsessed scribbling on my son's loose-leaf paper. My fourth-grade draftsman talents render a pair of narrow wall shelves bracing the fireplace, including a hand-routed entablature to match the room's existing millwork. Commensurate with my new obligations as gentry, I will wrap the baseboard molding around the CD cases.

All of July a fever rages in me to build shelves on either side of the hearth. By August I have taken a crowbar to the living room baseboard and molding and spend my evenings in the lumberyard and then the garage. Throughout my years I have spent enjoyable hours woodworking, but always I am impatient and forget something, leaving an amateurish taint. When I finish the pair of shelves I forget to cut the top edges completely flush to the side panel. When I attached the header, I can see a centimeter gap of daylight between the case and the wall.

Then more color storms rise to a hurricane. I force my neighbor's eyes onto my stairwell from the front yard for three days, after I take down the front door to remove the black paint, getting out the heat gun for the edges where the panels meet the stiles. I then stain the door "Early American," but it comes out too brown. I tell myself that I should have tried "Gunstock," a name I adore, which has more orange and blond. The surroundings and my improvements stir a weird mash of memory and emotion. Whenever I walk across the street to admire the porch columns and the door's contrast color, I keep hearing snatches of music ping-ponging between my ears. It's always

"Panzerlied" from the *Battle of the Bulge* or the "Horst Wessel" melody from the thirty-nine-volume Time-Life World War II book series commercials from the 1970s.

After a few months there and noting the armies of landscapers, electricians, plumbers, remodelers, and roofers, a demon gnaws at me whenever I notice my dilapidated, skewed roofing shingles or the ripples bubbling underneath the drab white trim paint. I was discovering that Homeland is a never-ending, noisy contest of maintenance and upkeep. The next year, after my accountant reveals the mystery, I take out a loan to repair the roof. Adhering to the legally binding building regulations of the homeowner's association, I contract with a Pennsylvania Amish company to replace more than five thousand dilapidated shingles with North Country unfading black slate. Even though their fee was immodest, the sober Amish have a reputation for fine work. The bearded men struck me as adhering to the renunciation of modernity in tiers: some craft masters were fully committed to the old way of life; others who occasionally used a cell phone and dragged on cigarettes were in a middle range of fidelity to the discipline of tradition, family, work, and sacrifice; and then there were people they knew or were related to who lived in the world and performed the raw labor and drove the trucks. On their weekends the sullied raced motorcycles and juiced crank. In the process of replacing every piece of slate and copper, the foreman identifies about seventy feet of rotted wood, and in the attic one eave that has slipped away from its rafter. Holding off this leviathan of repairs any longer would have been skirting disaster. My son inserts a picture of an Amish man for my contact on his cell phone.

With the remains of the loan money, I hired my homeboy and his Guatemalan crew to repaint the exterior. The trim work would be khaki and the shutters and the three wooden gable ends would be olive drab. These are the field uniform colors of Edward Bland, my uncles Wilbur and Harold Macklin, and John

Kinloch during the last war in France. The colors, like the roof itself, require the written approval of the homeowner's association, an awkward, time-consuming process. When the painters commence the prep work on a side porch with a copper shed roof, they reveal even more substantial wood rot than the roofers had earlier. I told them I would take care of it myself, so that we wouldn't have to slow the work down scheduling a carpenter. Even with my trusty toolbelt, the job morphed into a three-day marathon that included rigging a circular saw to rip the rotted plywood behind the trim, which never should have been so close to the ground to begin with. I needed sixty feet or more of everything that went down and fetched materials from stores like I was going to the refrigerator. I mistakenly blended plywood sheets of different widths. To replace the exterior trimwork required a lot of handmade molding, followed by the real trouble of squaring it up and camouflaging the mistakes. But the errors of my skill did not outlast those of my effort. I was happy I had done the work because I could control materials that came in ground contact with water. The best achievement turns out to be one that never meets the eye.

Six towering arborvitae shield me from my southern neighbor, who sits on a double lot. Another six stand between me and the dog-walking brigades in the alley. The evergreens were once privacy hedges, but they have grown thirty feet now, and they have lost all of their sight-level branches. One lone Green Giant overhangs the front of my house, the branches splinted into a unity with thrice-wrapped garden hose. The tree shields a dinner-plate-size metal disk in the upper right-hand corner near the roofline, which reads "United Firemans In Co" and features an embossed twin-masted steam pumper. Other houses have an insignia bearing clasped hands and the year 1794. There is a small beech tree in the front and a massive one in the back. The rear tree has been pruned before, so that in winter a perfect upturned cone is revealed, the branches splaying twenty-five feet from the barrel-size center trunk. I lop off the branches and stems from the first eight feet of the beech tree out front to maximize the sunlight lancing through the canopy and onto the southern chunk of the lawn, split in two by a flagstone path. Closest to the house is a weeping birch tree, with a trunk that snakes into two boughs entwined like lovers. *Betula lenta* produces the saddest, most scabrous green-brown leaves, though it willows gently in the breeze. At the northern edge is a gigantic scarlet oak; the bough hangs menacingly over my neighbor's house. The heavily shaded yard has known better days. The thin front grass is mottled and speckled, stippled with moss and dogwood, scattershot by clover. This seedy part of the front is bracketed by a Virginia pine that must have stopped flourishing when I was a boy.

Tree-lined, thick-blade grassy fields are palpable, olfactory-replete sensations of memory for me. They return me to early adolescence and the aroma of freshly clipped broad-blade fescue. My urban elementary and junior high smelled of asphalt, paste, and varnished linoleum, but high school in the country with the Jesuits oozed chlorophyll.

At my secondary school, named after the Basque founder of the Jesuits, Ignatius of Loyola, I was a conscientious student—blandly pious, mildly athletic, and patriotic. I can recall conscripting my neighborhood friends in the fight against what was "un-American." Less Sino-Soviet villainy, it was a betrayal that I connected to the languor of old Europe, and the reluctance to struggle mightily or withstand fatigue. I was captivated a lot more by a wooden Horatio Alger than an impresario Jay Gatsby. I sought security in order. My top college choice was the military academy at West Point; the framed acceptance certificate is still at Mother's. At home and in the neighborhood, I worked avidly cutting grass and shoveling snow (though in 1977 I had failed to stop the threadbare bad-boy Wookie from stealing our shovel from the porch). But, I was ingenuous enough to blush with embarrassment at the sight of the ragged black men who comprised the grounds crew at school.

My understanding of the life of black outdoorsmen was remote. They reminded me of the disheveled men who bunched around the entrance to the car wash at home. The Jesuits didn't teach anything about New World slavery, probably for the best, and I was what black people called too "sheltered" to need the groundsmen in a real way—for physical safety, a ride home, or food. And yet, there were only thirty of us black boys at the school, making the landscapers impossible to ignore. I never then nor today saw black families in that part of Towson near Ruxton. I only knew that I didn't want to be classed with the school's yardmen, as was one of the poorest, unkempt black students, who only lasted a year. At the same time, the men reminded me vaguely of my grandfathers and country relatives, the long-lived Virginia Ethiopians.

A thick gauze shielded us from the manual labor our predecessors endured. In my Dad's care on the way from school or to church, the same places where I pigeonhole my own children, I never learned about what my father's father, who grew up in a slave cabin, had done as a "helper" before he died. My grandfather's efforts for the Wytheville, Virginia, contractor McDowell & Wood, or the ten years he spent as a farm laborer on the Sandy Creek place his father rented, or in the fields of Mr. G. K. Hall, were from another time. That rural world of plain tools, mother wit, and simple machines was the world my own college-educated parents rectified using the glossy public life of the Kennedy family as a model. About my grandfather's service overseas in the military in 1918, I knew a single bitter proverb. "All I ever did in the army was dig ditches," Grandpa Jackson admitted to my dad, undoubtedly right before my father went to Texas for basic training. A life of humble service was like a sentence.

The groundskeepers at my high school seemed only woe

betide. But somehow their sincere journeyman methods clung to me. They used to hotwire the mowers in some kind of jerry-·rigged machine shop. They would solder a grate over the top of a canister, tack that to an old sheet metal deck with wheels, and then paint it all gray and take the fixed height cutters to work. There were no riding machines, just a phalanx of gum-booted men with over-repaired bladed sleds. In those days of rakes and brooms and shovels, grunts and high-pitched black English blared out from grounds and practice fields. Around that time I started to use my dad's battered Korean War fatigue cap when I cut the grass at home. My girlfriend used to call me Elmer Fudd but I didn't mind. I was giving myself over to yard.

It's curious that my feeling for outside work evolved at all. Late one summer evening before *Nightstalker* my father ran over a rock with the electric lawnmower in our backyard and the missile hit me in the eye. Perhaps that's why I could even appreciate the pleasure of working the grass with hand tools, a child weeder from the "Trash Gang" whose duty it was to keep the yard tidy. I came to love the hand weariness of the spring-loaded grass clipper, the *thwack* of the hedge shears, the pole edger tearing at the sod spilling onto the sidewalk, the scraping whistle of the steel-tine rake. The electric equipment that came later, but especially the fishing line trimmer, has the possibility of speed (and the likelihood of error) on its side. But any barber who uses electric shears achieves real precision only with a razor and scissors. No young person I ever knew as a child shared my enthusiasm. Certainly not the children next door, whose father's business as a landscaper, with a gated trailer containing self-propelled mowers, rakes, and gas cans parked alongside their house, was always on display.

But it is my confidence as a keeper of yards that makes me feel at home in Homeland. Naturally, I go further than my usual maintenance, and I shovel out a narrow trench between the grass and the mulch beds. The sound of a motorized engine ruins the pristine serenity of our cottage park, and I am chagrined even to run the gas mower or trimmer. I try to use the blower, the most loudly irritating instrument known to humankind, sparingly. Although we do bring a heavyweight tiller to bear one year, running it until the cotter pin sheared off from holding the axle together against three barrels of tree roots, I usually use a pick against these evil subterranean hands of the trees. From an extension ladder I prune the beech tree with a variety of handsaws to help in my battle against the moss and the shade. In the process my neighbor's yardman pays me the highest compliment I have ever heard. He is ultraefficient, tackling the double lot, leaf or lawn, with tactical speed and vigor. He tells me that in his decades of labor and in spite of the obvious mottled brown peeking through, he has never seen the grass on my place look so healthy.

The compliment, yardman to yardman, makes me wonder if water does indeed know its own level. Across the street is a neighbor who is rarely outside save for the daily luge run to the car. He walks a serenely friendly older dog before work and sometimes flicks a lacrosse ball with his boy. After the battle between the roots and the tiller, when I am hand sowing a specialty blend of grass seed, a semiannual task, he offers brightly from his side of the street, "Sod's faster!" Another man, clean-shaven and tall, walks by my house every day dressed in a desert hat and fatigues. From time to time he stares in our direction, but, even if I'm outside, he never says hello.

I belong to five generations that have made a home in this city. In 1930 my great-grandmother Maude Jones Macklin left her husband on the farm and moved up to Baltimore. She was soon joined by her preteen children and five of her adult children, most of them married. One tangible Monumental City advantage over Virginia and Washington, DC, was open seating on buses and streetcars. They all seemed pleased by what they found. My entire life, all of my grandparents and great-aunts and great-uncles, and my mother and her first cousins pridefully recalled "Nineteen-o-one" McCulloh Street. The three-story rowhouse was the urban homestead of the Macklin troop. Their clan arrived in the city about twenty years after a colored attorney named Ashbie Hawkins bought a house at 1911 McCulloh (which he rented out), breaking the color line and sending the city into a convulsion.

In those early days of black West Side city life before World War I, plenty of people had a living memory of blacks and whites residing on the same blocks, usually among the urban poor on alleys. Black Americans had lived on the narrowest streets of West Baltimore, like Woodyear and Whatcoat, Brunt Street and Etting Street, and the comparatively grander Division Street. They were wedged onto abbreviated blocks on the cross streets of Robert, Laurens, Presstman, Lanvale, and Dolphin, generally after the 500 block of Druid Hill Avenue. Druid Hill Avenue was the boulevard of black American aspiration, from near the downtown Lexington Market to the blocks beyond the city's old boundary at North Avenue. It offered spacious rowhouses with convenient indoor bathrooms, modern plumbing, electricity and probably even gas. Thurgood Marshall's striving family operated a corner store. But on prestige roads like McCulloh Street with its keyhole houses and posh Eutaw Street with mansions and tree-and-fountain-filled medians, the dispositive race barrier set up like cement.

For most of the nineteenth century, my Macklin ancestors had lived in Mecklenburg County, Virginia, in Bracey, north of the Roanoke River. In May of 1860 Nat Macklin bought forty-seven acres of land from the Bracey family for $312, and he donated a portion in 1883 for the St. Mark's Episcopal Church. Nat was born free, like his mother and grandmother, and was described on the free registry at the courthouse in Boydton as "bright" in complexion. South of the Roanoke River in black kin neighborhoods along the Jerusalem Church Road, his youngest son,

Joseph, would buy land and raise my grandmother and her nine siblings close to where his wife's father, Lewis Jones, had a sizable farm. The older man had to swear an oath before the county clerk in Boydton to attest to the legal age of the groom wedding his daughter Maude. Landholding, churchgoing free ancestors meant nothing in comparison to the saga of slavery. After the *Roots* broadcast I was persistent asking my grandmother about her parents and grandparents and bondage. She admitted to me that Lewis Jones and his wife, Amanda Farrar Jones, explained to the children that they had been beaten during slavery. I had anticipated a tale of triumphant escape or bloody defiance and I did not understand why Gramma was downcast, bitter and brief. When I knew little, I thought slavery and Africa were in the long ago.

My grandmother Christine received more formal education in the rural South than any of her siblings, at a Normal and Industrial school called St. Paul's in Lawrenceville. The campus was purchased by Xinhua Education Investment in 2017. She was born to young parents almost nine months to the day from their marriage. My gramma admired her father, Joseph Macklin, a great deal, or so it seemed from the venerative stories she told me during our time together in the 1970s. After a stint in NYC, she married a younger man named Vernon Mitchell from South Hill, the biggest town nearby. He and two brothers moved to Baltimore; another sister and brother moved to faraway Philadelphia. In 1940 my grandparents bought a house at 303 Robert Street, a surprisingly integrated block just beyond Eutaw, at Linden Avenue, during the heyday of racial segregation. They lived there with my two-year-old mother, a boarder, and my great-aunt and -uncle. They worked and saved, ironed their clothes, cleaned their front steps, and kept their business indoors.

My grandfather, known to us as "Pops," worked as chauffeur and butler to Moses Hecht, the builder of a mercantile powerhouse in Maryland, who, in the middle 1920s, lived at 2442 Eutaw Place. I don't know if my grandfather ever served in that house, but, if he still did in 1940, he could have walked home in four minutes or so. The Hechts, an immigrant family from Heidelberg, soon moved to Greenspring Valley, beyond the Jewish-friendly suburb Pikesville, as black migrants surged east of McCulloh Street and onto lower Madison and Linden Avenues after World War II. Samuel Hecht, who took over his father's role as chairman of the clothes and home merchandise chain in 1947, was the same age as my grandfather but lived a mirror-opposite life. He graduated from Johns Hopkins in 1928. I sometimes wonder if they have a picture of their colored butler tipped-in a scrapbook passed down in Samuel or Henry's or Harry Schloss's family, which recalls the glory days of the Eutaw Place home or the Greenspring Valley mansion. A sweatered Yale bulldog stuffed animal of theirs found its way to my mother, and to my own children.

My mom's parents countered the Depression with migration to the city and joined the black middle class through homeownership and steady work. But in an odd twist of fate, soon after 1940, the power play of race and law caught up. Wherever they went, the ghetto soon followed. White Baltimoreans of means were taking up the final lots in Homeland and Roland Park, as the suburban vision took hold. More ordinary white families followed the streetcar lines to leafy streets of single family homes from Catonsville, to Windsor Hills, Forest Park, Woodlawn, Randallstown, Owings Mills, and Mount Washington. The affluent were leaving behind the fifteen-room, high-ceiling palaces of Eutaw Street and McMechen Street, and the speculators carved the once glorious townhomes into apartments and stuffed them with tenants. Two blocks south of the house where my mother was born, Linden Avenue became a den of "pestilence," occupied by "low-income Negroes and transient Southern whites." White men not long from Appalachia fought shirtless drunken battles among themselves until they were bloody. To realize its potential for "gracious" downtown living, by the time my mother had finished college and married, the Mount Royal Improvement Association lobbied to have the complete corridor "demolished and rebuilt." And they succeeded. My grandparents took the mayor and the city council's offer on September 13, 1965, and sold their improved lot at Robert Street and Linden Avenue and bought a house in Park Heights. They joined the Great Society, slum clearance, urban renewal project.

Leaving Robert Street and Linden Avenue for Pimlico was moving in the same general northerly direction as Pop's employers. My mom and dad enlisted in the migration, too, and made their first home in the large, freshly integrated northwestern swath of the city, in an apartment in Forest Park, off Liberty Heights. Many of these enclaves had been the homes of working-class Jews, who then moved just beyond the northwest city limits into suburban Pikesville, sometimes hanging on to their old houses and renting them to black families moving in. While a hearty contingent of German Jews immigrated to Baltimore before the Civil War, the port city did not become home to the nation's third-largest population of Jewish Americans— primarily from modern-day Poland, Lithuania, and Russia—until the final decade of the nineteenth century. Their migratory pattern out from the seaport slum areas was to follow that of their German predecessors. The large African American group living in Baltimore's riverside neighborhoods throughout the nineteenth century notwithstanding, rural southern immigrants like my family moved into twentieth-century Baltimore, following closely the residential inroads made by the Jews. The best mid-twentieth-century black neighborhoods on Madison Avenue or Auchentroly Terrace had a synagogue nearby.

But if the move from Robert Street to Pimlico Road had at one moment gotten my grandfather closer to work, the 1960s' new terms of existence and the protocols of integration unraveled him. My grandmother, a registered nurse, had stiffened as the public protesting and defiance crested and tradition fell away. The chaos of the era jeopardized the class standing she had cemented during the 1940s on account of her professional ambition, home ownership, skin color, and Episcopalian restraint. She always reminded me that when she went to work, she walked through the front door.

Even as a child in the early 1970s, I noticed a kind of residential despair shrouding my grandparents' neighborhood. It must have been gallingly similar to what they had abandoned on Linden Avenue. To my kindergartener's eyes, Park Heights was filled with bullies, and was a bit pockmarked, bottle-broken, and litter-strewn. After a verbal tussle with a group of the Sumter Avenue boys at the alley fence, I preferred to play in the house. To me, there was a tangible difference in empathy and in exposure to malice between the children who lived next door to my grandparents, and the equally poor children I played with on the street beside the Crispus Attucks Center where my dad worked in York, Pennsylvania. The Pennsylvania kids were cheerful and generous to strangers. In Park Heights outsiders were targeted. I think even my grandfather, who passed away in 1974, was mugged walking back from Hoffman's bar. Living alone, my grandmother's main act, on a block of daylight rowhouses with sixty-four square feet of fescue in the front, was to put up a chain-link fence between her yard and the neighbors. For me the acme of pleasure had been jumping down two feet from the concrete block ledge to the sidewalk. Her fence was the first of its kind on their street. By the end of the 1970s, everyone had one.

Twenty years later, I lived as an adult in my grandmother's house. By then, heroin and crack cocaine, incurable disease, and two generations of cheap handguns had scarred the neighborhood in a way that, twenty years earlier, industrial layoffs, failed marriages, weak schools, and rented abodes had not. Men were shot down in the yards, in the gutters, and on the sidewalks. Women sold themselves in the alley and on porches; they knocked on doors with their children begging food. My next-door neighbors, who had moved there when I began junior high school, both succumbed to heroin addiction. The belles across the street ran a shooting-gallery-cum-brothel. The teenagers gave themselves over fully to the rigor of the cartel wars. The police installed quadruple klieg lights in barrel-size canisters, like at a stadium, to brighten the darkness along Sumter and Wylie Avenues. I won a stipendless appointment to Harvard for a year, and was told by Howard University that I would be fired if I did not cut the sabbatical to six months. I pleaded for money with Professor Gates, the man later invited to the White House to reconcile his unhappy encounter with the police. He recommended that I resolve all of my financial woes by turning my grandmother's place into a bed and breakfast.

Almost twenty years after that, in the months following my move to Homeland, my mother sold the Pimlico house to a childhood friend for $5,000, or about 15 percent less than what my grandparents had paid for it in 1965. Even at that price, he couldn't afford to both buy it outright and finance the needed renovations, which he was doing with his own work crew. Although he redesigned and beautified the interior of the house, the first thing he did when he gained ownership was demolish the fluted cement columns that held up the porch. They were the house's only distinctive feature and a unique detail in the neighborhood. He's trying to sell the daylight rowhouse now, and he is perpetually borrowing to pay the interest on the hard money loans he secured for the renovations. The whole process keeps threatening to drag him under. In my experience people nod their heads with understanding about the reality of life in poor black neighborhoods, but they are oblivious to the deadly undertow of its economy.

When I have my family, neighbors, and friends over to celebrate a *New York Times* review of one of my books, a friend from across the years can be overheard musing to himself, "So this is where Larry ended up." A much closer friend from the old neighborhood will deliver a judgment with wrenching sardonicism, "Not all of us can live here." He means I am an Uncle Tom, the sort of black person willing to erase any vestige of their ethnicity to win white approval. Some of my new white colleagues will also feign surprise when I reveal my address, telling me with their eyebrows that I have forsworn a tangible solidarity with "working-class" or economically "diverse" communities that they find more appropriate. I always think that these allies are slyly comforted by the glacial pace of black property acquisition, ever at the mercy of bank or council. Even though I do not make them privy to my rage, I resent their presumptuousness, which so easily erases the property struggles of the seven generations of Americans that I can name to which I belong. Indeed, I have to labor strenuously to recover those forebears at all.

Of course, as a Homeland resident, I want to believe that there is something heroic in becoming the black person who lives with his class, "integrated, with power," as Martin Luther King Jr. encouraged. I don't want to fall prey to the trap of opposing my own interests, the best amenities that the tax dollars can provide. But, more so, I reckon that it must be worthwhile to work for the position to transmit some slight generational wealth to my children, something that, as far as I am aware, has not yet happened in my family. It would also be different if I were directly from the Caribbean or Africa. The increase native to the immigrant is foreign to the native. Nonetheless, I worry that I am trying to have it both ways, the material world of the white middle class and perfidy to its core value, aggressive, dispassionate accumulation.

At the first Charles Street entrance to my new neighborhood there is a plain white wooden signboard with black Times font lettering that reads "HOMELAND." With better than seasonal frequency, some jolly delinquent steals one, some, or all of the

letters. Every time I see the sign in disrepair, I chuckle aloud
until the tears come. I guess I think the irony is funny, the attack on the snobbery that I desire because the snobbery implies
an economic security that I crave but have every reason to believe is a chimera. My real thought about Homeland had been
the same as any ancient one: patrimony. I could convey an inheritance to my heirs. Mirthful it may be, but bequest was the
color storm that started to rise when the invitation came for the
job. My vassal's wage and toft and croft, the home and the land,
might allow me to conduct patrimony. Imagine that.

The world of ambitious American universities, the one I have
pursued since the 1980s, is emphatic on this point: black patrimony is a labyrinth of folly. Yearning to pass on the house
and its land, the sinecure that dutilessly endows the children
not just as bequest but as a constitutive, has been declared a li-
ability from the last century. This folly is ecstatically true, and
ecstatically enunciated, in the place I am from and the place I
am going. Homeland belongs to the great tragedy of Baltimore,
one plantation land where they just couldn't make slavery pay.
Maryland, in fact, was the only state where it remained legal to
own people through the Civil War, and, between 1790 and 1860,
the population of the enslaved declined both by percentage and
in raw numbers. Something about that disdain toward increase
and the reproof of the instruments of coercion had gotten into
our black behinds.

Between the Eastern Shore and Potomac River plantations
and Philadelphia freedom was a netherland of farmers in the
forested saddles along a prehistoric ridge declining toward the
Chesapeake Bay. I am unsurprised to learn that the original
English name of the place where I decided to live reflected that
condition: "Job's Addition." English people, Irish people, even
Scottish people went to Maryland's Eastern Shore and became
quality. But only a scapegrace in the good ole days wanted to

settle between the Patapsco and the Susquehanna. The land wedge between the rivers dropped five hundred feet to reach the sea. Unlike the serene pastures of southern Maryland and Tidewater Virginia, the northern turf granted Cecil Calvert was steep and needed to be cleared and terraced and the giant stature Susquehannock battled against. After the French were vanquished, western lands glittered the horizon and more sweetly enticed the settler. By and by, English colonists started moving to the town at the Patapsco River basin and claiming the land alongside its many tributaries: Jones Falls, Back River, Middle River, Gunpowder River and its Falls, Winter's Run, Bynum's Run, and the Bush River.

In 1695 when Job's Addition was patented to Job Evans, the clerk Thomas Hedges would have begun the indentures like so: "This Indenture, made the Tenth Day of July in the Thirteenth Year of the Reign of our Sovereign Lord William the Third by the Grace of God of England, Scotland, France, and Ireland, King Defender of the Faith." The western Chesapeake wilderness still lay beyond the comforting aegis of the sovereign's Supreme Being. Perhaps that blessing had to do with slavery remaining "tangential" to the economy. The colonists never brought legions of the enslaved to work the Patapsco; whites remained a substantial majority throughout the state; and in the northern counties, free labor ruled.

Two lifetimes after the land was surveyed and sold, in 1832, a thirty-eight-year-old Baltimore clerical prodigy named David Maulden Perine bought Job's Addition. The tract had been owned by his stepfather, William Buchanan, who in 1799 had acquired the land from James Bryan, who came by it from the family of Colonel Charles Ridgely, who had received portions of Evans's kingdom. The original tract was more than 150 acres, and Perine added another fifty to it on April 1, 1835. When Buchanan started putting up buildings there before Perine was born, the records suggest that in the realm this far north of the

Patapsco basin there was one log chamber, twenty by fourteen feet, as well as a few "old negro houses," some of the earliest documentation of African people. Ridgely and Thomas Deye Cockey were the guiding hands of north Baltimore County, and different parts of the land bear their names today. Perine became the epitome of a husband of property and its declension to heirs. He sought fellowship with the early Maryland pioneers and he christened Job's Addition with a new name, "Homeland."

A city boy from Baltimore Town, Perine had studied at the John Deaver School on Fayette Street before boarding in Baltimore and Harford County for more learning. By 1810 Perine worked as a scribe alongside Buchanan, the court clerk and register of wills. In 1811 Buchanan suffered a paralyzing stroke and never returned to the office, launching fifteen-year-old David in a job for life as the Baltimore County clerk and register of wills. From a headquarters in the city courthouse, Perine devoted his career to organizing the legal documents upon which inheritance and generational property succession would be conceived for the entire region. Prudent of speech, he would become the wizard of patrimony.

He traded his desk for a uniform and officer's braid in the perilous summer of 1814, when the British naval squadron and 4,500 troops invaded Baltimore. Perine served under Captain Richard B. Magruder in the Maryland Militia's Volunteer Artillery Company. Artillery men were noted for physical size, since it was necessary for them to manhandle the cannon, which could weigh nearly a ton, after every discharge. His unit was in line for the battles at Northpoint and Hempstead Hill in the second week of September, simultaneous with the more famous bombardment of Fort McHenry, where Francis Scott Key penned the lyrics to what later became the national anthem. As they had done during the Revolutionary War in Maryland and Virginia, the British deployed black troops, two hundred Colonial Marines, Maryland escapees fighting for their freedom.

Considering the conventions of the time, Perine himself could have been accompanied by an enslaved black rider, laboring at the margin between groom and bodyguard.

In 1818 the officer married Mary Glenn at her parents' home called Glen Burnie, a southern suburb of Baltimore County on the road from the city to the state capitol at Annapolis. By 1825, the year before young Frederick Douglass was sent to Baltimore, Perine owned a house on Queen Street (or Pratt Street today) in Old Town and a more impressive one worth $381 that was also his main residence on Liberty Street. He had accumulated enough household goods that his furniture and plate silver alone were valued at $202, the price of a good house. He accepted election to the board of directors of the Bank of Maryland and when it failed he got into hot water as a silent partner guilty of schemes of speculation, inflated interest rates, shell companies, and circulation of bank notes that couldn't be redeemed. Any monies supervised by the court he steered into his bank and promptly made himself an uncollateralized loan. In August of 1835 his friends at the bank, prominent men—Reverdy Johnson, William Glenn, J. B. Morris, and mayor Evan Ellicott—had their furniture and homes burned. But he bounced back from scandal and moved up from pew no. 122 to pew no. 5 at Old St. Paul's Episcopal Church, the white parent church to the black one I grew up attending, St. James.

Perine had a knack for setting up trusts so that estate or inheritance tax didn't ravage the increase. He handled perhaps the most important single estate that came through Maryland, the bequest of the Declaration of Independence signer and main owner of the land that became the city and county, founder Charles Carroll. It was Carroll who paid for the mansion Homewood ("Carroll's Folly" he called it) built and occupied by his son Charles Carroll Jr., a profligate man who menaced the enslaved women at the Folly. Despite his talent for intricate legal accounting, Perine preferred a vision of himself as a country gentleman.

In his prime, Perine maintained a town home at 39 N. Calvert Street, a block below the famous Battle Monument that was erected in 1846 and commemorated the very battle in which he had served. It was the city's second-most picturesque square, but he knew that squiredom would ever allude him without lands in the country. He bought north of the city from his mother Hephzibah, who had inherited Job's Addition from her husband, Buchanan. He was flush. He and his friends were rumored to have turned a profit of $450,000 out of the ruined bank.

To reach Homeland, where I live today, from his downtown Baltimore houses, Perine rode a horse or drove a carriage along the York turnpike road, through the village of Waverly and, just beyond the Cold Spring Inn, the village of Govans. Towson was farther to the north. The old two-story farmhouse he found at the addition didn't suit his objectives and in 1839 Perine replaced it with an opulent honed-stone, five-bay-wide Federal neoclassical mansion. The Homeland manor house boasted a six-column portico capped with a faintly sloping pediment. The estate included mammoth outbuildings like a six-carriage livery, winter dairy, and a two-story, five-door Roman stable. Only a short time after Benjamin Latrobe's final work on the White House, his engineer son John and his local pals were creating enviable, even ostentatious wonders in the Greek style. In England, it would have been impossible to both amass this level of wealth and purchase lands for an estate. Fifty years after the nation's first president was elected, Americans were like Romans, taking the Greek model and expanding it beyond their wildest dreams.

The house had its dressed stone hauled from a quarry at the northwestern edge of his property, where there is a bowl today. The process must have appeared like a grand enunciation of some kind of timeless principle, all of a piece with the 178-foot-high marble homage to General Washington in a square on Charles Street that opened up in 1829. But Perine's enemies, probably disgruntled mechanics from Baltimore who had lost their savings in

1834, robbed his temple and set it on fire on March 7, 1843. The insurance would only replace half the dwelling and all the furniture was lost. After surveying the damage on the next day, Perine wrote to the architect Robert Cary Long to design a new house on the property in exactly the same location.

All that remained of the Homeland chateau were the two-foot-thick end walls ninety-seven feet apart. Long's new draft plan seemed less inspired by Andrea Palladio's *Four Books of Architecture*, Thomas Jefferson's good book of design, than had his first neoclassical marvel. The replacement house uttered a repudiation of the James River Georgics in favor of Italianate inspiration. By year's end of 1846, Perine had rebuilt the destroyed home, and his architect had transformed Perine's old dream of a Greek neoclassical temple to another vision of sophisticated style. The Italianate villa had low-pitched hip roofs, high lower-level windows, a front gallery porch, and a hint of a belvedere upper floor observation room. The house had hot and cold running water. Perine resided permanently now at Homeland and, in 1851, he refused to be considered for the job he had held in Baltimore for four decades. A very rich man, Perine paid taxes on more than twenty-three lots and their improvements in Baltimore, valued at $102,000.

Perine's choices shaped the moment. A few years later in 1852 and about three miles southeast of him at Clifton, the merchant prince of the city Johns Hopkins completed his revision of the Captain Henry Thompson stone house, transforming it into a pink-hued, stuccoed Italianate mansion complete with an eleven-arch veranda. The Hopkins belvedere was five stories high.

Living out the ideal of Roman splendor required the comfort provided by servants. All of the buildings at the intersection of modern-day Saint Albans Way and Witherspoon Road, where the manor once stood, would have been built with some enslaved labor, like the notched stone pillars in the bowels of the nation's Capitol itself. Perine needed the workers to dig a foundation, mortar the stone, frame out the two-story building, and then put up the stone walls, and, for the final two houses, dress the stone walls with a coat of stucco. But Perine almost certainly went to his neighbors or even free blacks for a heavy workforce. He wanted to become a gentleman squire, not a hard-edged planter who kept squads of people in thralldom. He could think of himself as tolerating, or acquiescing to slavery. Even mild Quakers like Johns Hopkins owned their domestic workforce. But like those in the class he aspired to, he didn't want to be linked to the obvious brutality of the slave trade, the shackles, whips, jails, gore, the parade of indecencies that gave holding people in bondage a bad name, a quality not to savor.

But partly, it would have been a problem of appearances. No successful member of the gentry was without devoted servants. After all, it had been Perine's man William Anderson who rode the nighttime turnpike down to Baltimore Town to deliver the devastating news to the family. That trip would have been risky for a rider unused to the roads or not a coachman, but it might have been riskier still to have awaited the safety of morning. Among the usual suspects when arson was reported were inevitably the enslaved, and arson was the cosmic leveling weapon of the basely aggrieved. In the city, on German Street and a block or two away from Perine, black women like housekeeper Sarah Young were accused of setting fire to the houses of employers they disliked.

The scrubbed record shows Perine always at his best. He subscribed to *Maryland Colonization Journal*, which sought to remove freedpeople to Africa. In that era Perine had living in his house one working-age freedwoman, and he seems to have owned only a single man, younger than twenty-four, possibly the night-riding Anderson, who boarded with Perine's family from 1820 until his death in 1892. Other black people worked the Homeland Manor and the city townhomes in the same capacity as any number of my own Virginia ancestors. In February of 1840, a black man named Charles Rose was found guilty in the City Court of stealing a shawl that belonged to "a black girl, a slave of David M. Perine, Esq.," probably a woman who worked in his house downtown. Being part of his household brought the benefit of the law, if it left the enslaved nameless.

Considering that, in the half century between David Perine's declining years and the property's sale, Homeland kept at task the coachman Charles Berry, the teamster Charles Wilson, John Foreman, and general laborer Henry Upshur, it stands to reason that more people than just Anderson lived at Homeland during the antebellum era. The 1860 census for Baltimore County shows Perine's Homeland household as containing a family of four daughters and two sons, and two free black people: "servant" Laura Gambrill, who was thought to be forty, and "laborer" John Coward, who was thought to be sixty. (Black people's ages coinciding evenly with the decadal census was a regular practice in the United States during the nineteenth century.) These workers almost certainly lived in the townhome on Liberty Street downtown at Lexington. The county 1860 census may hold an intriguing part of the archive pertaining to the black people who worked at Homeland. In the neighborhood that included Perine's Baltimore County lands, the 1860 "Slave Schedule" pages include an entry that is oddly rendered and thought by the digitized registries to be that of "David McGuire." But the scrawl could also be the name David M. Perine. The record shows this person with two houses for enslaved people on his land, and what looks like one family: a sixty-year-old woman, a couple in their early forties, and a group of children ages seventeen to nine born about two years apart, and with a baby seven years younger than its nearest sibling, suggesting that illness perhaps took the lives of other young children. What if the couple was William Anderson and his wife, and she had been the person whose shawl was stolen so many years earlier? Anderson, known to his owners as

"Uncle Bill," and a family connected to him, including someone old enough to be his mother, seem very likely landed at
Homeland.

In the later 1840s the founder of Homeland began to reap the
harvest he had sown. To coincide with his original Greek revival
mansion, he had planted 555 apple trees in symmetrical ranges
north of his house and peach trees in lots to the west. When he
had fully refitted the second manor he started to enjoy the fruit.
He tended toward yellow skin and yellow meat fruit apples that
were "subacid" in taste: fifty Long Island Russetts, fifty Newton
Pippins, forty Prince Harvests, fifty Gilpins. He paid homage to
his mother's Lord Berkeley, New Jersey, origins with Winesaps,
forty trees with dark-red fruit, good for cider, dessert, or for
market. Bellflowers, Boughs, English Redstreaks, and Codlings
rounded out the bunch. One hundred and one pear trees completed the larder. The barn was home to Scotland, an Ayrshire-
bred bull who took the premium prize in Maryland's 1853 fair.
With the help of a French botanist, Perine and a neighbor maintained piles of vegetable compost to compete with animal manure for soil fertilizer. Homeland, a farm of 238 acres with ample
outbuildings and a caretaker's cottage more elegant than the
homes of many of the local grandees, was a gigantic fruit garden. The bucolic country estate consisted of a mélange of orchards, cleared fields, woodlands, meadows, springs, and ponds,
the largest called "Banjo." (The springhouse water at Homeland
was so good that son Glenn was reputed to have carted barrels
down to his house on Cathedral Street.) Perine, whose "nature
and tastes have always inclined me to retirement," had finally
become a country squire.

Perine was modest about his professional attainments and
yearned to have hunched over the scholar's desk a bit more.
"Having left school at the early age of fourteen years, I became conscious that my education was defective," he admitted
in his diary. Perine had only gotten as far as the "Second Book

of Latin" by then, and he thought that the classics were important enough that when he had spare time he engaged a tutor. The place between the adoration of the Roman pastoral life as it was revealed in the pages of English translations and those feelings of desiring intellectual improvement led Perine into the important camaraderie with fellow Marylander Roger B. Taney.

Although Taney was fifteen years older than Perine, the men remained friends for more than forty years. Taney, the oratory prize winner of his Dickinson College graduating class, was a scholar. He left his autobiography and his opinions on the Dred Scott decision in Perine's trust. Taney had seen and known the most eminent of eighteenth-century Marylanders, like the soiled state attorney general Luther Martin and the corseted, doeskin-glove-wearing William Pinkney, thought unsurpassed in the courtroom. Taney admired Martin's powerful writings, but disliked both his personal appearance and his use of "vulgarisms which were never heard except among the colored servants, or the ignorant and uneducated whites." Taney had stood with Andrew Jackson against corporations and banks as US attorney general and then as chief justice of the Supreme Court.

The friendship blossomed in the years after Taney had become noted in Maryland for his success in arguing for the freedom of Jacob Gruber, a minister charged with inciting enslaved black people to revolt. In his remarks, Taney had called slavery "a blot on our national character." He became much better known to posterity, though, for his decision in *Dred Scott v. Sanford* in 1857, in which the chief justice decided that since the Declaration had freed no slaves it did not consider "these unfortunate beings" as "created equal." In the years before his death he went even further in his opposition to Republican centralism, going toe-to-toe with Lincoln in 1861 after martial law was declared in Maryland and Cockeysville's insurrectionist cavalryman John Merryman was held in Baltimore. Taney visited Perine's villa to relax and to quote sayings from his favorite book, Boswell's *The*

Life of Johnson. A year before he died, when Taney had become a convalescent in his own home, he "often thought of the pleasant days" at Homeland. He wrote to his old friend Perine that he frequently reminisced about those visits "enjoying the fresh country air & walking over your grounds."

In the company of men like Taney, Perine could swing away from his Whig sensibilities and become rather democratic and antagonistic toward the government in Washington. He claimed a friendship with Albert Bledsoe, the Old South's architect of the Lost Cause mythology. Bledsoe authored *An Essay on Liberty and Slavery* in 1856, the longest defense of slavery then known. When guns were silenced, Bledsoe made haste to Jefferson Davis in the casement prison at Fort Monroe in Hampton, Virginia. He mailed Perine a twelve-page letter describing the interview and decrying the Union's "scheme for turning the world up-side-down" and placing "the poor vulgar upstart over the charmed people of the South." Homeland's origins belong to a wealthy man not above fiduciary crookery whose clan of Baltimoreans showed "a good deal of Southern sympathy."

In 1854 the legislature approved a plan to take Charles Street through Perine's property, directly through the apple orchards. Well connected enough to have altered or delayed the route if he disliked the idea, Perine seems to have favored the graded macadam. His well-to-do neighbor Samuel Wyman, who had purchased the Carroll farm that would become "Homewood," was experiencing the same trouble of having the F. C. Crowly Company's heavy labor force striking the road through their lands. Once Charles Street was finished, Perine's property would be accessible on two sides. He would lose the sedate buffer between the public road and the marble footrests of the mansion. Perhaps the new circuit and the possibility of traffic seemed completely inevitable, the cost of progress as the city population stretched beyond two hundred thousand, and the county having tripled in size since his boyhood. The Maryland and Pennsylvania narrow gauge railway would open for business, complete with a station at the bottom of his eastern land at the Stony Run and another depot called Homeland, at the northwestern edge of his property, in 1876, six years before he died.

By the time Perine could get a train between Homeland and his Liberty Street townhouse, the world was changing in other startling ways. Like the Roman dramatist Terence, black Americans were taking freedom into places that impinged upon the social class ideals of Lost Cause white southerners. In July of 1877, African American Richard Greener, the first black man to graduate from Harvard, class of 1870, gave a rare-book lecture in Baltimore at the brand-new Johns Hopkins University, then downtown on Howard Street. The occasion was the ninth annual meeting of the American Philological Association, which Greener had been attending since 1875. A professor of moral and mental philosophy at the University of South Carolina, Greener served as the university librarian and faculty secretary, and he regularly taught Latin classes. He was a highly accomplished, bookish man, but his intellectual achievement was not indicative of his distance from the bare-knuckle fight for black survival. The year before his philology lecture, the light-skinned black Republican had faced the zealously murderous Red Shirt mobs of South Carolina Democrats at Wilhala and Pickens. Greener fearlessly stumped for Governor Chamberlain in the fight against the Confederate general Wade Hampton. Hampton's violent victory and the successful disenfranchisement of the black majority electorate set the course of American history for more than a century. Greener would shortly be forced out of his positions at the university and resettle in DC as law school dean at Howard. But the mark of excellence that he set, the Latin professor who often-enough graded white students unsatisfactory, was a volcanic natural rights riposte to the white supremacists. After the war, Albert Bledsoe and his ilk held fast to the idea of the "intellectual and moral debasement which, for so many thousand years, has been accumulating and growing upon the African race." Greener reacted hotly to such calumny, telling his listeners, "If eloquence and pen fail the Negro must use pistol and bludgeon."

The new university in Baltimore that hosted the mixed-race band of philologists was based on the radical German model of the seminar and its reading materials and busting up tradition. Hopkins president Daniel C. Gilman believed that black people could be "uplifted," and he supported the enrollment of a black polymath named Kelly Miller at Hopkins in 1887. In the 1890s as a trustee of the Slater Fund, he groomed Booker T. Washington and W. E. B. Du Bois. Sometimes, Gilman favored the Harvard model of education over the German, and in 1894 he directed Du Bois back to the United States from his degree at the University of Berlin, so that he could "devote [his] talent and [his] learning to the good of the colored race." He even cut off Du Bois's stipend to hasten his return.

The week of the Philological Association conference, Gilman was out of town, so the school board president, John Morris, called the meeting to order, thankful that the "sectional, sectarian or political purpose" was dormant. Baltimore's mayor, F. C. Latrobe, descended from the US Capitol's architect, checked in on the proceedings. Professor Haldeman from the University of Pennsylvania presided officially over the conference, but much of the public and organizational work was handled by the association's vice president, the Hopkins Classics Department chairman, an ex-Confederate junior officer named Basil Gildersleeve. Gildersleeve doubted that blacks could be uplifted, and he wrote during the war that northerners were offering to blacks "the privileges of social position," which they scorned anyway, and nothing of "material guarantees" or "the present or future profits" that might be derived from the war. Gildersleeve did believe in drawing-room exclusivity, and he may have had something to do with Greener's presentation being omitted from the official secretary's journal of the conference.

But the *Baltimore Sun* recognized suave professor Greener, ninth among the "experts in the science of language." He was and more. He went against Frederick Douglass and proposed black migration from the South. Greener aimed sarcastic barbs at southerners when he told an audience in 1879, "It is true the Northern people do not love us so well as you did, and hence the intermixture of races is not so promiscuous there as here. This we shall try to endure, if we go North, with patience and Christian resignation." Baltimore had contained the largest number of freedpeople in the nineteenth century, and heeding Greener's advice to renounce the dream of owning the land where they farmed, its black population was on the verge of surging again.

Black Americans moving north for better lives must have seemed a bit rich to Perine, in the same way that Richard Greener's analogies comparing black Americans to battle-scarred Greeks or Frederick Douglass to Victor Hugo were a bit rich. The richest thing Perine ever did was to give nine of his Homeland acres, and a seventeen-room parsonage, to found Redeemer Episcopal Church. The Episcopal (which means governed by a bishop) church that I grew up in was one my grandmother started to attend in the 1930s. She had married my grandfather in Douglass Memorial Methodist, and that was the church her mother preferred. My church was originally called St. James African Protestant Episcopal Church. The name changed in the 1930s, as the final generation of black church members born in slavery were laid to rest. The church's origins go back to a "talented old colored man" named Jacob C. Greener, who was a lay reader and communicant at Old Saint Paul's. Old Greener lobbied the bishop for a black Episcopal house of worship, sometimes holding services in his own house. One was established in 1824 with the help of a load of bricks and a land gift from St. Paul's, where Perine had been moving up his pew. To the envy of Perine, Baltimore had a handful of black classicists who knew Richard T. Greener's grandfather Jacob. Among them were the black priest at St. James William Levington, abolitionist William Watkins, who ran a school, and William Douglass, who left Baltimore in the 1830s to pastor an Episcopal church in Philadelphia. Although a freedman, Jacob's son Richard Wesley Greener left the South in Baltimore for the liberty of Philadelphia, too, where Richard Theodore was born in 1844. That patrimony was a locale, a situation.

On the occasional Sunday when I am feeling particularly like I don't want to drive and add an hour to our devotional obligation, I walk with my sons over to communion with the white Episcopalians at the most affluent parish in our entire diocese. My youngest son, Mitchell, slyly put our names on a register so, if we choose, we can even wear Redeemer buttons with our names, obviating people's ability to ask the nonwhite parishioners if it is their first visit to the sanctuary. But I never wear the name tag and am indifferent to history and manner because the church has exactly what I am looking for: a crisp sermon and communion after a seven-minute walk. Without any organizational effort on my part, I can work beside Redeemer members on Habitat for Humanity projects on McCabe Avenue, or find a willing audience to listen as I describe my books. What's more, when I put a farthing in the offering plate, I feel no guilt.

But most Sundays I feel guilty enough to get into the car and burn fossil fuel on the way to St. James in Sandtown. After I have settled into my house, Mrs. Roslyn Woods, a ringing soprano and my mom's contemporary, spins around one morning from the pew in front of me, where she has been sitting since the church interior was rebuilt following a terrible fire in 1989. She regards me with an understanding strangeness, although I have known her my entire life, have gone to school with her son, and dated her daughter. Whenever Mitchell visits from Atlanta, I invite her grandchildren Chandler and Wesley over for pizza. She shows me a photograph of herself as a smiling girl with her hair curled and next to a clean-shaven man in a three-piece suit with his hands thrust into his pockets. She points to her father and says, "He worked in your house."

From the 1830s until he died in 1882, Perine lived at the top of the Homeland oval, about a field's length away from my doorstep. The road between the old city and the increasingly densely populated county contoured his imagination. When the sawyers brought down the apple orchard to make way for Charles Street, they roughly dressed and stacked the fruit tree lumber. Besides the orchard, Perine had also planted ornamental trees: silver oak, silver leaf poplar, copper leaf beech, Norway maple, American aspen, horse chestnut, lindens, and red flowering maple. In 1922, understanding himself to be at the end of his life, Perine's son Elias Glenn sold the family acres to the Roland Park Company. As the estate left the hands of the family who had known it for more than a century, the surviving Perines recovered the lumber and routed a few pieces to a finish carpenter who, in later years, made two decorative chairs. In the splat of each chair was carved either of Perine's mansions, and on a fluttering scroll the motto "Homeland." Then the workers, using ox teams, pulled the house down.

Take away rights created by emperors, and then who will dare say,
That estate is mine, or that slave is mine, or this house is mine?
—Augustine of Hippo, *Tractate VI*, 25 (410–430)

We cling to our oppressors as the objects of our love.
—Martin Delany, *The Condition, Elevation, Emigration, and Destiny of the Colored People of the United States* (1852)

Christmas: Long Quarter at River Bend

The feast day chimes of the Catholic cathedral across the street are the first thing to adjust to on Albion Road. The sounds and smells and sensations along Perine's old lot confer on me another kind of identity as a person born and reared in Maryland, a place I had returned to after school in California, before leaving once again for married life in Richmond and Atlanta. Now I was serenading a third time. When I had previously given any serious thought to ancestry, I had been prone to lyrically investigate Pittsylvania and Mecklenburg Counties in Virginia, and, when not focused on that rural past, my sense of life as a Baltimorean. Never as a Marylander.

My third reverie home opens me up to haunting by two great Old Liners, who were also Baltimoreans, Frederick Douglass and Billie Holiday. I focus my graduate teaching on these two figures that I know so little about, beginning with Douglass. I agree to write a short chapter on Douglass's city youth and, in the process, I make some discoveries afforded by unusual juxtapositions. To showcase the results for lay audiences, I decide to make a visual aid, a digital map with the archival material embedded upon it. When it is finished, I present the work at the African American theme museum in Baltimore, and at the area archival repositories, and to a group of enthusiasts in Annapolis.

Douglass has been with us so long here in Maryland as to be contained within his legend. Our homage to him, which began for me at home with his image emblazoned on the Black History Mystery game, continued onward through my dutifully shuttling the Howard undergraduates on the subway over to Anacostia to visit his last home. My mother had graduated from Frederick Douglass Senior High. Black History Month was February because it was Douglass's birth month. Even though he had the mystique of Harvard connected to him, black classicist Richard T. Greener seemed a tangible, proximate person to me, one who worked for the federal government in Russia and Japan and was a diplomat to India. The personification of emancipation, Douglass was closer to a holiday my grandparents would have celebrated, one known to my generation, but far off. I don't think it ever even occurred to me that there might have been naysayers to Douglass's vision of how black people ought live in America, until I read an unpublished manuscript of Ralph Ellison's from the late 1940s. A radical character, cut from Ellison's famous novel, counseled more "responsible civic action" on Douglass's part: that would be the insurrectionist violence of Nat Turner.

In our tradition Douglass was forever on the right side of the question because he emancipated himself and favored uncompromising struggle to break the hold of the enslaver. But was it possible that he had not driven the bargain hard enough? Was he as earthly a mortal as King and Mandela? I did wonder if the Homeland house and my pressing desire to raise my children in the undisputed middle class was connected to an unseemly fondness for ancient white power. Sensing that Douglass was somehow involved, before the end of my first summer back, I would visit the "secluded, dark, and out-of-the-way" part of Talbot County on Maryland's Eastern Shore where he had learned what slavery was all about.

Frederick Douglass left Maryland at twenty, fleeing to New York, Massachusetts, to England, and settling at Rochester before fleeing again, and then back to Rochester, where he could help people escape slavery and where he himself could get away to Canada. Then he took government positions and lived in Anacostia, across the river from downtown Washington, DC. At the very end of his life, Douglass was building a house not far from Annapolis that would look out over the Chesapeake Bay. His perch from the western shore would have allowed him to gaze across the water to Talbot County, the peninsula of his childhood.

In his boyhood, Douglass's imagination had lingered over a windmill on Long Point, a tongue of land separating the Miles from the Wye River on Maryland's Eastern Shore. But the real landmark haunting Douglass was Wye House, the home of Edward Lloyd, the fifth in his line to roam the New World. To the manor born, Lloyd, who governed Maryland at thirty, was by far the wealthiest man on the Eastern Shore. Tall, white-haired, laconic, and firm-handed, Edward Lloyd the fifth enslaved at least 565 people according to the 1830 census.

The owner of a bushel of prize farms—Wye Town, Davises, Newquarter, Blisland, New Design, White House, Hopewell, Forrest, Woolmans, Four Hundred Acres, Home House, and Wye House—Lloyd pressed his black "family," an Eastern Shore sobriquet for bondmen and -women, into grueling slavery. He did so at a time when slavery in Maryland was being regarded as a crime against humanity, even by its supporters like Roger Taney. Lloyd the fourth had been compelled to respond to "Accusations" in 1793 that he overvigorously beat his enslaved family, levied by an intrepid Episcopal reverend. Rough treatment, even by slaveholders' standards, certainly seemed possible: when Douglass was a lad, Lloyd held in bondage more productive working-age adults, many more, than he could remember by sight. Nearly a dozen overseers, throughout Talbot County, plied the lash to ring profit in his name.

In three autobiographies over thirty years Douglass enumerated and condemned the murderous brutality of day-to-day life at the Wye House farm, including multiple accounts of acts that he did not personally witness. These brutalities and murders had taken on legendary status among the enslaved, and the foul deeds wound their way inside the boy. It surprised me that, in 1881, fourteen years before his death, Douglass crossed the threshold of Wye House to "live over in memory the incidents of his childhood." By then he was a distinguished American with a US cutter at his disposal. But the fact that the world's most prominent escaped slave and hector against the ancient regime sought an afternoon chair and sweetmeats at Maryland's cardinal plantation in the immediate years after the end of Reconstruction and the overthrow of the black franchise in the South disconcerts. What's more, the Lloyds reminded him in a subtle way that his genteel fantasy would always be just that. Douglass was handed his sideboard wine by a teenager and a nine-year-old boy. Edward Lloyd VII had taken his carriage into Easton.

Edward Lloyd the first told people he was from London, though some estimated him born in the early years of the Virginia colony. That Lloyd, a Puritan, had gambled about which edge line of the English Civil War to toe. He dissembled in the Catholic colony, backed Oliver Cromwell, seized colonial government between 1652 and 1658, and made conciliation pay dividends. In 1659 he claimed the rights to three thousand acres of Eastern Shore land. He called his tract by a Welsh name, Hîr Dîr Lloyd: Lord Lloyd's.

The Chesapeake Bay that dominated Lloyd's and Douglass's life and the Wicomico, Pocomoke, Patapsco, Patuxent, and

Choptank Rivers retained their Algonquin names. But at the country seat that would be occupied by his descendants, Edward Lloyd the first christened the rivers and places after the stripe of water separating England from Wales, the migrants from the natives, the Wye River. Edward Lloyd the first returned to London to mount his campaign as a factor—a mercantile dynamo in tobacco, finished goods, and slaves—in the final third of his life, a move that helped to ensure the success of his line for three hundred years. But one key experience making his progeny Americans instead of Englishmen was the "traffick"—the "execrable commerce" in the language Thomas Jefferson pruned from his draft of the Declaration of Independence—in Africans.

Lloyd's white, wood plank, two-story, double-winged manor called Wye House is a national historic site, still occupied today by his direct-line heirs. At first glance, Douglass's final nostalgia for the "grand mansion" and what it represented seem at odds with the principles he developed over a lifetime of public service that culminated with his contributions to the Emancipation Proclamation and Thirteenth Amendment to the US Constitution ending racial slavery and the Fifteenth Amendment enabling black men to vote—even before white women. Maybe because I had grown up in Baltimore, knowing of other hardy black Marylanders like Harriet Tubman and Matthew Henson, while blithely unaware of David Perine, I was annoyed when I read about Douglass's afternoon at Wye House. Lloyd had inspired his detestation and horror at the slave system, and Lloyd had been the employer of his master Aaron Anthony, almost the owner of the owner. Harriet Tubman had never seemed of the sort to go back to table, glad to share tea and a biscuit with those people. In graduate school I had imagined a dissertation project that included Douglass the writer and his short story "The Heroic Slave," but I always found more fascinating his invisible mentor, the revolutionary pamphleteer David Walker, or his rival, the physician and explorer Martin Delany. Granted,

those men, like Richard Greener, were freeborn. Alongside John
Mercer Langston and Sojourner Truth, who took it as her duty to
ridicule Douglass's "efforts to speak and act like a person of cultivation and refinement," several prominent black voices had expressed dismay about Douglass's willingness to cozen. Yet it had
been Douglass's writings alone against the barbarism of Lloyd
and slavery that had at least forced Lloyd's chroniclers to acknowledge even the possibility of brutality during enslavement.
Then again, the slightest softening on Douglass's part was an
opening to the defenders and sycophants of the old power on the
Eastern Shore. After the 1881 trip, they decided that Douglass
viewed people like Lloyd and Thomas Auld, paid in gold to re-
linquish his claim on Douglass, "in terms of great admiration
bordering upon veneration."

Was my new job an equivalent plea to the sideboard, the
hope for victuals and kind chatter? A stitch of unease started to
direct me back in time to Talbot County.

Driving to the Eastern Shore from the middle of Baltimore
required me to choose my approach to the Bay Bridge: the eastern or the western route. I went east for the first time in my life,
driving across the Severn River and the larger Patapsco River on
the Francis Scott Key Bridge, which we just call the Key Bridge,
in a way that fully disassociates it from its historic namesake. It
costs four dollars to travel this eastern path, the main reason I
have never before taken it. An even more exorbitant fee has dis-
suaded me from using the tunnels that course underneath the
harbor. A young Baltimore writer, a retired street hustler, causes
me to pause now at Key, whose anthem was adopted by the nation when my father was an infant. "The Star Spangled Banner"
was written on board a truce ship in the harbor during the 1814
invasion, and the ditty originally contained an unpleasant third
verse: "no refuge could save the hireling and slave / From the
terror of flight or the gloom of the grave." In grade school we
certainly saw many colored drawings of Douglass, soulfully re-

cited the poetry of Paul Laurence Dunbar and Langston Hughes, and sang "Lift Every Voice and Sing." But I don't recall ever learning any of the spirit or context behind the national anthem.

Teasing out Key's slaveholding bias just adds new dung to the pile, however. The state flag represents the marriage of two houses, Calvert and Crossland, two sides of the Civil War. The official state song, "Maryland, My Maryland," opens with "The despot's heel is on thy shore." That boot belongs to Abraham Lincoln and the Union Army. Emancipation in 1864 is the culmination of the tyranny the song deplores. As it would happen, Key married Edward Lloyd's daughter, and the poet visited Wye House during the time Douglass wandered the yard. The man Key visited, Edward Lloyd V, had voted in Congress in 1807 against the abolition of the African slave trade. Baronial Lloyd's maiden speech in the US Senate in 1820 insisted that Maine and Missouri be admitted together, one free state to balance one slave state. A day later, he voted against excluding slavery north of the thirty-sixth parallel. "Beguiled by the siren slavery" is how his apologists describe him.

One bridge down, I skirt past Annapolis and the Naval Academy, and out to the same water again. The Chesapeake Bay Bridge is four miles long, most of it sunk in marshy lowlands, but reaching a significant kind of utilitarian, Cold War–era, iron monstrousness where the road rises to 186 feet above the water. At the western edge of the bridge is Sandy Point, the Maryland beach designated to permit blacks in 1956, and which shortly thereafter became the black or "city" beach. It was the place we went most frequently throughout my childhood. Baltimore is the sort of place where seasonal whimsy is significant, and visits would be marked by different parodic fashions, like the dime-store captain's hats, or the billed caps with spinning helicopter blades worn by children and adults alike. And always a blaring song for the summer, like Maxine Nightingale, Anita Ward, McFadden and Whitehead, or Junior. When I was a Cub

Scout, and had no idea of Douglass's connection to the region, we walked across the bridge, a daylong event. Mainly, I recall being hungry. The beaches on the Eastern Shore at the Atlantic ocean remained the customary preserve of the whites.

A month before, one of my homeboys from my old neighborhood near the Preakness racetrack, a retiree who had logged twenty-five years as a city police officer, had an accident on the Bay Bridge, and had to be helicoptered to the Shock Trauma Unit at the University of Maryland hospital. I visited O'Donald on the secure floor. While his body was broken, his mind and eyes were alert and he recognized me. He passed away a few days before I left on my trip.

I stop the car at Wye Mills, only a few miles beyond the bridge, a neighborhood convenience once owned by Edward Lloyd IV, near the site of the Old Wye Church, and the downed Wye Oak, which had been Maryland's oldest historic tree. The still-grinding mill, with a two-thousand-pound millstone leaning up against the heavy rock wall, is an oblique signal to the passerby that in Douglass's time Maryland's agricultural past in tobacco was overtaken by wheat for cash and corn for the animals. Not long after Wye Mills fed the Continental army at Valley Forge, a total agricultural change came to the land. Douglass worked on a farm as a teenager planting wheat and corn and chopping wood, but he never worked a "cash" crop like tobacco or cotton, the most demanding and scrutinized of the agricultural tasks.

Inside the mill, the proprietor presents herself by way of a reference to a Beach Boys song. The miller and I banter about the variety of grains of wheat and corn and the comparative coarseness and fineness of the grinding, as well as traditional units of measurement, like a "peck," a term she is unfamiliar with. I don't, but I should be thinking back to my mandatory Chaucer 101 class: "The millere sholde noght stelen hem half a pekke / Of corn by sleighte." At the time I read those lines in college I could not have imagined the pure connection between the people of the territory around this mill and the English pilgrims swapping tales as they trudged along the road to Canterbury. But they sounded similar. The natives of Maryland's Eastern Shore carol in a unique dialect, a product of extreme isolation. It's a place where after the Englishwomen and -men got off the boats, few people from the outside, beyond a sprinkle of Scots and Irish, ever joined them here again. Of course there were some they didn't want. In 1669 English colonists killed every one of the Wicomesses they could find; the Nanticoke were treatied off the peninsula; the Choptanks intermingled into oblivion. The people who did come and stay were mostly from West Africa and had spent time "seasoning" on an island called Barbados—a rocky breakwater in the Caribbean as much like the prison at Alcatraz as a farm.

I tell the miller that she is selling one-eighth peck parcels of meal. Four pecks to a bushel. During slavery a peck of meal was the common weekly ration in Maryland for field labor, and children were expected to draw from their parent's portion. When I get the meal home, I will make small loaves to go with a breakfast of fried apples. I work through my half of a quarter peck at about six tablespoons per loaf of cornbread; my pan is about the size of a half brick. But unlike my baked sundry with egg, milk, baking powder, soda, and sugar, nineteenth-century cornbread was made only with three ingredients: meal, water, and salt. Harriet Bailey, Douglass's mother, needed twice as much meal, maybe three times as much, for her dense concoction to reach a similar stature. But I think that they were as likely to have folded the batter into corn husks and made something closer to a tamale, like the Natives would.

The miller smiles at me pleasantly, despite the fact that she said she was planning a brief adjournment when I stepped across her threshold. The marking of race on the Eastern Shore is immediate and active. The miller says that I resemble someone she knows, a friend of hers, a woman who is "real, real light skinned, like you." She signals an intimacy that I did not wish to invite. Black people can be touchy about references to race or color from whites—even from other blacks—that distinguish us as if we were unusually different. Since we also come from a culture that, with a few exceptions, values the community over the individual and strives for equitable balance among its members, we resist descriptions that rank us as belonging to a different nation or clan. If there is too much precision, we suffer by being made exotic. I feel like I would be out of my mind if I said, "Why, you're almost as dark as I am! Are you sure you don't have black ancestors?" Maybe she thinks I am trying to pass myself off as a white person, and she is gently remonstrating me? I would think, What is the point? But, even that might only indicate the level of what I don't know and can never understand.

Little of this was an issue for fatherless Douglass, who lived his life with a single standard. He sought out white people and he enjoyed the company of bright white women especially, who were eager to exchange erudition with him in a way that white men were not. Sometimes Douglass's appreciation for life north of the color line peeks through his writing. People at Lloyd's like William Wilks seem to have been "very fine looking" because they were "about as white as anybody on the plantation." What disappointed Douglass about the people he knew who had the appearance of Wilks was the cleft of the bar sinister, theirs and his and our sad origin. But I choose to ignore the miller's clarifications as an insult. I buy several housewarming gifts to go along with my cornmeal, five dollars for one quarter peck. The crockery I buy is gray with blue lettering that says "The Ole Wye." I notice the heavy lids that fit overtop containers for butter or salt or honey. I learn that the couple that makes the pottery is from Pennsylvania. The containers seem like farm niceties, and remind me of the crocks and jugs my Virginia-bred father appreciated. The miller's family moved from Appalachia. I banter protectively with her in a way that makes it easy for her history to evade conflict with my own and for our conversation to continue. Is it patience, resignation—or yearning—seeping into my life?

A good stone's throw up the road from the mill is one of Maryland's oldest Anglican churches, renamed the Episcopal denomination after the successful revolution against England. Prior to visiting the mill, I had attended religious services at the Old Wye Church. I had taken a few days to work on a manuscript in isolation, and I thought that Talbot County would give me that. At the church, I was feeling conspicuous, but in awe in the way that pilgrims can be at shrines to colonial architecture, an American's only English-based antiquity. Rebuilt very early in the eighteenth century, the brick-floor church has a pulpit off to the left, and seats its parishioners in marvelous, high, inlaid wooden boxes with brass locks. I visited on stewardship Sunday and in lieu of a sermon three congregants publicly account for their personal journeys to Christ and this small chapel of ease. The parishioners originate from Pennsylvania and New Jersey and other enclaves where economic competition is keen. They have come to the water's edge after a lifetime of foraging to retire in comfortable historic peace. To my mind the Eastern Shore natives seem represented by a man with a crew cut and a mustache who comports himself with the directness and affability of someone who earns their living by holstering a sidearm.

After the service, the minister and the sexton, energetically courteous, show me the artifacts and discuss the history of the church. I know that it's hard for them not to see their courtesy to me as a simple gesture of magnanimity and recompense for the still-recent era that would have made my visit uncomfortable, if not impossible. My mother had a beloved teacher named Waters Turpin who was from and wrote about Maryland's Eastern Shore, but like fellow Marylander Ron Karenga, or the fetus

James Baldwin of Deal's Island, he seems not to have shown much interest in return. I am doing some stretching not to see the gesture as a cloak hiding suspicion, unease, rejection, and the heightened surveillance directed at a possibly malignant foreigner. But probably I would take their ignoring me in the same way. For the sake of that weekend sojourn, I decide to let it all pass. We all concur concerning the simple elegance of the church, whose beauty emanates from its puritan simplicity and craftwork. It seems to me to surpass the more elaborate cathedrals with their emphatic representations in glass, marble, and paint of a Nordic God. I am also fortunate to be visiting the revised version. Wye Church was restored in the latter 1940s to a classic style it had not known since the eighteenth century. I ended the visit with a march up the stairs to what is still called the slave gallery, where an elite group of enslaved blacks would have worshipped above their owners, and then I walked out alone into the church's cornfield on the other side of a stream.

Of all of the mesmerizing items in Old Wye Church I studied most curiously a flag I had never seen before, one that marries the King's Colors to the black-and-gold banner of Cecil Calvert, the second Lord Baltimore, the main ingredient of Maryland's contemporary state flag. The King's Colors, or Grand Union flag that existed when only England and Scotland formed Britain, rests in the canton, the upper quarter of the flag. I assumed it was a colonial French and Indian War curiosity, but the flag probably never flew at all. The one in the church was special ordered in 1976 and made at the women's prison. The better-known Maryland emblem of today, agreed upon in 1880, represents the reconciliation of Douglass-era politics. During the Civil War, Confederate Marylanders like the Lloyds had flown the red-and-white knobbed cross of the Crosslands to distinguish themselves from the Maryland Unionists, flying the black-and-gold standard. But contemporary Eastern Shore Marylanders prove to be less interested in symbolism so subtle. Before I leave Tilghman

Island, where I spend the night, I will be assailed by gigantic representations of that other nineteenth-century red, white, and blue herald, which rips something out of me.

I want to believe I have my bearings set better on the second journey. After a short drive through morning fields towering with corn and bristling with wheat I arrive at Schroder's boat shop. From prior experience, I do not trouble myself with asking for the proprietor or owner, but prepare myself to start addressing whoever is nearby. When I get out of the car, a man in old khakis and a T-shirt, smoking a cigarette and holding a beer can, gives me his attention and tells me he will help me get the boat. He interrupts a conversation with another river idler wandering in and out of a large aluminum outbuilding. The accent of these Eastern Shore men is strong. "Arn" for "iron." "Far" for "fire." "Ague" for "egg." "Danny" for "down to the." "Creeyun" for "crown." While the local twang grates against the rather Elizabethan sounds of the James River Virginians (which would sound more like "Jamez Rivuh Vuhginyuhnz"), both accents connote the same distinction. They are peculiar to early settlers in the English colonies adjusting to remote historical conditions of life, and they try quite hard to exclude any Africanisms at all. It is difficult for me to imagine a white person who so much as has the ambition to travel to Pennsylvania as wanting to talk this way, but the desire to see Pennsylvania has been such an ordinary part of my life. It makes me wonder what Douglass sounded like when he spoke to his Eastern Shore bride Anna.

My trip to the skiff is a minor tragedy in the making of men. I intend to spend about four hours going up and down the Wye River, and, in the back of my mind, I think of steering the boat for St. Michael's, the seaport Douglass knew as a teenager, maybe six miles south by water. But my clumsy approach to the prow of the fiberglass long boat forebodes possible disaster. With a computer-stuffed backpack, water bottles, binoculars, and the receipt from the boat company in hand, I tumble into the slender craft, meriting fully the boatman's mirthful bark: "First thing you want to do, buddy, is make sure you don't fall in to the water."

He puts his beer on the dock and unhooks the line and tosses it onto the deck. The oddest thing I can think of regarding the legacy of slavery and segregation among black people is the lingering suspicion that despite what your mother wit tells you, the white people are giving you valuable advice.

Being dubbed "buddy" is, of course, special. In Chester Himes's novel from 1945, *If He Hollers Let Him Go*, the character Pigmeat chides the hero, Bob Jones, for calling him "buddy," which Pigmeat connects to the legacy of slavery and subordination. "Don't you know what a 'buddy' is, Bob? A 'buddy' drinks bilge water, eats crap and runs rabbits. That's what a peckerwood means when he calls you 'buddy.'" Although I am an energetic biographer of Himes and committed to the freedoms he fought for, I let it pass with a smile and a chuckle that are not at all heartfelt. Perhaps I am drawn to the fact that the man who talks to me has bags under his eyes, a mark of immense dissolution that I know from my grandmother's second husband from Arkansas, who smoke and drank unrepentantly and kept a firearm and ammunition in every room. Because he was not related to us, my sister and I called him "Tommy," and I suppose he had an origin story similar to Douglass's or Ferdinand LaMothe's. Besides, what do we really know about any of it at all? Tobacco smoke harms the throat and lungs, but it also helps to move the bowels. Every day I spend more time on the "seat of ease," so who knows for certain the instrumental remedy of our ailments and aches?

Wanting badly to show myself agile and a quick study, I respond to suggestion and pull in the ten-pound, bullet-shaped, six-pronged anchor, and am then directed by the ancient pilot to the engine and the choke. I don't spend much time looking around or settling my belongings. On the four-stroke Tohatsu I can see well enough the rip cord, which will pull the engine to life like any gas-powered lawn mower. I can't observe any other switches on the motor.

My belief that I would be untroubled by a motorboat is supported by a slender thread. In the mid-1980s I worked at a tourist electric boat rental at the Baltimore Inner Harbor. From time to time I occasionally piloted the Chase boat, a fiberglass craft with a cockpit, steering wheel, and throttle, and an Evinrude outboard motor. I have no memory of starting her up.

My job at the boathouse during the summers of 1985 and 1986 was my introduction, at $3.15 an hour, to the world of adulthood and unskilled wage labor, but also, much more fretfully, race relations. I was a good student at a Jesuit high school for boys, the same one that the boat owner's sons had attended, and on weekends, the men, in their late twenties, would take off their Jos. A. Bank suit coats and run the business for the summertime crowds. I can't explain why I expected better familiarity with the owners than what occurred. It might be captured by the caption underneath the photograph of John Carlos and Tommie Smith at the 1968 Olympics in the history textbook we were assigned, "Misuse of the podium." I am nearly always under the impression that white people favor two types of blacks, those who are completely housebroken and unctuous flatterers, and those who, whether by language, bearing, or expression, evoke animal ferocity. I fall somewhere in between; I think, like most of us.

I regularly came to work on time and did what was asked of me without complaint, mainly putting life preservers on children and making sure that no one rammed the boats into the docks when they returned after their half hour was up. By the second summer I had begun to chafe at the job, which wasn't an easy one to come by. But there was no way of improving the condition, of earning a raise, no fantasy of advancement, and plenty reality of being scheduled less and less or having fewer and fewer hours, until your name didn't appear on the handwritten schedule at all.

The only other loader I can remember was an anemic, childlike woman in her twenties, who I presumed was of Polish descent but looked as if her origins also included Mongolia. She spoke with a strong Eastern Shore accent, which signaled her living in a community of shipyard workers to the east of the Inner Harbor in a place called Dundalk; or Highlandtown; or Brooklyn; or Hampden among the descendants of millworkers—all hearty enclaves of Ku Klux Klan ghosts. If we didn't know anything, we knew that. Her accent and that she was eagerly working minimum wage meant I had very little to say to her. Then one summer day I found that she was getting $3.50.

The one youth who stood between the owners and the other loaders was a boy named Tom who seemed to have life figured out, between ample measures of meaningful professional ambition and experiencing worldly pleasure. We were the same age, but blond, tall, Towson Tom was being taught how to repair and maintain the boats, the simple engineering of the batteries and propellers, and he was also responsible for managing the schedules. Because he sought company with the elite, Tom's accent was typically neutral, like a person from a national television program. He taught me how to use Dutch snuff, which got me high and helped pass the time and which I shared with the fellas from my block. From time to time Tom would take me with him in the Chase boat, propelled by the hefty Evinrude, to haul in the boats that wandered out beyond the Pier Six Pavilion. A handful of times when he was away and an electric boat ran out of juice or its occupants had run over debris and fouled the propeller, I made the rescues in the Chase boat alone. At night, a green light attached at the helm flickered as the boat whisked along the river.

Which is perhaps why I tug the pull cord with gusto, starting the motor as instructed, and noting accurately that the throttle is on the tiller, which I have in neutral. For forward power, the pilot has only to twist the lever. However, lines off, motor on, anchor up, and boat underway, I am uncomfortably drifting backward toward the embankment pocked with softball- and bowling-ball-size rocks. The pilot barks instructions at me, clamoring about the forward and reverse, which I had imagined were more directly connected to the throttle. I am made to understand by the severity of his command that the gear switch is lodged on a more obscure part of the boat. I am told the controls are to my left. "It's on the motor!" he cries forcefully, though not in desperation. I look to my left and see nothing. I look to my right in case I don't know my left from my right. I scan the motor and see prominently the thumbscrews used to moor the engine to the stern. With embarrassment, I touch them to make sure they don't have some more recondite meaning. I am an expert, it seems, only at appearing confused and befuddled. The craft is steadily drifting backward. In a few seconds the propeller will bite into a lunch of stones.

The ancient mariner rests his beer on the dock and begins yelling to me, "The lever!" and, at the last moment before running the boat a-rock, I see a lever shaped like a C-clamp, on the far side of the engine. It is painted the same black as the motor cover. I flip it back. The motor reverses.

The hydrants of sweat ease and I escape the stony embankment and the menacing dock, shamefaced, and at what seems like an aggressive speed, relative to the sound of the engine. I steer out into the river to get underway, splashing water into the bow and unconcerned about my knapsack and Coast Guard maps I have printed on copy paper that are slopping onto the damp boat floor.

At the edge of someone's property, which the state has lovingly gabionaded from erosion by reinforcing the shoreline with metal wire mesh cages of granite boulders, the motor starts to cough and shake. I am spitting distance of a bunch of reeds when it dies out. I can't seem to get the motor restarted and I worry that I have inadvertently broken it. I think that I could wade ashore and walk back if I had to. My worldview can be encompassed that way, which is an unfortunate bit of fake self-reliance. I hesitate to fly because I am not sure I could land the plane in an emergency, that sort of thing. I feel most comfortable within the orbit of my expertise. I'm hardly the sort to have run away from slavery.

Using a paddle to push away from the reeds, I yank the cord and the motor catches. I notice that it sputters and shakes whenever I approach the shore. The Wye East River is shallow at the rim, sometimes getting to ten or twelve feet in the dead center, but more regularly only a foot or two toward the slope of the land. My four-horsepower Tohatsu sticks a foot down beyond the keel, and I will work all day to keep it from raking the mucky river bottom. Whenever I edge the banks the engine bucks and flips. I anguish over how much to manhandle it, or if it will break and I will take on vast fees. When I worked on the water at the Inner Harbor, we were mainly concerned about plastic nettings and bags snagging the electrically driven motors. In the Wye shallows, the concern is digging the propeller into the soft mud.

Happily, I note the motor gaining courage away from the shore, and I test it fully by heading north on the East River. The perky boat surges forward up water. I am elated, feeling confident, driving swiftly. The river is pocked with duck blinds at the river's edge and miniature estates up off the water, with footpaths to docks tucked down by land's end. Like eight-year-old Douglass on the sloop headed to Baltimore and away from plantation slavery, my adventure on the water to the new world inspires a vision of a completely different life for myself. It is an imaginary one shaped by my recollections of the characters in the novels of Ernest Hemingway, *Island in the Stream*'s Thomas Hudson and *Across the River and into the Trees*' Richard Cantwell, those impassioned treatments of white men, guns, and reels. Although I am a pescatarian, I experience the urge to plan fall outings to hunt and roast waterfowl. I look for an uninhabited bend in the river and relieve myself off the side of the boat.

I ride the length of the Wye East River, getting my dander up, and wide-berth-passing the fishermen so as not to disturb their sport. It seems a mystical, wonderful part of my Maryland nativity that I have forsaken. The terrain reminds me, minus rice and palm and palmetto, of the lowland river estuaries of the other coastal places I have befriended: St. Helena, South Carolina; Tybee Island, Georgia; and Grand-Bassam in the Gulf of Guinea. When I think I have explored the totality of the creek, I come about in four horsepower might and plan my course for the rest of the journey. I decide I will circumnavigate Wye Island and spend time exploring Lloyd's Creek, the waterway where Douglass bathed as a child.

Twenty-first-century people are known for their fickleness, their inability to envision (or determination to reject) a grand goal and unify their personality to accomplish it. But from time to time I capture a neat, tidy vision, and relying upon the paper maps and circumnavigating Wye Island is one. In colonial and antebellum times, the island was mainly the residence of William Paca, Maryland's third governor and a signer of the Declaration. Wye Hall was his home. William Paca the second loved the Union so much he shot and killed blood relatives in a Civil War disagreement. The danger around Paca's isle on this journey seems negligible. If called overboard, I am wearing a life vest, but I think I could freestyle however far I needed to go if it came to that. I know my judgment is sometimes faulty. A few weeks earlier I had convinced myself I could swim from Tilghman Island's Black Walnut Point to the western shore. Later I learned that the distance was three miles, and which possibly I could not have done. I had to swim with my son against the current once before, so I have some reason to imagine myself as a competent swimmer, but it is not an experience I would seek again. I know that to live life fully you must accept risk. A friend at work has already counseled me to be on guard on the Eastern Shore in the wake of Trump rising, presumably a national ethic that returns us blacks to the misery of Hattie Carroll, and edging in on George Armwood's public burning in Princess Anne County in 1933, the "last" lynching in Maryland. But to win, or, really, even play the game, you have to operate on the margins of the rules.

South of Wye Landing the real journey begins at a waterside estate called Wye Heights Plantation, a mildly raised escarpment at the confluence of four waterways revered for centuries as "one of the finest sites on the Eastern Shore." Wye Heights's immense brick dwelling was originally built by Douglass's Colonel Lloyd for his heir Edward the sixth, and he owned another of the old spectacular Eastern Shore mansions midway between Wye Heights and Wye House, Gross Coate. That name evokes permanence and scans to me like a stand-alone poem. Today Wye Heights Plantation is pleasantly called a "family run farm," breeding Black Welsh Mountain Sheep for gourmet meat markets. The bowling green beneath the brick estate has scores of unattended fat woolly sheep grazing in contented splendor. Fat black sheep absentmindedly waddling the sward, while, a rod in front of them, watery mists spray from an underground sprinkler. The word "plantation" is used proudly, without any irony, in the same way that Edward Lloyd and Aaron Anthony used the word "family" to describe the black people they bought and sold. But the transcendent effect reminds us of a passage the better educated of the Lloyds would have known: "His chaste house keeps its purity; his kine / Drop milky udders, and on the lush green grass / Fat kids are striving, horn to butting horn." Virgil's *Georgics*, his paean to the bucolic life, is the single strongest cultural model the English had when they created their own version of a Roman redoubt, dragging Africans in chains from Negroland's Bights to Barbados and then Baltimore. The image of the flocks returns us to 29 BCE, crucifixion time.

As I edge along, thirty feet from the shore, I am surprised to keep being caught in spider webs as thick as human hair that cling to my face. Waterborne arachnids spin out silk threads that snag the skin of the river traveler. The sky is sometimes quite brightly lit up but not a striking blue. The water is a placid gray and, from time to time, the dismal muddy brown Douglass recalled. At the Wye Island Bridge several boats pass me and I enjoy rolling in their wakes, which course like deep tubes shooting along the surface of the calm water. At first, from the distance it seems as if there is only a single throughway under the bridge, but as I approach I can see multiple passageways. My main task is to avoid the shallows.

At nearly 3:00 p.m. I understand myself as gaining the northwestern edge of the island, itself shaped like a wily amoeba, with a fatty nucleus center and flaring pseudopodia arms. I am not fully confident that I have rounded the edge of all the limbs. Repeatedly, I have anxiously anticipated my boat a distance well beyond what I have reached, and I keep misreading, distorting the features of the map to conform to contours of shore that I am seeing. Wye Island has several "lochs," hooks and promontories that call the unwary back into a forested shore lagoon. Several times I have had to curb the impulse to pilot the boat into an inlet or channel that simply could not be the river's natural bend. But the Christmas-morning hopefulness, the anticipation of fulfillment, is so hard to quell. Douglass said that he knew more theology than geography in his years here as a belligerent teen, and I too feel impelled more by what I feel than what I know.

I have been out for three hours, motoring steadily, burning gas. If I am where I hope I am, the Tohatsu has needed a full hour to reach beyond the island's northwestern boundary. A part of me had been hoping to go farther south to the Miles River, the north side of St. Michael's, where Douglass lived between 1834 and 1836, but at my rate I have to give up that folly. I find myself fighting down a kind of panic, not a mortal panic, but a panic of

humiliation, that I will have to be rescued, "buddied," and un-
manned further. I try to assess how much of the island I have to
cover before I start heading east again, and back to the landing.
If the trip requires another two hours, will I run out of gas and
either need resupply or to be towed in? Even if my fuel holds,
I might not reach Schroder's before their 6:00 p.m. closing. The
muddling adds the edge of panic to my expertise in befuddle-
ment. These inadequacies strike me as needing to be overcome.

I satisfy my qualms with a rough estimate, based upon the
Coast Guard map, which has pile locations, duck blinds, river
water depth, and topographical landmarks. I tell myself I'll be
solid as a ship with a benchmark to key the map.

Two kayakers paddle nearby the shore, and as I drift into the
shallows and my motor starts kicking, I ask them plaintively a
question that does not have a lot of yield: "This is Wye Island
to my left?" They affirm it, looking like recent retiree weekend-
ers with a lot of new gear, and I head away from them trying
not to brush waves over their cigar boats. I manage to convince
myself that I am skirting the huge knob known as Long Point. I
am falling forward into the world of mirage, where I keep hoping for every marsh and mudflat to be the opening of a branch
and a tributary to the Wye East. My motor isn't hearty enough
to allow me to head out and double back in case of an error. A
person whose strength is more meringue than muscle, I have to
triumph in a battle of mathematics: reduction, distillation, ab-
straction, and probability. I am covering the island at a rate of
about four miles an hour, which puts me in the neighborhood of
a four-hour trip, if I never meander, never once lose my bearings.
Despite the disappointment, the point of land that didn't bend,
the river that turned out to be a creek, I decide gas and time be
damned, that I can make it. Figuring I have rounded Long Point,
I turn left, back toward the mainland, at what seems to be a wide
mouth of river, and adjust my position on the map. Shaw's Bay,
a little socket west of Lloyd's Creek, should be due south. I must

now be very near the place where Douglass scrubbed himself as a child.

Self-taught literacy is Douglass's most famous experience. But reading and writing did not get him out of slavery as much as a boldness bordering on arrogance, and tempering that to join the crowd when it suited him. By the time he was sixteen years old, Douglass considered himself able to "do as much hard work as some of the older men" and the combination of power, endurance, skill, and acceptance by his fellows is what freed him from the "slaveholding priestcraft." He forged that mental victory, immediately, into a route to escape.

Douglass had connived a plan to flee the farm of a man named William Freeland, about ten miles south of where I am, by paddling a large canoe with the Harris brothers, his uncle Henry Bailey, Charles Roberts, and a conjure man called Sandy. The weekend before Easter in 1836, the team would stroke the canoe to freedom without any kind of Bay chart whatsoever:

> The plan of escape which I recommended, and to which my comrades assented, was to take a large canoe, owned by Mr. Hamilton, and, on the Saturday night previous to the Easter holidays, launch out into the Chesapeake bay, and paddle for its head,—a distance of seventy miles— with all our might.

Douglass was ambitious and committed but limited to a world within the circumference of his own eyes. He admitted that Canada was "simply a country to which the wild goose and the swan repaired at the end of winter" and that he "really did not, at that time, know that there was a state of New York, or a state of Massachusetts." But as a plain farmhand he still knew more about northern geography than he knew about a fisherman's ways on the waters of the Chesapeake Bay.

He planned to begin the journey at night, the last week in

March. Typically, the water at that time of year is in the mid-forties. Even if it could be done physically, I don't see how he would have found his way. Douglass just seems like a headstrong eighteen-year-old, risking the lives of others on account of the odd privileges he had grown accustomed to: running the streets of Fells Point, writing graffiti on fences and walls as he mastered writing, chucking rocks at the white boys from Old Town trying to cross the bridge onto the Point, blabbing incautiously on the Eastern Shore that he could read, carrying around books he had used in oratory contests with freedpeople in Baltimore, and, to top it all off, fighting grown white men. Douglass was always recklessly angling for something more, living in danger, and playing both ends against the middle. He refused to believe that the rules and laws of society applied to him.

More than ten years after Douglass's botched youthful attempt, Harriet Tubman did escape in 1849 from a farm south of Cambridge, Maryland. She cut a land route through the corn and wheat fields to hike to freedom from the Eastern Shore of Maryland to Delaware to Pennsylvania. She left her free black husband, John, at his hoe in Dorchester County. Her route seems one that could at least be grasped if it was even more likely to have encountered opposition than the one Douglass imagined. The Choptank and Chester Rivers funneled her toward towns carrying posters with her image and advertising rewards. The abundant creeks from the bay knifed her onto heavily traveled roads, easily patrolled by horsemen with bloodhounds. But Tubman, even with a price of $40,000 on her head, came back to the Eastern Shore every year, and run off people she did. What she accomplished was so outsizedly humiliating to slaveholders that their heirs continue to relegate her to obscurity wherever they can.

But running off from slavery was a bit more ordinary than what is suggested by remarkable figures like Tubman, who understood the work as an ordination, and Douglass, who reveled in his capacity as a professional "instigator." One of my favorite advertisements is for a man named Arnold who knew what purpose to put religion and absconded with himself after a camp meeting on Church Creek. This Arnold had "several acquaintances in Baltimore." Describing the person he owned as "quite tall and black . . . [with] a pleasant voice and manner, and good countenance; very white teeth," James Steele offered $100 if Arnold was captured out of the state, a considerable sum in 1827. William Matny was worth only half as much to Stewart Keene, perhaps because he had "beads in one of his ears," almost certainly a sign that he was born in what everybody called Guinea. Will Matny had had two ears pierced at one time, but "the hole in the other is filled up." Even though he was afraid of people "direct from Guinea," Douglass married a woman born near St. Michael's whose father was called "Bambara," which probably puts his origins in Mali. I took a DNA test that seemed to point to Mali as the origin of one of my own Chesapeake ancestors. If William Matny was originally from West Africa, he had conspicuously adapted American sartorial manners, fleeing in "a white and red striped cotton over Jacket, ruffle shirt, red silk cravat, and a pair of blue cassinett pantaloons," plus a fur hat. When Douglass sarcastically asked in 1852 "What to the slave is the fourth of July?" he might not have had the red-white-and-blue-bedecked Matnys of the world in mind.

A white watercraft with a burping motor races by and I follow the speedy boat with my binoculars, watching it skirt the island coastline, and then dart back and forth from the island to the mainland, touching the docks. Then, in spite of fair effort, I lose sight of the boat completely. They have hung a sharp left pretty soon after making Long Point, but my reasoning brain makes little of it, especially the fact they never return to my view. I don't presume that they have continued in the only waterway that's circuitous. I quibble that they are gone for other reasons. My eye has missed them. I have miscalculated their location and they have speedily docked. Something. Perhaps I am just another landsman out of his natural order, looking for what Lady Macbeth called, trying to suborn murder, the "sticking place."

Thinking about Douglass's first plan to win his freedom, and the failure that nearly resulted in his and his comrades being sold to Georgia's cotton fields reminds me of my youthful misadventures with my friends from the old neighborhood. We went through so much together as young men that the bonds have proved enduring. When I attend O'Donald's funeral, after addressing his mother, I fall into my place on the pew with my other homeboys from my block. We always called O'Donald "OD" (long before we knew anyone who had overdosed) and he was a formidable player on his father's championship Little League Baseball team, the Reds. The guys from Dolfield, OD and his brother Arnold, Peter and his brother David, Buttons and his brother Gerrod, Timmy and his brother Chris, Keith, Christian, Ronald, and Phillip, all played for the Forest Park trophy under Mr. Sampson. I didn't make that team, and played instead for the Yankees. I sit next to a man named Tumas who moved to our street in middle school and is also outside of the championship clique. We have another link. Before football, basketball, track, and wrestling took over our ambitions, Tumas and I played guns together, which involved elaborate costumes and surplus military gear for me. "Make-believe" and "dress-up" held little for the other boys my age in my neighborhood, but by high school we all belonged to a neighborhood social club called the Oxfords, named after our preppy, upbeat, attire. The Oxfords was my avenue to strong ties with the fellas who picked sports over dress-up, as well as several other nearby clans. The club was a key reason I am at the funeral today.

My boy Tumas is judgmental and impulsive as well as loyal, accepting, and patient. Among us descendants of migrants from Virginia and North Carolina, he is at least a half Marylander.

His father's family descends directly from Harriet Tubman, Dorchester County, and the Eastern Shore. I only met his father's side once or twice, and his mother, from North Carolina, has more of a face shaped like the famed female emancipator, out at the cheeks and in at the eyes, that ancient octagonal beauty. Tumas has small features in a dark chestnut face, like the Assange masks. In school we had called him Fat Boy even though he only weighed about 180 pounds then; now he hovers near the weight of NFL linemen. He always calls me after a name-brand cracker, proving his alert repartee about physical traits, although some of his cousins are lighter hued. I have never heard him express unique pride in his Tubman ancestor's accomplishment, in the way that the advertisements for genealogy-research services extol the pride of being related to George Washington. A few weeks after the funeral, Tumas will astound me with a cask of moonshine, which he gets from his relatives for the holidays.

The other fellas obediently trickle in: Bone, chubby philosopher in childhood and now lean and able to wear his jeans as if they are dress pants; Gerrod, who resembles a Lumbee Indian; David and Gary, who are caramel colored and becoming stout; and Rondy, just showing his gray, but towering over us all and reeking of fitness. We look all right but whether or not we could take down a tree or bring in a crop is something else. Edward Lloyd described one exceptional African man in bondage as "hearty for his age" at forty-seven. One or two of Lloyd's people a few years older and still working were yet "good" for their age. But for most enslaved black men and women on the farm, a couple of decades of slavery's toil would put you in the class of "nearly dun," "past labor," "good for nothing," or "worth but little."

As the funeral gets going, a young woman sings an inspirational hymn, and we follow that song with "Blessed Assurance." Douglass and his homeboys the Harris brothers were "remarkably buoyant," singing hymns as they crafted their plan to run. Bone and I are fraternity brothers and have sung the same blue chain-gang rhythm pledge songs and Edwardian-tuned formal hymns. But after an awkward first chorus of "Blessed Assurance," the minister slowly understands that the younger people, well represented by OD's four adult stepsons, are unfamiliar with the venerable spiritual. There is only mildly rousing declaration at "This is my story! This is my song!" The choir director has to line out the verses loudly to Fanny Crosby's hymn that is Methodist benchmark. We resemble our forebears physically, but we don't buoyantly reanimate the body of their traditions.

O'Donald is carried out by his brother and his wife's sons. Although they know each other, the group is unaccustomed to working together. The young men would leave the room when Arnold, a correctional officer in Anne Arundel County, and O'Donald, a city police major, came around. Those enforcing the law and those working the edge of the law. That's the combination that carries you home.

It all comes to mind as I pilot the skiff. I imagine my squad in Mr. Hamilton's stolen canoe trying to row to freedom, or even in my small skiff circumnavigating Wye. I wonder when the arguments about decision making would begin. We have inherited a tradition that sees a readiness to follow orders and obedience as a sign of fecklessness. But another side of what we are is a people always ready to reconsider first-order principles, always attempting to cut a side deal, always uncertain about when to put it all on the line and who with. There was another choice too, during Douglass's time. The year before Douglass tried to escape, a forty-six-year-old black man named Jacob Gibson from Bayside, Talbot County, who knew his ABCs, sailed with Captain Pascal on the schooner *Harmony* and "returned" with his wife and seven children, to Africa, to Liberia. Arthur Wilson from Queen Anne's County, Talbot County's western neighbor and the last Eastern Shore landmass before the open water of the bay, wrote with delight when he described his African return: "I like this country very well, and expect to end my days here. When a person first gets here, he is for getting back, but after remaining awhile, this feeling wears off. Tell all the coloured people that can come, come! come! come! to a free country." For a time, Maryland had an independent republic with a capital at Harper, Cape Palmas, West Africa.

I guide the boat toward the southern shore, attempting to keep Wye Island on my right. I am looking for an elbow bend to show me just when I can start heading east, but I also hope to at least glimpse Lloyd's Creek, which is the obvious extant marker of the old plantation. Douglass spent several years in the orbit of Lloyd's Long Quarter, a barn he described as "a very long, rough, low building, literally alive with slaves." There was also "a very tall, dilapidated, old brick building—the architectural dimensions of which proclaimed its erection for a different purpose," inhabited by enslaved people. Douglass slept in "old master's house," "a long, brick building, plain, but substantial" that was occupied by Aaron Anthony, Colonel Lloyd's superintendent, Anthony's daughter Lucretia, and a boarder, a sloop captain named Thomas Auld. At night, little Fred tucked himself into a ground floor pantry in the indoor kitchen, wrapping himself in a gunny sack. He felt like a cast-off person, and several historians have liked noting his identification with whites in his earliest years. Lonely Fred was in the company of Aaron Anthony so much that he believed he "really understood the old man's mutterings, attitudes and gestures, about as well as he did himself." As an adult, Douglass thought of his childhood as including moments of being indistinguishable from Aaron Anthony, the man he thought was probably his own father. Twentieth-century black writers, conceived in Maryland and writing through Douglass's rich ore, would similarly lay claim to the ideal of farm cottage America through patrimony's shards. The mixed blood was the same as the blend of people on the land.

Although he lived there with his brother and his sisters and other kin, Douglass's memory of Wye farm was principally of four people: two enslaved black adults—Aunt Katy and Uncle Doctor Isaac Copper—and two whites—Mistress Lucretia Anthony and Master Daniel Lloyd. He greatly preferred the latter. To Douglass, Aunt Katy was a tyrant who carved apart the flesh of her own children. Not much kinder to Douglass, Doctor Copper, a black man who had exhausted himself working for Lloyd, was a healer, armed with castor oil and epsom salt and who needed crutches for mobility. He taught the Lord's Prayer and loved to stroke children with hickory switches, the "all in all." Douglass figured that so much beating took place among enslaved people because of the pride and self-esteem connected to having even a minor role in the hierarchy of brutality that glued the slave system in place.

Although his recitation of the brutality of the slave regime contributed mightily to the end of slavery, Douglass never exactly warmed to the idea of being classified as an African. Unlike whites who claimed to be disgusted by African racial features, Douglass resented the protocols of deference and the cost to the flesh. Douglass said that Africans made perfect gentlemen, because "there is not to be found, among any people, a more rigid enforcement of the law of respect to elders." Isaac Copper and Katy Lloyd, who could see the favoritism from some whites Frederick received and singled him out for punishment, yet obtained his public deference. And then there were people like the runaway William Matny, Africans identified by marks on their ears. According to one descendant of people enslaved by Edward Lloyd, "a tribe of them Africans, they had a mark on one ear, some kind of mark in the flesh." This kind of tradition that ritualistically and volitionally tore the flesh and downplayed innovation and pragmatic alliance was abhorrent to Douglass, a new kind of man.

I know I always viewed as barbaric excessive deference and ritual scarrings. I liked the freedom to make my own assessments too. My schooling always competed with my tribal life and I kept choosing to pay the tuition over the intoxicating bacchanals of burning flesh.

No ruins of Anthony's cottage or Long Quarter, nor any other Wye farm building, appear visible through the brush and trees from the river. The map I am using is now simply inducing a plain quandary. I consider the possibility that I am reading it backward. I drift within a football pass of a leisurely trawling speedboat, but I don't ask for advice a second time. Who wants to be thought lacking situational awareness? I can't imagine being so wrong since the body of water has, at the very least, opened up. Still, as I meander the Back Wye farther, looking for the eastern inlet to the Front Wye, I just keep nudging along the reedy shoreline, down a narrow, forested creek with shallow depth. I want to know if it will become a tributary.

At about 4:00 p.m. I break down and open up the telephone, with its satellite position in the map application. I have an ambivalent relation to the technology, but with my orientation secured I learn incontrovertibly that I have mistaken an inlet for the river. I failed to pick out the terrain from the shape on the map or factor in the disappearing boat and adjust the course. The good news is that I have spent half an hour meandering the shoals of Lloyd's Creek, the place where Douglass bathed himself before heading off to Baltimore in trousers. I can't see Wye House on account of the summertime foliage, but I have been trawling along the banks of the story I was looking for. For Douglass the baptism and the rebirth on the Patapsco rested on crucifixion. Lloyd's Creek was the site of heinous murder, where young Bill Demby was shot dead by the overseer Orson Gore.

The black man had refused to be whipped and sought refuge in the river. Though I can't see them, the headstones of the African graveyard on the property are just behind the brush at the inlet.

In Douglass's time, both sides of the creek, Shaw's Bay, the first inlet when you break back to the east and, really, all of the land adjoining the southern Wye River was Lloyd property. Daniel Lloyd, his early playmate and five years his senior, would own the land when Douglass had last been there.

After three hours and having only made it to the rear estuary of Wye House, I realize the impossibility of a journey to St. Michael's in this scrawny motor skiff. To sail south from Long Point and down to the Miles River, a mile across, losing sight of land, seems akin to a journey across the open sea. Douglass's plan to propel a crowded hand canoe up the bay past Havre de Grace to freedom seems no more than foolhardy, the same kind of braggadocio of any of Baltimore's legendary teen badmen like Dontay Carter. It makes me think about all his actions and plans in reverse. Was he a charlatan narcissist, opportunistically stirring up a crisis with Robert and Henry Harris that could only have led to their doom? Plenty of single people ran away, but a gang run like he proposed would have been considered insurrection undoubtedly. Wherever they went, talking their own country talk and Douglass writing "Hamilton" for "Hambleton," they were sure to arouse suspicion. Mrs. Freeland called him a "long legged yellow devil," and while calling him yellow was a debatable description, she certainly wished to make it known that the neighborhood understood him as marked on account of patrimony. In the 1850s, Douglass was considering that instead of Aaron Anthony as his father, the man who petted him on the head and called him a "little Indian boy," Thomas Auld had conceived him with his mother. Douglass visited Auld at the end of his life, and he apologized to the bedridden man for depicting him as cruel in the first two autobiographies.

When Douglass did escape, it was partly owed to his beautiful wardrobe and soft words. A Baltimore freedwoman, older than he, lent the dandy wages she had been saving for seven years. Industrious Anna Murray "devoted all her energies to assist" her young beau. Anna Murray Douglass had, in the telling by her eldest daughter, who resented the white women—Lucretia Mott, Julia Griffiths, and Ottilie Assing—her father brought around, "enabled with others to make my father's life easier." Some men wouldn't have taken the nest egg from their fiancées, no matter the benefit.

Douglass always claimed that the original escape plot was betrayed by Sandy, the "genuine African" who "had inherited some of the so called magical powers, said to be possessed by African and eastern nations." Sandy Jenkins was noteworthy to Douglass because he was a herbalist who practiced a form of Obeah. Because Sandy declined to go with them after having been involved in the initial planning, he seemed the obvious traitor. In the nineteenth century, Sandy was a common given name for black males who may have simply been long associated with the daily task of scrubbing brick floors with sand. But even while being called Sandy hinted at the ordinary birth of men like Douglass's comrade or the father of my father's grandfather, the name also possessed a Moses-like quality. It was sandy at the river's edge. The Sandys of the world were associated with crossing the water. If Sandy did betray the band, his reasons might have been connected to Douglass's Protestant Christianity, his reading the Bible aloud and encouraging others to read this book of the slave owners, or his obvious English ancestry. Did Sandy consider the big, unmarked, bronze-colored boy dangerous, unreliable, or a fake? Douglass had an enhanced sense of himself. For a while, he reckoned he was "loved by the colored people" because he was "persecuted" by the whites. Local blacks living free around Pot-pie Neck respected the boy's literacy and admired the panic he stirred in the whites. Douglass's moods and aspirations for freedom must have been keenly scrutinized after his legendary fight with Edward Covey and the cyclical passion to escape bondage must have been more transparent to the professional slaveholding class of St. Michael's than Douglass could have imagined. But what if his freedom dream was spoiled by his own vanity?

After the Civil War, Douglass was roundly criticized by other blacks for his office with the Freedman's Bank, his compromise with the withdrawal of troops from the South, his public encouragement of blacks to remain in the South. But his heart wasn't in doubt: he had escaped from slavery, harbored fugitives and gotten them on to Canada, and then written the most effective rhetoric in the service of abolition. Was it all a part of his stature? How much distance was he able to place between himself and Colonel Lloyd and Wye House? Did he wind up loving the immensity of the tradition that Wye House represented? How did he reconcile his words to Auld—"both of us . . . victims of a system"—and yet belong to the system so heartily?

Douglass was "greatly affected" and "deeply moved" when he returned to Wye House on June 12, 1881. Fearing to have been thought to have forgotten the brutality of slavery, he sought pardon "for speaking with much complacency of this incident." But more than the opportunity for social equality with the heirs of the plantation aristocracy of Maryland, his afternoon on the veranda, in the dining room, and at the cemetery was one where Douglass "agreeably" marveled "to find that time had dealt so gently" with the ancient estate. It was a lesson in the durability of structures and the evanescence of people. Time flowed rapidly ahead and stood completely still. It was the aura of the national American story winning out against the most ancient labor model. It was his revenue cutter steaming from Baltimore to Wye Creek in the same time it took me to circumnavigate Wye River. It was a kaleidoscope view of a future showing the for-profit Chinese education company purchasing my grandmother's Normal and Industrial School in Lawrenceville. "In all its appointments," he recalled, Wye House "was so little changed from what it was when I left." Sixty years had preserved the buildings and grounds as before. "Very little was missing except the little squads of black children . . . and the great number of slaves in its fields." They were all gone, like machines wheeled out of a garden.

When he had lived in Baltimore as Frederick Bailey, it was possible to reach Fish Street, the locale of the activist, independent Bethel Church, by crossing through Old Town. Off Aisquith Street, between Fayette to the south and Gay Street to the north, which both had bridges over the Jones Falls, was Douglass Street. While the Scottish name was known to him there, Frederick Douglass swapped his surname of Bailey for Johnson after he escaped in 1838, so that his pursuers would be confused. In mid-September of 1838, Nathan Johnson of New Bedford, Massachusetts, welcomed Frederick and his wife, Anna, into his home. Douglass had used the surname Johnson, even on his New York marriage certificate, but now believed all of the escaped Marylanders in Massachusetts had overworked the name. Nathan Johnson was reading Walter Scott's poem *The Lady of the Lake*, and dubbed Frederick Bailey with the name of a feuding Scottish earl, Douglas. In the poem, the king, James Fitz-James, who sometimes masquerades in Lincoln green as a knight, reconciles with the chieftain. King James redeems Douglas, but the sovereign calls himself "Lord of a barren heritage."

Since I have broken the spell and used the telephone I call the dock to let them know where I am. The pilot gives a pebbly chortle when I tell him that I am motoring rather slowly back. He knows my four-stroke speed perfectly. About five-sixths of the way, as the Back Wye broadens and there is less navigational misery, I again overtake the two kayakers. They had given themselves the same circumnavigation mission, but taken a surer course. I have no problem getting around the rest of the island.

When I make the dock, I see three men in shorts and shirt sleeves, their skin translucently white, drinking beer under the overhanging corrugated tin roof. I know that if I took another kind of DNA test these are the English-descended people I would share some lineage with. The meager fact of my line helps me to understand Sally Hemings, Elizabeth Keckley, and Harriet Jacobs succumbing to the gentry a little better. The dockers seem of a piece with the unaristocratic world of St. Michael's Douglass had recalled from the 1830s: "dull, slovenly, enterprise-forsaken," where the wood dwellings had "never enjoyed the artificial adornment of paint, and time and storms had worn off the bright color of the wood, leaving them almost as black as buildings charred by a conflagration."

I ease off the throttle and use the oar to bring the craft in and tie on to a cleat on the dock. I drop anchor easily enough, but am confounded by the motor once more. I see no switch on the Tohatsu to end its sputtering life. The motor churns relentlessly while I look at the cover and choke, in a duplication of the searching panic five hours earlier when the journey began. A wee black trunion next to the red button choke gets my best attention; I pull it forward and the churning dies. I plan on telling the idlers about the foibles of the journey, the sort of self-deprecating narrative most people enjoy. Just as I pull up I hear one of them spout "That black guy!" which, while a decided improvement over "nigger," makes me self-conscious of the old cut. I decide to leave "ahoy" alone.

I drive thirteen miles to Easton for dinner, but my path takes me off the main roads and through Unionville. Douglass journeyed to Easton from St. Michael's once, his wrists roped and the lead tied to the pommel of saddled horse. I mistake the scattered houses for those of rural whites in love with guns and religion until I see the sign for St. Stephens AME Church. Across the Miles River and into town, a helpful passerby sees me gazing at a large sightseer's map and presumptively makes some recommendations. His solicitousness strikes me as the same courtesy from the Old Wye church, equally warm and suspicious, and the man warns me away from the high post French restaurant in town, "Unless that backpack of yours is full of money!" The yeoman whites have been, friendly is not the word I want— solicitous isn't it either. They have been ubiquitous. In Easton, I see black people driving by in flatbed trucks, but everyone on the river and the walkers along the historic brick paths are absolutely white. During slavery time, at night or on weekends, the entire Wye must have been exploding with Africans casting nets and dropping lines and dredging with baskets, lighting fires and eating unsupervised, singing songs and inquiring loudly, "Oo dem got cwaby?" But not anymore.

The passerby turns out to be the owner of a tavern, where I dine al fresco. From a harried young woman, straddling a position between waitress and assistant manager, I order the rockfish on couscous with tomato. The cloverleaf rolls are hot from the oven and so delicious that I request a double order of white bread. The fish comes out quickly and I eat a native dish with an African twist. The owner returns and tells me about his hero Jeremiah Banning, a local pirate who gained a fortune and then freed his enslaved people, creating a place in Easton called "The Hill." He believes it may be the oldest community of freed blacks living in the United States.

After dinner, I walk to the courthouse, unprepared for the encounter with the enormous new Douglass bronze, heroically in front of the door behind which he had once been imprisoned for a week, accused of plotting escape. Douglass believed he was then returned to Baltimore by Captain Auld because the local white men were threatening to shoot him on sight. I gazed and reflected, and then I noticed the division. Douglass strode and pointed on the right. And balanced on the left was another bronze hercules, a full and powerful rejoinder to the "heroic slave." "The Talbot Boys" monument showed young men racing

over the battlefield, rifles in hand, for the Confederacy. One reason the monument agonizes is because probably more Talbot
County men served in the Union ranks, but he who pays the
piper calls the tune.

I wander over to Goldsborough and then to Washington Street,
window shopping at the downtown boutiques housed in the
Federal-style two-bay brick rowhouses with middle dormer windows. An antique store has a light on and, pleased, I walk in,
startling the owner who was getting ready to close. In her mind,
she had probably finished the day. I briefly tour the aisles, and
we talk. I learn she is from Illinois and has been operating since
my days in the Cub Scouts, my earliest memory of the Eastern
Shore. She tells me my visit is the nicest thing that has happened
to her that day. After leaving I amble down the street, admiring
scrollwork and cornices and masonry bond patterns, until am
slightly startled to hear someone intoning my surname, among
the most African English in the country's history. It is the shop
proprietor and she presents me with a small piece of china, delft,
the ballast of many of the nineteenth-century boats, cast off and
used by the enslaved during meals. We had had a conversation
about the crockery a few minutes earlier in the shop. We em-
brace. I follow that joy with a coffee at the Tidewater Inn, and
wonder if it is just me or if the waitress is deliberately ignoring me? It just goes on, the ebb and flood, the "fiery curse, his
tainted frame devoured" Georgic tide washing over Douglass's
"grand possibilities of a glorious future."

Then said the judge, "Of what family or race are you?"—"What does it concern you," answered Alban, "of what stock I am? If you desire to hear the truth of my religion, be it known to you, that I am now a Christian, and bound by Christian duties."—"I ask your name," said the judge; "tell me it immediately."—"I am called Alban by my parents," replied he; "and I worship ever and adore the true and living God, who created all things."
    —Venerable Bede, *Bede's Ecclesiastical History of England* (731)

Then he gave him a parchment roll, and there was written within, "Flee from the wrath to come."
    —John Bunyan, *The Pilgrim's Progress* (1678)

The natives of the countries bordering on the Gambia . . . the body of the people, both free and enslaved, persevere in maintaining the blind but harmless superstition of their ancestors.
    —Mungo Park, *Travels in the Interior of Africa* (1799)

Epiphany: Sunday Boys

My toft and croft in Homeland has obliged me to drive other roads to church. Now my Sunday morning duty to "defend the faith of England, Scotland, Ireland and France," as the Maryland property ledgers from the seventeenth century used to remind the pilgrim, takes me down the Jones Falls Expressway to exit at Mount Royal and North Avenue. The western skyline of the intersection is dominated by the Maryland Institute College of Art dormitories. The field where we had run riot so many years ago hosts a four-story MICA housing complex. Recess at my old elementary–middle school has become a tepid, corralled affair. The traffic pattern is restrained too. The city has installed a bike lane on North Avenue traveling west for the people who do not live here quite yet but it wishes to attract.

If we catch a crowded light and a boy comes to the window with a squeegee in his hand, I decline the windshield wash and press dollars and coins into his palm. There is a debate over whether or not the guys are entrepreneurs or villains, but I admire the gritty boys hustling and working together inside their age-group. They are at least momentarily declining the vigorous exploitation of the drug corners. My dad's voice comes back to me about the intrinsic value of venture work that he called "hustling." Critics of the squeegee boys, a venerable occupation since the 1980s, have long remained hypocritically silent as truant children in desperate need of minimal education relay narcotics and dodge maniacs and bullets. Their loud objections come when poor boys and girls make themselves obstreperous in public trying to improve their condition by legal means. Baltimoreans of today rarely recall that George Herman Ruth was such a boy. Nor do we wish to face the reality that our city can easily contain the living conditions of the first, second, and third worlds, or the seemingly incompatible epochs of feudalism and capitalism, in a single space. I tuck change and small bills into the compartments of the car for them, and go out of my way to palaver encouragingly. I can be as fearful of strangers as the next person. But with just a little verbal courtesy, even when my purse is empty, the Sunday boys strike me as somber and reflective, adept at some Bible verse, eager to share a prayer.

Between the assassination of Martin Luther King Jr. and President Obama's final days in office, I would ride to St. James down either Liberty or Park Heights onto Reisterstown Road to Pennsylvania Avenue and merge onto Fremont and then Arlington. Sunday church was, by the time of my teenage years and my schooling on the outskirts of the city, a quixotic task. My family belonged to a denomination that had outlived its heyday. Cerebral and well connected perhaps, the stiff Episcopal Church and its ornate ritual was unsatisfactory to most of the black people we knew. The rare converts were attracted to the church as a place of refuge. As the AMEs and Baptists built stadium sanctuaries for their congregations in the suburbs, we were still driving downtown past the winos and junkies on the corners. Instead of tethering our future to the county, we drove back downtown through mounting black desolation. I chafed at mandatory attendance and the interminable wait at the post-service reception or my parents' guild meetings before returning home. My father compelled me to join him when we put up the annual Christmas decorations and, by the time I could imagine the pleasure of friends at the shopping mall pizzeria, I loathed the long foodless Christmas Eve under his discretion. One Sunday, in teenage frustration at having been forced into the pew alongside my ever-more-devout parents, and whose view on the neighborhood, shaped by their childhood in the 1940s, wildly contrasted with my own, I stalked out at the moment the service ended. Walking past the bars and the corners, the Foxes Den nightclub and sundry abandoned buildings, and feeling conspicuous in church clothes, I was surprised that once I had gotten as far as Mondawmin, my footwork was nearly done. Home wasn't far away.

It wouldn't have made any difference to me then that the original name of the church included the word "African" in the title. St. James African Protestant Episcopal Church. We had been founded in 1824 by a New Yorker trained in Philadelphia named William Levington. To be ordained, the black priest had to have learned a good deal more Latin than David Perine. While such skills would have made him oracular to a learned few, they were no guarantors of popular appeal. "The colored congregation of this city are or stood Accused of [being] indisposed to him, but support him for his Piety & good conduct," thought the bishop of Pennsylvania, before his black acolyte received approval from Maryland bishop James Kemp to preach in Baltimore. Levington obtained, shortly after his arrival, gift deed from James Bosley and five thousand bricks from George Warner to build a church at Saratoga and North Street. Just up the road from city hall, the lot was a couple of hundred feet down the hill from the grantor, Old Saint Paul's. As a young member of the St. Paul's vestry, David Perine had a say in sanctioning this unusual new quantity, a trained African American priest.

Even though he was heading into the teeth of the slave regime and was already considered by Philadelphia whites "unfortunate in Point of utterances" (whether he was loose in doctrine, overfond of black idiom, or an open abolitionist is not known), Levington impressed the white slaveholders of St. Paul's. Plenty of them were latching on to the dream of emigration to Cape Palmas, West Africa, south of Monrovia, for the free blacks who were flocking to Baltimore. Levington even brooked opposition from his congregation to permit enslaved black people to join and to vote at St. James. In short order, the new priest traveled to Boston and raised more than $500 for this spectacular venture, the first black-run congregation of any major denomination below the Mason-Dixon line. He speedily opened a free school out of the church, teaching about sixty primary school pupils. By 1829, when Edgar Allan Poe and Frederick Bailey were nearly neighbors in Fells Point, Levington was in his prime, leading a black church a block downhill from where Perine worshipped. Levington would die after a short and painful illness in 1836, probably a victim of the recurring cholera epidemic, but, even though the sanctuary he built brick by brick was condemned in 1889, the congregation lived on.

The Episcopal Church, established after the War of Independence to shear it fully from the Church of England, is the most hierarchical and economically conservative of American Christian denominations. Founded on the right of divorce, it differs from Catholicism by dispensing with private confession and having no special place for the intercessional mother of the Savior. Like all Protestant denominations, it will offer communion—the host—to anyone at all. To reach paradise, the church doctrine proclaims it is unnecessary to do good works, receive signs of your destiny, read the Bible, or choose baptism as a conscious act—all you have to do is accept God's grace. We use scripture, tradition, and reason to boost the individual climb up the rungs of salvation's ladder. The perfection of the soul is a private affair. As the English queen Elizabeth, the founder of the Church of England, reputedly said, "I would not open windows to men's souls." While only rarely performed in Latin, the service prides itself on a crisp, uniform liturgy, with much nodding, bowing, cross making, genuflecting, and kneeling. The priests can have fairly elaborate robes and shawls and head coverings for feast days, but they wear black with white collars during typical business hours. While not always faithfully observed, the Episcopal service privileges quiet reflection and literacy. There are also creeds, prayers, and psalms read aloud, sometimes in unison. Bereft of opportunities for bodily movement or much vocal expression beyond English hymns and sixteenth-century chants, in the 1970s and 1980s, we were a rare home for a black congregation. We are even less so today.

A couple of times a year I load up my station wagon and take my teenager to clean the street outside of the church. Perhaps, as a permanent resident of Homeland, I notice the litter more now? Maybe I don't want my son to make an unthinking association between white Americans and clean prosperous neighborhoods and black Americans and dirty streets and decaying abandoned buildings? I am not sure that what I am feeling could be called survivor's guilt, because Sandtown is not where I consider myself as being from, any more than I would say I was from Ashburton, which I lived across the street from growing up. Nor would I allow that my current assignment is so secure that I have achieved the lofty plateau of a survivor. More and more I am convinced that in a few years I will be selling my house to pay for college for my children. Part of me is inclined to believe that I work on the street mainly because I have the right equipment for the job.

When I lived on Pimlico Road in Park Heights in the late 1990s, a neighborhood portrayed in the news as undesirable, I wrote a couple of editorials decrying the deadly violence against children, the failure to support schools, green spaces, and adequate recreation. It was the whole righteous liberal shebang, the same mantra of Patrisse Cullors and #BlackLivesMatter today. One Labor Day the city declared it would clean up, and brought T-shirts and bunting and a whole lot of talk about what might be done. To the credit of the public sanitation department, they donated brooms and shovels to the residents, and I took a giant push broom and a flat edge shovel to war against a generation's worth of alley garbage and overgrowth that bred strong rodent infestation. I have seen rats the size of cats climb a chain link fence and jump into garbage. I have walked alongside them digging their tunnels the circumference of paint cans and the length of the yard, warrens that would be the envy of soldiers engineering combat trenches. The broom and shovel were the same as I remembered from my own childhood, when men used to walk city streets with a wheeled metal can, edifying the city one push of the broom at a time.

Besides helping to remedy the rodents' nests, I enjoyed the day of shared purpose that brought the neighbors together: Mac, the retired postman; Harvey Sr., a dutiful mechanic whose adult son was a flashless operator; and Sheila, a mother who lived with her parents. I was commuting three times a week to Washington for work and had mainly my memories to guide my sense of things beyond my own painting and hammering to make the house livable. What I mainly recalled from childhood left me feeling guarded. I had taken a few lumps from the Sumter Avenue toughs. I had to prove myself against a big boy at the church camp run by a neighbor at the end of our block, the sort of camp where the counselors got high on the park trips and shared street-corner jokes. I was told the one where the contest hero responds to the provocation, which involved a "grass" and "ass" rhyme, and triumphs at the end of the epic tale by telling his ofay foe, "I'm coming through the walls, beating my balls, do you hear me?"

The first day as an adult on Pimlico, I was cutting the wheat field of grass when a tall disheveled girl recovering from a spree wandered down the alley trying to scrounge up money with a come-on, which would involve me watching her undress. I gave her all the money in my pocket and wished her well. But once I had tidied up my place, even though the back gate had been stolen decades earlier, few wild entreaties came my way. "To make us love our country," thought Edmund Burke in his ungenerous reflections on the French Revolution, "our country ought to be lovely." What probably gave me the most joy from my own swept front was the way it seemed to inspire the neighbors. I felt strongly enough about the appearance of the place that I attempted a massive repair of the front porch, which involved removing the rotted header and roof flooring and tar. I often performed the work late into the night. One amenable yeoman, who did a good job of managing his addiction and disdained the four-and-one rule for balancing a ladder, helped out for a few dollars. But once one person gave their home some regular deliberate effort, more people went beyond just washing their cars and started to pick up the trash, pull the weeds, and keep the grass clipped. This led me to a friendship with a beautiful and spiritual young woman named Angel. I brag to my son about my contribution to porch architecture in northwest Baltimore, taking credit for introducing an additional third post to support the header beam.

What it takes to rake and bag the litter, trim and edge the grass, and sweep the street at St. James is not backbreaking, but it goes beyond custodial work. There are hazards, like bloody syringes, feces, odd pieces of rusted, sharp-edged metal, and broken glass. With some small efforts I am able to convince a group of young brothers from the university to clean and weed the Arlington Avenue memorial garden to slain children. Usually the job takes about two hours, if we haven't let it go too far.

I am not the only one who loves the idea of service imperialism. A young black woman with an Eastern European surname recently launched a political campaign by exploiting the street mess in Sandtown. Reddish-brown complexioned and flaunting Indian woven hair, she becomes a favorite of the president and the zealots backing him, numbers of whom drive into the city and collect trash for a few weekends.

But unlike the trash can missionaries, I have a flair for sweeping because black working men, starting with my adoration of the garbage men on the back of the truck, have always fascinated me. The labors also connect me to my parents' fathers, Pops and Grandpa Jackson, slavery, and the grounds crew at Loyola High School. I never saw Pops at his mop on Baltimore Street, but I saw others do it whose manner reminded me of him. At my elementary school stoop-shouldered, humble Mr. Robbie, head and face completely shaved and togged in worn gray coveralls, never-endingly mopped the floors. At the Giant supermarket on Menlo Drive, home of that marvelous pickle barrel, a tall Hershey Bar–colored, toothbrush mustachioed man with a cigar clenched between his teeth drove the mop like a horse. When I lived in Oakland, I had observed a homeless man obsessively servicing the litter on Lakeshore Avenue, guiding bottle caps, gum, and cigarette butts into the trash can, even while he rallied to help move the black market commerce along the bus routes in innocuous-looking bags with his comrades. I ached to join him. Their single-minded purpose and duty seeped into my pores.

Ten years later I worked as a journeyman to a carpenter at my house, aiding with the measuring, carting, framing, and toe-nailing. The long process of home-breaking—divorce—was underway and I would stretch from the pry bar removing a window frame to change Mitchell's diaper. The best skill I could offer was to keep the work space clear, sweep up the sawdust, and stack the waste neatly for reuse. It was only busywork, and in those circumstances all that I could undertake on my own initiative, but he commended me for it. When my ex-wife withdrew my youngest son from a neighborhood school for a charter school across Moreland Avenue in Atlanta, I borrowed the safety cones from the golf-cart-riding security patrol and took the boys with me to hack down the feral wilderness between East Lake Terrace and the crosswalk at Bible Way Temple of God. I just wanted my children to have a clear path walking to school. I remain a person less interested in how than in what— outcome over process. So, I am always driven to clean as much of my own street as I can, whether it's the neighbors' side or not doesn't make that much difference. Refuse blows in a whirlwind and I like a clean street. Like the tax paid to the Sunday boys, the work is a general contribution to the commons, a publicly shared space where we all have the option to practice the good in spite of or indifferent to claims of property rights. Although we are often enough told that our democracy doesn't work because it has narrowed the electorate and silenced certain voices, I think it works better with fewer voices and more brooms and dustpans to tidy up the commons.

The balance between what is owed and what is shared is as vexed as the concept of private property itself. Conceiving of the ordinary natural right to own land was not just a feat of English political theorist John Locke but also of the original theologian St. Augustine. The African bishop thought Adam and Eve's expulsion from Eden transferred divine right to human right, through the agency of an aristocratic earthly power. While it may be that "the same earth supports alike the poor and rich," he observed, "God has distributed to mankind these very human rights through the emperors and kings of this world." "Take away rights created by emperors," Augustine continued, "and then who will dare say, That estate is mine, or that slave is mine, or this house is mine?" A prelapsarian imperative lurks on the outskirts of the sentence's sheltered conditional "if." Take away the emperor's right. If we take away right, there was a time when the house belonged to us all.

On any given city block, residents will display differing degrees of conscience about property upkeep. Sometimes renters see themselves moving on to greener pastures, and believe that any committed work only slows that leap. Others certainly have the spoiled idea that any work that goes toward the commons is personally unfair. But the well-to-do in my neighborhood can also be quite selfish. In controlled experiments, the upper middle class and wealthy have proved to be more prone to lying and cheating than other Americans; they are the prime inheritors of a mentality that authorizes strong greed. To boot, in Homeland we benefit from privately maintained commons. Our ponds, dug in 1843, and green spaces are maintained by annual homeowners' dues that bring in about $450,000. Excepting a small field where our neighborhood sign stands, these perks are mainly aesthetic. Our real recreation is conducted on privately held common spaces, enclaves informally borrowed by the more-or-less elite public, like the public lands on either side of the Stony Run stream that meanders from Northern Parkway down past the Homewood campus. At my cross street at Saint Dunstans the wooded trail is accessible only through the private athletic fields of the Friends and Gilman Schools. The combined prep school lands constitute a minor Olympic village. My son and I go there to play baseball, basketball, tennis, track, and football. Our baseball game involves my hitting the ball to him, at a distance of maybe seventy-five yards, requiring pretty much a field to ourselves. Once or twice a security guard will shoo us off of a field that is being reseeded, or politely refuse us use during a graduation ceremony. My behavior to everyone we encounter is as polite as it is presumptive of access to the private ground.

One Sunday in February during Nathaniel's fourth year in

Baltimore, my mother telephones at 8:00 a.m. to remind me that the bishop of Maryland was coming to St. James and there would only be a single service at 9:30 a.m. I had been asleep for four or five hours, having folded my rest around a weekend of my son's events that concluded with a series of dances. Studying at the same high school that I attended thirty-five years earlier, he is connected to the students and the extracurricular life in a way that I had half desired but had not imagined possible at what was the early morning of racial integration for my family. My son lives in the same neighborhood as white classmates he has known since middle school, and is invited and sometimes even chauffeured from a pre-party to the dance, and then even to an after-party. And where in my experience, tobacco, beer, and wine were always in a trunk or a pack, the younger breed seems in a loose confederation with every single "Mothers against" group. The elaborateness of these events, which sometimes conclude at hotel ballrooms with disc jockeys and involve games with light wands and strobe lights and where the tables groan from the weight of the sodas and chewing gum, and the inconsequentiality he associates with formally accompanying young women to the dances who are not African American, strike me as powerful inducements to belonging to the school culture. My experience at his age was a world apart. I remember standing in the doorway in a school sweatshirt that I had crookedly sewn my felt junior varsity letter to, waiting for a neighbor to arrive to take me back to school for an awards banquet. My parents were busy at work, school was far away, and no boys from my neighborhood were enrolled there. I scanned the approaching cars for two hours, but she never appeared.

Mom and I have an ancient dance of distortion on the telephone, a disorienting technology to us both. She claims she can't answer the iPhone or send a text message, and I think she just doesn't want to. I field the same indignation or suspicion from my own children and younger colleagues, dismayed by my reluctance to clamber aboard the digital train. I'm not on Instagram, Twitter, or Facebook, which struck me from the outset as self-implemented surveillance tools for Big Brother. But even if my mother and I communicated only by letter there would be this difficulty; she would consign her best energy to the preamble. When she talks I impatiently push her on to the main point. When I tell a story she mishears me and so my tactic is to sternly deliver the vital information all at once, in an importunate staccato flurry. Then I am chagrined to hear how grumpy it sounds. I try to atone during our miscues on the phone, and let her know that I understand as soon as I answer that it is she and of course I want to hear her news. I want to be with her, but I am uncomfortable to rely once again upon her exclusively. I resent the profundity of our tie. I hear her small voice in my own cough and style of expectoration.

I get off the phone with my mother before promising to join her at the service. I had been considering strolling to Perine's 1856 offering to the neighborhood. The tie resonates powerfully today since the church serves as the technical home of the neighborhood association that collects our annual dues and supervises the appearance of our houses. If we walk to church, usually we make the Redeemer 10:00 a.m. service, the only church in the diocese allowed to meet at that hour. The later mass is in the new church, which was built in the 1960s, and resembles a kind of sprawling one-story rancher-sanctuary, concealing an interior that is both vast and remarkable and culminates with a gigantic abstractionist motif stained glass apse. Redeemer's service is always efficient and crisp, the sermon sentimentally appealing and full of literary allusions, the music professional caliber. The resonant sound of the organ and choir, and brass on holidays, suggests to me that the newer church devoted most of its design budget to world-class acoustics.

An early service is held at 8:00 a.m. and lasts fifty minutes. My son is always in favor of the abbreviated prayers and on one occasion we'd gone to gratify my ulterior motive: 8:00 a.m. mass is held in the original church, which duplicates the box seating from Wye Church on the Eastern Shore. Barely fifty years separate Perine's plea to his children "that 'Homeland' may be retained in my family and not pass out of it . . . even at the sacrifice of pecuniary interest," and the sale of his estate and the destruction of his property. A few weeks before Mom's call to me about the bishop, I had desired to see the one remaining building connected to the Perine bequest up close.

Most Sundays our nerves are frayed by the level of coercion it takes me to produce the result of a clothed teen in the church pew before the Gospel has been read. But on that Sunday, we actually walked over in good humor, treading over small residential streets instead of the alley. Our mood is good and I have time to notice that some stone cottages are actually built quite modestly without a center window over the porch. Standing at the large Methodist church we see on the other side of the parkway the huge political banners to joust for the congressional seat left empty by the death of a popular local congressman. When he began hearings that would lead to articles of impeachment, Congressman Elijah Cummings had been condemned by the president as presiding over a rat-infested war-torn barrio. The congressman's Seventh District is surgically drawn to exclude Homeland and the northern, affluent sections of the city from the majority-black parts of Baltimore, like the neighborhood where I grew up and the one that includes St. James. The Democratic Party, which controls seven of the eight congressional seats, has used the gerrymandering to empower itself but also to limit black Marylanders to choosing two representatives, one in Prince George's County, and the other in Baltimore, the areas with the densest concentrations of black people. But by deliberately carving out the upper middle class and zones of suburban business redevelopment, and giving me the same congressperson as someone living in Annapolis, thirty miles away and on the

Chesapeake Bay, almost in another land entirely, they also succeed in alienating nearby citizens from each other. The huge blue Mfumè sign at the intersection of Charles Street and Northern Parkway is aimed at the black commuter traffic driving through the needle of Homeland affluence.

Old Redeemer, joined to the new structure by a system of breezeways and a covered plaza that serves as an auditorium, has a modest Gothic exterior, a stone building with a forty-foot spire and can't be sixty feet wide—four rods—at the transept. It was conceived as a country church, catering to a few families like the Perines, the Alders, the Wilsons, the Secords, and the Prices. The interior bespeaks English Romanesque simplicity. Most of the stained glass windows follow unadorned geometric repetitions; one features a Gabriel-like figure stretching a hand skyward. The stained glass clerestory behind the altar reveals a crucified Saxon Christ and the robbers on the hill with three Roman soldiers below. Redeemer seems made of fieldstone, dark-colored occasional granite, probably quarried from the dell two furlongs away.

Old Redeemer's oaken doors open directly into the nave of the church; the sinner is frankly exposed. My son immediately ducks for the grace of seated anonymity and I walk past him and up to the middle rank and steer into one of the numbered pews, about no. 17. Eventually he comes up beside me, his hair still damp from the shower, and he's sniffling from his illness of last week. I try to stop thinking him willfully negligent to walk outside with wet hair in winter. I spoke to him about it on the way over, but didn't want the remonstration to overtake the togetherness of the morning and our work outdoors the day before. On the northwestern edge of the wing is the applewood carved plaque to David Maulden Perine and Mary Glen for donating the land and the parsonage. The plaque shows more chisel marks than the applewood chairs at the Maryland Historical Society.

The minister conducts the entire service in Rite I of the

Anglican Church, which is the older "ye and thee" version of the sacrament first codified in the Book of Common Prayer of 1549. His sermon explores John and James's leap of faith when they decide to follow Jesus. I just keep thinking to myself that the disciples were fleeing bad marriages and they abandoned their wives and children to follow some bright, homeless guy they met on the beach. I always pick up an interesting point from the Redeemer liturgy, and over the years I note a difference in tenor between sermons there and at St. James. At my home church, often enough, I shake my head and scribble myself notes, sometimes despairing at the loud and long doomsday sermons, the preoccupation with sin and obedience. It takes about three years to break my back, and I come to admire the stentorian marathons, which by then include forceful eruptions against the chatter during the service from the pews. Redeemer, on the other hand, is a uniformly quiet congregation, excepting its children.

During the Peace nearly the whole Redeemer church shakes hands with polite reserve, as warmly as the tradition allows. I wonder which of them I would entrust with my medical or financial well-being, the weighty, decisive moments where I have encountered this ilk before. No women in the church appear under sixty years old. But the sharpest contrast between 8:00 a.m. Redeemer and 11:00 a.m. St James is gender; the early goers are skewed in favor of men, six out of every ten. When I kneel at the communion rail I note from the inscription carved on the stipe of the footpace that the entire altar has been dedicated to Rebecca Perine, David's daughter who died in 1879.

But on the Sunday of the early call about the single service, rousing the boy and making the coffee happens easily, so I decide to join my mother downtown. I debate the shower and then simply don the uniform that I sometimes leave on the back of a chair, a sweater with the shirt inside it, a leftover from the day before. The outfit is a dignified coveralls that greatly simplifies the hectic race to church before the reading of the Gospel, an

ancient ritual prerequisite to receive communion. I need help
to minimize the interferences. A quarter of the time I am disinclined to stop reading the paper and watching the news. The
press shows seem invaluable in the Trump era, though the predictable "copy" that he provides them has made the producers,
writers, and newscasters lazy. Sometimes I just refuse to miss
the English Premier League, which is sort of like religion for
me. The skill and speed of the players aside, I get to see West
African names like Touré, Diallo, Sissoko, Kamara, Coulibaly,
Soro, Keita, and Koné put to West African faces. One player
from Brazil looks like a twin of my younger self. The advantage this day is that the newspaper has arrived on time, so I can
drink the coffee and "do my mornings," while I read the paper.

My boy is up and ready to leave. I know he has reason to be
even less keen for the service than I was at his age. In my high
school class there were a dozen regulars. Younger children were
taught in the basement of the church, but the upper grades were
instructed in a rowhouse on Lafayette Avenue. Today, St. James
has a parish center with a reception room and classrooms, but
only one single regular attendee with infant children; my son is
often the only person in Sunday school in his grade. Typically,
he accompanies me into the main church for the entire service.

My classmates from Sunday school were a regular part of my
social life, invited to birthdays and graduations. The boys were
Daryl, a child of prodigious memory and speaking ability; Joel,
heavyset and wearing old-man's clothes even then; and Benjy, a
thin, slightly mischievous boy with close hair. And while I can
still see some of them in those rabbit fur coats, the girls were
far more mysterious and by the time I had begun to be curious about them, they were nearly women. Tara, Charlotta, Lisa,
Michelle, Yolanda, Gail, Kelly, Amy, and Sonji were all in my
class. I became notable in my neighborhood because I invited
them to attend my middle school graduation party. Cereta and
Jennifer, Harry and Eddie were a year ahead, while Carmen,

Nicole, Julie, Cecilia, and Raymond were a year behind. My parents taught the high school class, a circumstance that made me seem, somewhat, like a priest in training. I resisted the role as well as I could, refusing membership in the acolytes who served on the altar. At the time, male and female adults subjected small acolytes to what we children called "touchy-feely." I thought the casual groping was un-American. Tara and Charlotta, enrolled in a historic Catholic girls' school down the street from Hopkins, dated my homeboys David and Arnold. Kelly, Amy, and Michelle all went to the same high school as my older sister, and they transformed from girls to women and had steady boyfriends. I enjoyed the company of Sonji, talkative with a big personality, but somewhere between high school and her going on to Howard, she just disappeared.

Although we get the car on the road after 9:20 a.m., we make most of our lights with only mild tailgating, and, after I cut the red light at North Avenue, I am angling onto Gold Street and then coasting the speed bumps on Division Street in fine time. I drive creatively, in the way that I would dance, and forever take the road less traveled, the alley and the ditched gulley, over the surface road with its stoplight. Motion is my principle because I mastered the automobile in trials of mounting peril. I took my driver's test on a condemned 1971 Beetle, and the state trooper failed me when the shock spring tore through the rusted cargo compartment housing. An inoperable door handle on the American Motor Company Hornet once saved me from a street beating. I achieved race car speeds on the tight streets off Walbrook Junction to flee drug dealers who smashed the windshield of the car. Sleep deprivation begat a headlong collision on Dukeland. I kept the wheel steadier than I did my bladder when assaulted by undercover police detectives. I turned the then-rare wheelchair access of a sidewalk into a passing lane for a service van, in the rain. Wrapping the front end of my best friend's Dodge Colt around a chain. Spinning a two-wheel drive truck in the snow into the rail. Rear-ending a sedan jumping in front to turn. Carjacked by the brigands in the Old West End. Swerving on the highway to foil the sheet of airborne metal slicing toward the windshield.

But an even greater influence were the steady emendations made to the laws by drivers in my part of town. Red stoplights can be considered stop signs or even green lights under certain provisions, like, after dark. Right on red is a privilege extending to the second or third car at the light. If the first car at a stoplight is not turning, it is permissible to drive across the yellow lines, into the opposite lane and drive around the inert vehicle. Any lane of parked cars also doubles as a passing lane. The unceasing motion of the buggy is my favorite brand of success; it's like Ellisonian moving without moving. A passenger in a healthy rain-skidding smack against the bumper of the car in front of us along the long stretch of road leaving Murtala Muhammed Airport in Lagos, I learned that it was not just Baltimore, but the preferred mode of African travel, not gridlock or streetlight, but polydirectional flow.

The dozen adult men that we slide past on Division Street selling drugs seem to be the same people we saw last week. A lean, short man in an undershirt, an Italian designer belt keeping his jeans from bunching at his knees, counts a sheaf of bills in the middle of the block after Robert Street. I observe a wayfarer in a heavy, butter-colored, leather sheep's-wool-lined jacket of the type that was in vogue when Ill Al Skratch was bard. I wonder what this betokens, men of my vintage out on the corners again, their wardrobes preserved while they were away thirty years. I cut over to Pitcher Street and lance across Pennsylvania and Fremont to get to Arlington. I ease the vehicle into the first empty space beyond Mosher. It has been a little while since Nathaniel and I have policed the trash on Arlington, and I still feel like those squares of Sandtown are my personal responsibility. But the sidewalk is pristine on the south side of Arlington, and the alley is clear.

The week before, a commando on a 250cc dirt bike roared up and down Arlington Avenue as the parishioners filed out from the service. Waving his hand like John Wayne up in his saddle, the motorcyclist redirected pedestrian and automobile traffic as on one wheel he pivoted 180 degrees to charge north from the church intersection at Lafayette. He repeated his Rooster Cogburn a few times. An exercise in recreational bravado for the boy and *Democracy Now*'s Amy Goodman notwithstanding, teenagers on unlicensed high suspension motorcycles look like only one thing to people leaving a church on Sunday morning: bedlam. What to the youth is a momentary respite from the banality of the corner, looks to us like flight from the wrath to come.

The congregation and the Arlington Avenue dirt biker are mutually scurrying from an awful fury to be sure, poverty, the police, crime, structural inequity. But the Hollywood studios aren't making films celebrating our teeny band. Liturgical Christianity, as in one whose main Sunday rituals involve reading selections from the Bible interspersed with specific prayers, chants, and responses read out in unison, will never be but so popular among people whose main identifying glue is the mythology of New World slavery. By now, black Americans have had inaccess to literacy sanctified into a testament of authenticity. Nonetheless, I think black Episcopalians have an important role to play. We are supposed to be the readers and people of reason, the Levites of our tribe. We are the House of Stuart squaring off against Hanover, our written history and ritual and organization the brake against the army of Methodist and Baptist passion and autonomy. But I belong mainly because I am accustomed to the service and the people and I love to reinforce the discipline of attendance and being around the black elderly onto my children. I suppose if it irritates them it is at least not boredom. Shared suffering, sacrifice, and fear are so much more memorable and effective to me than communal pleasure.

While few academics are inclined to religious worship, it is not uncommon in white Christian countries for intellectual blacks, Muslims, and Jews to express their devotion. Fidelity and self-defense go hand in hand. For black Americans it is generally purported to be simple piety, while the other groups are acknowledged to have bigger fish to fry. Of course, I have never met a person who did not pray or meditate or swear, and attendance offers me a weekly occasion to express all three devotions. I can easily become irate at doctrinal deviations from the pulpit, especially around the question of the relation between good deeds and salvation. I am an unsparing judge of the quality and choice of the musical selections, and I recognize that my affinity for one church member over another is based on only the most trifling personal grounds.

In my life, religion is a disciplining force. I donate to the church a tenth of my income—which is used to run the building, the weekly food pantry, and school programs. The tithe essentially demands austerity in my household. I set aside one portion for church, two portions for my children's education, two portions for the house, one portion to my ex-wife, one portion for food, water, heat, and light. Emperors, federal, state, and municipal take three-and-a-half portions, and retirement and health care take a half portion. Despite the comparative opulence of my new address, my lifestyle resembles the one I have known since graduate school. The fact that I am in control of where I live and where one son is educated and maybe what we eat also insists upon quite a bit of prayer.

Sad to say, despite my regular participation, I am really a sort of fellow traveler Christian. The debates about the consensus reached by different councils of bishops over the years can unsettle me, and I don't read a lot of evidence for resurrection in the four gospels. In three of them, I don't really read any evidence. As in everything in life, it's always the people who come later who want to tell everybody what happened. But my desultory questioning is enveloped by black faith and togetherness. On certain holy days at church, the words and the music, the people, and their connection to me and the past and my earnest prayer for union turn supper with the Lord into a real event. For me this is ecumenicism defined. During the Tabaski feast in Bouaké, when the Senufo Muslim women said those prayers over their beads for my voyaging sons, I couldn't understand their words but I believed them. I have seen the pictures of the Milky Way from the Hubble Telescope and it looks to me a lot like the Twi sign for Nyame, which is God. Stranger things than a savior being resurrected have gained broad acceptance, like the world coming to an end. All in all, the people and the memories and even the building at St. James are sort of a catacomb and wellspring of my heritage.

The St. James Church edifice was originally constructed by a large and prosperous group of white Baltimore Episcopalians called the Church of the Ascension, offshoots from David Perine's Old St. Paul's. Cut from Maryland alabaster marble, another level of splendor compared to the blocks forming a country parsonage like Redeemer, the Church of the Ascension opened its quarter-acre main structure in 1869. At the time, Arlington Avenue was called Oregon Street and Lafayette Avenue was named Townsend, the farthest edge of the city. The parish raced to complete the 62-by-112-foot building that could seat a thousand. The cornerstone had only been laid in April of 1867, a few scant months after a federal garrison in the square had broken camp. The church design included an upper deck, a gallery, "for the use of colored people." Fashionable parishioners at St. James today pay homage to that group of pioneers, probably the servants of the very well-to-do, by sitting upstairs in the old balcony. The interior of the church was known for its wainscoting.

The church caught fire in 1873, and major parts of it, including the spire, needed to be reconstructed, but never were.

The church where I was baptized and confirmed is also a place where I try, nearly always, to forget what I am actually looking at. Sometimes I am lucky and my attention is called elsewhere or I can concentrate fully on the minister, clergy, or laity in the sanctuary. But if not, I have to actively repudiate my encounter with white Jesus, in the form of an imposing anthropomorphic tiled mosaic behind the altar depicting the ascension of Jesus the Light. I have long been fascinated and repulsed by the mosaic, and I know that it must be an object of professional curiosity to those more incisive and learned than I. Why does Saxon Jesus unnerve me and not Saxon tree worship at Christmas or egg-and-hare Saxon fertility rites for the goddess Eostre?

In childhood I presumed that it was Christ and the disciples, because in all, there were nine figures in the tiled mosaic and three cherubs in a clerestory stained glass window above. I thought it was the founders and Iscariot snubbed. But as I have looked more closely during the last decade, the hairless mosaic figures resemble women more than men, and are apparently angels, some glancing downward, and some carrying lyres. The about-face was helped by the loss of the cherubs, due to a bolt of lightening starting a fire that again threatened the church building in 1993. During repairs, the motif of the stained glass window was altered to feature an Abyssinian cross, one modeled from a relic we use during the service, which a parishioner brought back from Ethiopia amidst the Afrocentric uproar. I remember the avid interests of my dad and other members of the church at the long 1989 session led by Howard University professor Cain Hope Felder to showcase his underground best seller, *Troubling Biblical Waters*. Some other stained glass windows were repaired with brown-skinned representations of biblical figures. But the tiled mosaic was preserved. The interior building today shows the competing iconography depicting the early church.

The traditions of interpreting the English bible—a word for papyrus—to avow the prominence of Africans in antiquity, became the bedrock for black epistolary abolitionist arguments, but they were not new even then. Written by a tailor, David Walker's 1829 *Appeal* buttoned its coat by redefining Western learning, writing that it was "the sons of Africa or of Ham, among whom learning originated, and was carried thence into Greece." Maryland-born minister Henry Highland Garnet addressed impatient black people in 1848, explaining that Herodotus's descriptions of "the ancient Egyptians," as in the creators of the pyramids and the people of Jacob and Moses, "were black and had woolly hair." I first heard these observations, references sourced to the Revelation of John, from the Muslim minister Louis Farrakhan at a Morgan State University lecture in 1983. At the end of the 1980s, then Father Curry thundered with those black Jesus images from the pulpit at St. James. The idea of black biblical figures fascinated me and stirred not a little of my displeasure with the gospelteers of the civil rights movement. Martin Luther King Jr. didn't explore the Africanness of antiquity.

Even excluding the claims of the Afrocentrist movement, the rabble-rousing over the Ethiopian in Hebrew and Greek writings remains spirited. To commemorate the four hundredth anniversary of the Ndongo captives at Jamestown, I contributed to a panel presentation at the School of Public Health at Johns Hopkins. As soon as he got to the microphone, an alum and minister of a local church shouted, "This is all because Constantine made Jesus white!" That is, every single problem faced by black people in the city of Baltimore. The large group in the hospital auditorium, which included the region's prominent health professionals and many white people, took the pronouncement with easy aplomb and not a small degree of assent.

In the Western art tradition, representations of a long-haired, light-eyed Christ tend to lean on the apocryphal letter "Publius Lentulus" from the supposed prefect of Judaea describing Jesus, but that missive can only be traced as far back as Germany in the fifteenth century. Since no images at all of Jesus precede the fourth century, rather than following Italian or English tradition, it would have made as much sense to have begrudgingly reproduced the sacred iconography of the Ethiopian church at Axum, founded in the fourth century. Jesus might have been rendered as black all along.

Puritan and Protestant suspicion of the sacred iconography connected to the Catholic Church had stymied representations of Jesus in the colonial and early national era. When Native Americans like the Pequot William Apess were converted, they still read the Bible literally and thought themselves included in the sacred histories because Jesus, "counted by all to be a Jew," could not be separated from the fact that "the Jews are a colored people, especially those living in the East." (I have no idea how long European Christians have had an interest in European-looking Jesus.) But the textualists would be overwhelmed by the imagists. The conversion wave of the 1820s and 1830s, which saw the advent of mass organizations like Bible and Sunday school unions, was helped by new print culture outfits like the American Tract Society, which distributed eight hundred million parcels in the century. Abolitionists such as Harriet Beecher Stowe circulated simple engravings of a background Jesus figure in *Uncle Tom's Cabin*, amplifying the contrast to her black hero, Tom. The Providence Lithograph Company made considerably more graphic depictions with its Sunday school programs. The watercolor exhibition of *The Life of Our Saviour Jesus Christ*, by James Tissot, primed the pump for increasingly virile, Teutonic images of the savior. By the time of the public careers of reconciliation American politicians like Theodore Roosevelt from the North and Woodrow Wilson from the South,

Americans accepted a Teutonic image of Jesus worthy of the con-
querors of Memphis, Atlanta, and Richmond, the Great Plains
and the Southwest, Cuba, the Philippines, Nicaragua, and Haiti.

But black people did not abandon the literal interpretations.
The heavily symbolic and putatively permanent affirmations
of whiteness and divinity are indicative of the crisis faced by
some whites unable to ignore the black aspirants of the twentieth century, the New Negroes. New Negroes, gaining education
and professional expertise, threatened epistolary conventions
that had shored up race-based slavery. Black theologian Willard
Hunter published *Jesus Christ Had Negro Blood in His Veins*
and blasphemed at volume that if Jesus of Nazareth were "living in the United States of America to-day He would be called
a negro."

Literate black Americans repurposed esoteric Greek traditions with the same speed with which they had made Christ black.
In 1911, the year Hunter fought against the images of Nordic Jesus,
a similar idea about black belonging in antiquity and ways to
bring that about occurred to an obscure black man named Elder
Watson Diggs. Diggs brought nine other black men together on
the indubitably white Indiana University campus to found a service fraternity, steeped in Greek and Old English secret-society
protocol that has more than eighty thousand members today.
The initiation trial concludes with a ritual called "crossing the
burning sands of Phi Nu Pi." My dad crossed Alpha Iota chapter in 1953 and I crossed Theta Iota in 1987. Negroes generally,
not just Jack Johnson, Ma Rainey, Joe Gans, Aida Walker, and
Scott Joplin, were showing up and doing things that they hadn't
been considered able to do. During the same decades that Diggs
brought Kappa Alpha Psi to life, seven other bands of women
and men worked from a similar template to create other organizations, some with even more conspicuous overtures to ancient black life. There are also ultra-elite black honor societies
bearing Greek letters and suffused with Abyssinian lore, like

Sigma Pi Phi, "the Boulé." By the beginning of the twentieth century, the contest over the blackness of antiquity and the Old Testament was joined on all sides.

Jesus became white at the Lafayette Square Church of the Ascension on May 18, 1911. The vestry signed a pact to be "improved" and they paid $9,000 to the Sixth Avenue New York firm J. & R. Lamb for the "reproduction of the Ascension in mosaics" in "the space back of the altar." The ascension of George Washington had been completed in the dome of the rotunda at the US Capitol in 1865, and that conflation between Washington and Christ carried heavy symbolism throughout the nineteenth century. The Lambs had probably traveled to Catholic strongholds in France and Italy and seen Renaissance-era depictions of the crucifixion. Striving to keep their version of Jesus in tune with more contemporary and widespread commercial images, F. S., Charles R., and Ella Condie Lamb made Jesus and eight of the heavenly choir as aquiline, blond, and white-skinned as good taste and common Levantine sensibility would allow. The idea that it would be pleasant or even historically necessary to render Jesus as a Semite, resembling the Liverpool striker Mohammad Selah more than English sovereign Henry IV, was unavailable to the Lambs.

As the saying of the day went, elevating Jesus to Saxon physiognomy was "mighty white" of them. Thurgood Marshall's father grew up in a grocery store at Division and Dolphin Street, the same locale his son would know, and the elder man attended St. James when it was located on Preston Street at the corner of Park Avenue, the church's penultimate site before where it is today. Old Man Marshall was a head waiter at the Maryland Club at Charles and Eager Street and the Gibson Island Club on the Patapsco River. Marshall worked for the blue bloods, and he fondly used to reverse the joke and say to everybody, "That's mighty black of you." I always thought the irony was funnier for a black person saying the original, but I lived in another time.

The improvements on Townsend Avenue occurred under the energetic, aggressive management of forty-one-year-old Rev. Robert S. Coupland, a William and Mary graduate. The street was eventually renamed to honor the Marquis de Lafayette, the French soldier whose statue flanks the Speaker's desk in the House of Representatives and whose signature is etched on the glass of rebel John Merryman's home. "One of the events of Dr. Coupland's ministry has been the cleaning of the building, which now again gleams with its original whiteness," approvingly noted the *Sun* in 1907. Coupland knew the most ancient traditions of Virginia, and, in Baltimore as in Indiana, they were changing. The same year that the mosaic hoped to incarnate Anglican Christian destiny, the purpose for its creation was effectively undercut.

A few blocks north and a few more east from Lafayette Square, an African American attorney named Ashbie Hawkins bought a house on an all-white block of McCulloh Street, near where my great-grandmother would later live. Whites rioted and tried to drive the black residents out, but the movement east to McCulloh Street and north of McMechen showed the hearty will of a large black popular migratory tide whose channel would not remain narrow. Striving New Negroes like the Calloway Family lived up and down Druid Hill Avenue and Division Street, but McCulloh going east and Fremont to the west were informal apartheid boulevard lines.

Alley streets like jazz great Elmer Snowden's Whatcoat were the traditional province of black workers throughout the city. The terror of disease, vice, and brutality comes to our era through some of the casual observations of the sons of the merchant bourgeoisie like H. L. Mencken. West Baltimore's black Vincent Street housed "slashed" and abused ladies of Hollins Square and their beau, noteworthy because of their marked flesh, "an ear bitten off, or a nostril slit, or a nose mashed." Black people moved weekly from one hovel to the next to outwit

rent collectors. Colored women cooked in white homes and received leftovers and outgrown clothes. Colored men unloaded
the packets at the basin, beat rugs, or burned tar and resin
to fumigate the waterfront neighborhoods from disease. After
Billie Holiday's grandfather, a janitor named Nelson Holliday,
died from the deadly respiratory ailment tuberculosis in the
shadow of the Hopkins hospital, his wife, Mary, and young son,
Clarence, could only afford to live in a converted livery stable
in Numssen Alley, also called Biddle Alley. Their block had
the highest tuberculosis rate in the city. Black girls were "fair
game" for white boys on the prowl, who delighted in shaving
their heads. No sensible colored person went to a hospital, because the medical students were anxious for cadavers. And the
neighborhood "berserker" Irish policemen happily delivered
them mortal wounds. "When he applied himself seriously to a
bad nigger," Mencken recalled of one officer, "there was one bad
nigger less."

Plenty of black people tried to escape the miserable predica-
ment, and some dared to do so by moving into white streets. To
silo the black attorneys and postal workers with the audacity to
pay for comfort back onto Druid Hill Avenue, City councilman
George West introduced a swiftly adopted ordinance that was
designed to prevent any black from moving onto a block that
was majority white. Then city mayor Barry Mahool signed into
law the 1911 city ordinance that required "separate blocks by
white and colored people for residences, churches and schools."
But the US Supreme Court invalidated the code in 1917. The
city did what it could to segregate the races. Declaring eminent
domain, Mayor James Preston requisitioned swaths of the black
neighborhood due north of city hall, and a migration of black
strivers would redefine the urban geography west along Biddle
and Preston and Fremont Street to Lafayette Square.

By the 1920s, these growing pains were strenuous enough
to take a person over the edge. One ex-serviceman, Vannie Lee,

a waiter who lived on Lafayette Avenue, went berserk in June of 1926 and shot eight policemen, killing one. That must have been a sign to many whites that it was time to leave. Four churches tried to hold on, signing a segregation pact. "Lafayette Square Section Now Believed Virtually Safe From Negro Invasion," ran a newspaper headline. But the Church of the Ascension, positioning itself perhaps with progressive white elites who wanted the tuberculosis-prone blacks cordoned off and a rigid apartheid, was not among them. Only fifteen years into the marvelous mosaic and having cleaned the stone back to its original pure whiteness, they decided to sell the church to a well-regarded black congregation headed by George F. Bragg. At the sunrise service on Easter morning in 1932, the St. James African Protestant Episcopal congregation celebrated its first mass in Lafayette Square.

Educated in Petersburg after the war, Father Bragg was an ex-slave who belonged to the heroic generation that included Anna Julia Cooper, George Washington Carver, and Booker T. Washington. Their motto was basically, having survived life as chattel, anything was possible. Bragg carried the vaulting spirit over to the congregation and the city more broadly, during an era of a significant social class realignment, where the majority of the black population had been born after Emancipation and distrusted the conservative wisdom of ex-slaves. A journalist and historian, Bragg took the historic church from its nadir in Old Town on Colvin Street, then over to Preston and Park Avenue, to a summit in Lafayette Square. He published a newspaper, the *Ledger*, which he then merged with John H. Murphy Sr.'s newspaper, the *Afro-American*, creating one of the most important and long-standing black journals in the United States. Bragg used a talent for writing to bridge the world of the Old and the New Negroes. To demonstrate practically the value and character of those enslaved people in Maryland, Bragg contributed primers like *The Afro-American Church and Church Workers* (1904),

Men of Maryland (1914), and *The History of the Afro-American Group of the Episcopal Church* (1922). In 1899 Bragg took up the burden of the Johns Hopkins Hospital, which had been founded with a bequest insisting it provide an orphanage for black children, and he opened the Maryland Home for Friendless Colored Orphans. By taking the boys, he enabled Hopkins to fulfill a small portion of its original mandate, and the school continued its all-girls orphanage until 1915, the girls and boys both attending St. James. Bragg's ever-vested, formally surpliced cadre of priests and educators produced a world-class Baltimore generation that included Clarence Mitchell Jr., Carl Murphy, E. Franklin Frazier, Pauli Murray, and Thurgood Marshall.

My grandmother joined the church during Bragg's last years. She would have understood a Virginia-bred man well, respected his learning and success, perhaps particularly so since he was older than her own father. She had grown up in St. Mark's, a black Episcopal church in Bracey. In 1883 her grandfather, Nat Macklin, had donated land for the church, just a few years after the birth of her father, Joseph. A "free Negro" registered with the county clerk, Nat Macklin lived his whole life in Mecklenburg, but was never enslaved. Nor was his mother, Nancy. More weirdly to me, in May of 1860, Macklin bought $312 worth of land from Hugh Bracey, the territory between what might have already been a train stop and the St. Tammany Road, near where Interstate 85 is today. How he would have amassed that small fortune is a mystery. The black Episcopalians of Bracey erected a large brick church whose outstanding feature is a tower with a crenellated roof. Though they did install a prominent three-panel Gothic stained glass window, I have never seen any of the images on the inside.

When Ascension relocated to Walbrook Junction in 1932, they planned at first to bring with them "memoria, windows and mosaic reredos." The odd word "reredos" refers to the decorative artwork on the wall of an apse behind the altar and visible to the congregation. The white Christ that seems but a gaudy insistence on white divinity to me may have been a bargaining chip in another sort of battle. To the congregation my grandmother joined around this time the symbolism may have seemed powerful and necessary, a sought-after antithesis. "Slavery is the price I paid for civilization," wrote Zora Neale Hurston in the 1928 essay "How it Feels To Be Colored Me." White Jesus appealing to the congregation from the altar was getting that civilization to the nines. Even better, the mosaic was the antidote to that side that Hurston could delight in but not everyone did, the indelible part of her "living in the jungle way." Clad in a sky-blue tunic and draped in a rose-colored cloak, acquiline nose Jesus ascending with the angels could not be conceived of as jungle in any way.

White Jesus, only seventy-five, began to smart around the time of my Afro-American studies courses in college. From then on, and even though I sang in the Wesleyan gospel choir and was regularly praying not to be shot, go to jail, catch AIDS, or become a father, I went to church haphazardly. My grandfather's niece would drive up to my dorm on the occasional Sunday when I studied in Columbus, taking me to her church on the Eastside. On the day of my oral qualifying examination at the Catholic chapel on Stanford's quad, an extraordinary example of an outdoor mosaic, I knelt down at the altar in earnest. On that morning, after having sought medical consultation a week earlier for a racing heart, I feared the weight of the English literary tradition might be killing me.

When I moved up the Bay to write my dissertation, I began to frequent the 8 a.m. service at a church in West Oakland at Twenty-Ninth Street and Telegraph, regularly attended by a dozen senior citizens and myself. The service was conducted in the sanctuary, and the parishioners sat in the choir's seats, a choice intimacy. One Sunday I had consecrated the ganja chalice and after the service I went to a classmate's house near the flea market on Ashby and told her I had had my own vision of Jesus. We had gone to the St. John Coltrane Church on Divisadero in Frisco, so I knew she would understand.

But I also attended to sustain my relationships with older African Americans after my grandparents and their generation passed away. I wanted to find ways to keep their memory alive. It pleased me to make new friends among people born in the first quarter of the twentieth century, and the acceptance and tender solicitousness I received back were a tenfold reward. I relished the folkways and historical wisdom they gave out, extending my knowledge of people whose lives I studied and would later write about.

When I married and became a father, I needed an extramural structure to shore up my family life, one connected to a high ethical and reflective purpose, one looped into national holidays. In Georgia I was far away from family and living, at first, in one of the original "white flight" neighborhoods of the postsegregation era near work. Emphasizing decorum and liturgy, the black Episcopalian church badly lagged behind the other denominations in its services to young families. The Catholic congregations all had nurseries and nursery rooms. In Atlanta, the church that I attended was in the southwest on Peyton Road, inside the beltway and not far from the West End colleges Morehouse and Spelman. The people at St. Paul's, educated professionals, some of them quite well-to-do, Caribbeans and Africans alongside the Negro, reminded me of those I had known in Baltimore; indeed, the two worlds would sometimes collapse or meld.

Both of my sons were baptized at St. Paul's. But even though I entered the Sunday school teaching rotation, we never went to other children's birthday parties or entertained other families. I was attending with my young boys, generally with Mitchell on my lap, and more than once I perceived something like horror as I was sighted as the regular caretakers of toddlers. When my eighteen-month-old made his jail-break dash down the center aisle of the sanctuary, moving toward the communion rail, some members of the church grimaced. I had my own odd quirks when I served as an exacting monthly Sunday school instructor. I enforced age-appropriate behavior and learning. I tended to find real value in the instructional dimension of the biblical stories and having the children read and color inside the lines. And even though the children were five and six, I thought the ones who were able to pay attention and follow directions would go further in life.

I had two favorite joys as a part of worship. One Sunday I noticed that the porch alcove bench had had its legs cracked and might even be permanently damaged. Without saying anything to anybody, I just put it in the back of the station wagon and took it home. I cleaned out the joints, drilled some pilot holes, mitered some blocks as braces, glued the joints again, and clamped everything in place. The next week I returned the bench to the alcove and no one was the wiser. The other was new music. I met up with two of my funeral songs, vigorous tenor melodies, during the course of my worship at St. Paul's. I became a committed votary of "I Love the Lord" and "Lead Me, Guide Me." In Atlanta, "Lead Me" never failed to bring down the house.

The anthem that my father and I were moved by at St. James was "Prince of Peace," by Clara Ward, an Advent gospel hymn snuck into the service by Father Curry to appeal to the Episcopalians like my dad, born into the charismatic denominations. "Prince of Peace," which for decades I errantly referred to by the name of its first line, "Holy Night," was sung following communion once a year at the Christmas Eve midnight mass. To bring the appropriate rhythm and muscularity to the song, the choir director, Maurice Murphy, would move from the organ down to a piano tucked beside the communion rail. The song acquired cult, ritual status, like Heatwave's "Always and Forever" at a black American wedding, or Frankie Beverly and Maze's

"Before I Let Go" at a Memorial Day cookout. The sorrowfully arranged lament "Prince of Peace" brought the congregation face-to-face with its gut-bucket past and its ambitious future. The soloists, one tall, mascaraed, hair streaked with blond, the other squat, big-boned, and wearing heavy glasses, battled each other to see which woman's voice could achieve the pitch and vibrato of a ringing bell. As the chorus to the very adagio song crescendoed, "His heart is purer, than gold . . ." there was a beat, a pause, and the soloists climbed up a tall ladder to reach the uppermost octave. Then the two would strike their vocal irons with fortissimo and clang, "Oooooohhhh!"

It was our shot heard round the world. That sound brought to earth the celestial sirens and turned the mass of black Episcopalians stapled to their benches into a composite mass of crying, writhing Odysseuses lashed to the mainmast. Once, the congregation became so loud—stomping feet, clapping hands, and rhythmically chanting—that the indignant, conservatory-trained choirmaster removed his hands from the piano and silenced the sirens in midsong. Instead of ecstasy, he lectured the apostates Daniel Payne–style to cease the raucous rhythms and resist the urge to turn the spiritual into a cornfield ditty. Even at the most celebratory moments, the rhythm of possession need submit to the solemnity of reason in our liturgy.

When "Prince of Peace" rang out over the congregation in 1989 at St. James, I could claim to have experienced a shared spiritual presence, a palpable thickening of emotional connection with people who were not materially engaged. This is my main experience of transcendence outside of a nightclub dancing to deep house music, and only then on those rare occasions when I had sweated through my pants. Not so different from the narcoticist, I am always searching for that sensation of group elation through the catalog of mutual physiognomy, shared history, and adherence to cultural practice. Another thing is this: any culture, anywhere, boils down to storytelling, singing, cooking, dancing, and nighttime. Considering the obliteration of culture with the electric gadgets, the reign of teeny tinny, the screech culture at volume and the machine rap, black church is the last holdout for something akin to an original utterance. Some of the religious traditions in music and speech hold on. From time to time on Sunday, the pious bathe in unadorned soul, an echo of real sound across the generations.

On the east side of Arlington and getting out of her car is my mother. Though I shouldn't be surprised, I am. As misfortune would have it, we miss her on as many Sundays as we come. Either we're tired or elsewhere or she is, and, relying upon telephones, we never plan mutually or in advance. She tends to conclude that the only times we come are when she is there, and everytime we're there and she's not the other parishioners ask me for her location and I just have to say I don't know at all. I hold her by the crook of her arm as we chat crossing Lafayette, searching out the flesh between her elbow and ulna. Later that same day, after playing basketball with Nathaniel, I will lift the bar plus two of the plates, and will only get it up comfortably four times. From the time I was sixteen, I could lift that weight ten times in a row, and when I was sixteen, it was twenty pounds over my weight; now, I am thirty pounds heavier than the lift. My muscle is turning to fat, her fat is turning to bone.

In the narthex of the church the three generations of Jacksons learn that there are no more printed copies of the service. Our program is referred to as "The Call," and it has an Abyssinian Cross on the front, a kind of gentle cut to the Anglophiles that Ethiopians at Axum had been preserving Christianity prior to the conversions in England and Germany. For a church that typically has fewer than one hundred members combined at both services on Sundays, this is a heavenly sign. Our bishop is a deliverer. The choir is singing, so we head toward a pew that shares a window with three others, a stained glass pane of a somewhat brown-skinned Jesus holding hands with an equally brownish-gray child. On a plaque by the window are the names of my mother's relatives and my father, my sister and my own. It is, so to speak, "our" window, our customary pew.

We walk in by age and all sit together in a row. I understand that at fifteen, my boy, who is named after the greatest American insurrectionist, wants more distance. On most Sundays, he sits behind me, and I will turn around and glare from time to time to try to ward him off his phone. His mother bought it for him, and the tensions, difficult with any child-parent relationship, have intensified. My son has also developed, and is now roughly eight inches taller than I. In the space of about eighteen months, the two of us walking into church has come to resemble a reversal of roles, the son as the father accompanying his father-child into place. The main work of the fourth century Council of Nicaea was on this point, conflating and equilateralizing Jesus with his father God and, I suspect, revising out the female deity from the Egyptian system, which the bishops would also have been familiar with, and substituting a "Holy Spirit" for her role. Suffice to say that in our family, Jesus is the obvious standard bearer now. The conversations my fifteen-year-old has with adult men whom I have known the half century of my life, reveal the significance of this fact. People seem to be hardwired into mutual recognition with other humans that they look at directly in the eye.

Sometimes the service, the dwindling number of ailing people, the regularity of the loss, the age and infirmity of congregation, bear down and depress. Three of my former Sunday school classmates still attend services regularly. One serves on the altar and has become a lay minister. Another uses a walker and oxygen tank, and when he stands beside his father during the service they appear to be contemporaries, equally wintered, instead of a sere capable elder accompanied by his youngest son. The other has ended his hoop dreams to become the full-time sexton of the church. None of us men have created stable families or enduring marriages. I see much promise in the future for our children but already even in their young lives the painful breakings have left so much uncertain.

When I see one classmate the Sunday after she has buried her mother I simply can't recognize her, and it makes me think we can't possibly be living in a country offering any health care, at any price, whatsoever. The fates are despairing because they have aligned so closely to what was visible forty years earlier: the church wasn't offering enough discipline for some and not enough leniency for others. Possibly those who remained in its orbit would be the ruins. Putting distance between oneself and the past represented by the church was the strongest flight from the ever-circling wrath. My sense of uplift comes from the classmate who has apparently given her soul over to the church, and on the special days when she puts on her vestments and offers communion, I always ignore custom and go over to her side of the rail. Inevitably she beams at me like we are both nine years old and we are having our own special ceremony.

I rarely see more than a sprinkling of men at the service at St. James, the line held steady by timeless Mr. Lovick and Mr. Simms. But we are thin because several of the regulars, George Barrick, Franklin Beaird, Judson Wood, Bill Lambert, Mr. Savage, and John James, all of them my old friends, all military veterans, passed away in the swift years after my return to Baltimore. I knew Mr. Wood, an upbeat, personable slickster who seemed so much younger than his eighty years, mainly because he sat on our side of the church. Tall, long-faced Mr. Beaird, an avid sportsman who survived being shot in the throat at the Forest Park golf course, I knew my entire life. His name is on the dedication page of one of my books. Mr. Savage was a decorated World War II veteran, like my grandmother's brothers Wilbur and Harold, and he swung the incense decanter in smooth round arcs during holiday masses throughout my childhood. On the day that his ninety-fifth birthday was announced at church, he stood up and high-stepped at a clip down the aisle, showing off his vitality. I asked him once if he would allow me to record his thoughts on city life in the 1930s and 1940s, and he politely demurred. John James, my dad's cut buddy, remarried a beautiful divorcée. Mr. Barrick gave me frame carpentry lessons, from platform jacks to speed squares to floor joist hangers. Really, it was a privilege to be with such like men one more time.

However, the Vietnam-era males like Arschell Morrell, Robert Griffin, and Harold Easley join everlasting hands with the Lord too. I remember Easley's wife, Cynthia, with a card on her first Valentine's alone, having seen them fondly at the nearby eatery the Belvedere Square. The older I get the more uncomfortable I am made by this skewing, the increasingly dramatic dimension of mortality when you compare the races side by side, St. James to Redeemer. Black men sicken and die so early and, especially if they are educated and in the middle class, seem to spend so many of their predeceased years alone, that I wonder what precisely does the society extend? The septuagenarian and octogenarian white men seem to be doing quite well at Redeemer. Not knowing them at all of course makes me as ignorant of the interior of their lives as I am of the people who are just missing. The ignorance, the segregation, makes the space for the envy. I know you are supposed to simply let it all go, and it helps you now more than ever before if you do.

For the Gospel, the bishop's deacon, a statuesque, radiant woman who inspires the pride of the assembly, reads the story of Jesus turning on the temple in Luke. Her manner conveys a fine balance of expertise, professionalism, restraint, competence, and piety. But nicest of all, she modestly understands her role is to prepare the stage for the main event. The bishop of Maryland is a man who bears a strong resemblance to Tuskegee's second president, Robert Russa Moton, who claimed to his biographer that he was of undefiled lineage, Mandingo aristocracy.

There are a number of contemporary Americans like the actor Dennis Haysbert and the Baltimore-bred basketball superstar Dominique Wilkins whose physical resemblance connects them to this tribe. They are like the doo-wop group the Temptations, all men of unusual stature: the Mandingoes.

Since the election of President Obama in 2008, the national appetite for black figureheads has increased. Bishop Eugene Taylor Sutton was installed in 2009, around the time that Robert Wright, the minister of the church I attended in Georgia, won elevation to the bishopric of metropolitan Atlanta. These elevations are not unseparated from the fact that Maryland's Prince Georges County and Georgia's Dekalb and Fulton Counties host the largest numbers of middle-class black American households in the United States. Not many months later, St. James's former minister Michael Curry became the bishop of the entire Episcopal Church, crossing over from being minister of a church with a declining membership in a dicey part of town to marrying the Windsors and presiding over the remains of President George Herbert Walker Bush. Bishop Curry, a Yale man, brought high learning and passion into the pulpit. Curry understood the historical experience of slavery, and was capable of conveying an important synthetic black tradition—recovering it, really—that had existed in Baltimore during the earliest years of independent black churches led by Daniel Coker and Jacob Fortie and Nathaniel Peck. I gave the commencement address at the high school that his daughter completed. I will always cherish him because he buried my father.

But where Atlanta's Bishop Wright is a look-alike for George Johnson, the guitar player from the soul group the Brothers Johnson, and the Most Reverend Bishop of the Episcopal Church Curry cultivates an Abyssinian dervishness, Sutton, clean-shaven, appearing not a day beyond thirty-five, approaches representing the physical symbolism of the deity in a supremely comforting black paternalism. He achieves absolute authority without the appearance of effort whatsoever. Nor do I ever recall Sutton ever mentioning his race in any of the audiences I have seen him at celebrating the eucharist and delivering a sermon. His ancestry is the elephant that becomes the room.

Sutton offers himself for the homily by warming up with a corny joke about the rabbi, the priest, and the imam attempting to convert the bear (the rabbi began with circumcision). I had heard him before, not long after his installation, and during a strong winter season of my personal life. Then I had thought the comedy profligate and unserious. Today I find him connecting easily with an audience that he is responsible for but doesn't really know. His sermon is about the value of presentation and preparation in the Bible, and he uses as his analogy the formal qualities of Romance languages. Instead of faulting him for repetition, I enjoy his careful walking through the different language examples.

He goes on to share an incredible detail with us. Only the day before, his father had passed away in the ninety-fifth year of his age. The bishop refers to his parent as a simple man, a man who worked with his hands and fixed things, fixed horse-powered wheeled wagons, fixed iron machines, and raised his children. I find it incredible that the man can stand before us and calmly recount an experience that is so raw. I know something of what a man who was born in 1925 and lived much of his life in Washington working as a laborer would have experienced. My own life is sharply defined by the decision my own father made to go up to Baltimore from Roanoke and live beyond his cousins who had settled in DC. The bishop mentions praying with his nephew's American University basketball team and the complex of feelings about family, generations, the value of reflective meditation, and the manner of conveying it all. Bishop Sutton is from Washington, DC, the great Virginia metropolis, which connects him, again, to me and to Moton. I consider that his unruffled demeanor in the midst of personal pain could indeed rest upon the unshakable certainty of his belief.

During the sermon, my son asks me to identify the chapter of Luke from the day's gospel. I show it to him and he pores over the passage, something he's never done before, reading the scripture beside me in church. When I returned to Baltimore I learned from Reverend Alan Robinson that the first three accounts of Jesus's life were called the synoptic Gospels. I noticed that Matthew, Mark, and Luke touched rather lightly on the resurrection part of the story, and I became intrigued to read the accounts further whenever I am in church. Nathaniel's request immediately makes the moment unusual, the three of us aligned in the pew according to age, having walked in together, the family of one member alone representing each generation—ages eighty-one, fifty-one, fourteen—and that we each have a missing partner, spouse, or sibling, our losses there beside us. After a while I am stunned to realize that the woman seated behind me has lost her mother the day before, a long-standing member of the church who had taught me in Sunday school. Her husband was a prison guard who was stabbed to death at a correctional facility by a preacher's son, and she had known hardship raising three daughters. I had taken her oldest daughter to the prom, and Mrs. Tolson had been wheelchair bound and unable to speak for several years. Her daughter would position her near the communion rail at the appropriate time during the service, and the custom was to greet her when leaving the feast of Our Lord. She could move her hand and her eyes would shift in recognition and judgment, though I am self-centered and was slow to realize that while she was immobile, she was shrewd.

At the conclusion of the prayers following the homily, all of the men are invited politely to the front to pray and to lay healing hands on the bishop. Our new minister says something to patch over the brief moment of gender exclusivity, but I don't remember exactly what it is. At first, it seems as if the only men to pray are from the Brotherhood of St. Andrew, my dad's old group, but then, as might be useful in a small church, all men are invited to join and my son, who now glimpses his own acceptance in ritualistic adult male bonds, starts to jostle me forward in a good-natured way. There are three aisles, and as I head forward, our one Asian member heads down from the choir's seating behind the altar. A hundred years earlier, there had been a Chinese worshipper at the church, and though the most prominent white member of St. James passed away the year before, the wife of one of the assistant ministers, there is still one brave amiable white woman who sits in one of the first pews. As we pray, with our hands on each other's shoulders, I can feel the hearts beating of two men I have known and who knew and served with my father. The bishop is seated before about thirty of us, and, as a person who has lost a father, I grasp his forearm before I shift to the center aisle and back to my seat. On my way, a step from the bereaved man, my classmate lugging his green oxygen canister looks up alertly and clasps my hand in his rough dolorous manner and groans in response to my entreaty about his well-being. "I'm glad to be here," he tells me solemnly. His final steps on earth are but ten days ahead. When his homegoing ceremony takes place during the first wave of the plague about to sweep the land, I chuckle to myself upon seeing the pictures of him with a companion. I had never glimpsed that side of him.

I have three years before my own son reaches college age and, in fact, his birthday is next week. On Superbowl Sunday he entered the world in a hospital in Georgia named for one slaveholder and then exchanged for another. For six months he learned French and taught his classmates English at Collège du Bambi in Bouaké. He was the favorite of my colleague Vamara Koné, a djele. When the moment arrives for birthdays and anniversary blessings, Nathaniel goes forward to receive the laying on of hands from the bishop. As my son stands there, chest to chest with the distinguished man, I can see that my Sunday boy is taking a vow to the Mandingoes.

The Protestant Reformation rescinded marriage as a sacrament in Protestant churches. The original installation seems owed to concerns about clergy and their marriage choices in the fifth century by way of Pope Siricius, a letter writer, and Bishop Augustine's more explicit work "De Bono Conjugali." By the thirteenth century and the Crusades, the Catholic Church decided to place marriage in its sacramental order, right beside baptism. I can see my own wedding ritual as a great romance and myth and one not about me at all. I can also recall one of the last heartfelt things that my ex-wife said to me before we were married, prior to our ten years of two oars pulling hard in opposite directions. An otherwise modest person, she had a personality that enjoyed making an occasional splashy statement. Describing her five-year-old, she said, "She's falling in love with you too." I remembered those words after we were engaged, uttered not without an edge of wan sadness in her voice. Eventually I grasped the irony of all that her confessional tone had not quite hidden. Where there is love among three people there is jealousy. It is hard to avoid the idea that if you love him, you love me less. Expressing mutual love among three people, blood kin or not, can be hard in practice. Whenever two of us achieved an intimacy that left out the third, my wife would always trot out a classroom term: the devilish, aspish nature of the "triad."

My wedding day involved a series of hollow moments, some of them minor, some not minor at all. My life had conditioned me to accept hollow moments, even times that never end. But I had not acquired the skill to calculate the damage of their effects, and to know the difference between meaningful and pointless suffering, and to choose wisely. Meaningful suffering imparts a lesson, an axiom if you will, that guides future behavior and shapes future choice. Pointless suffering is closer to masochism, but without the possibility of any satisfaction.

We had wanted a small, intimate service, which mushroomed to accommodate the needs of extended family. (It made me wonder if I was the one wanting a small, intimate service.) Of course, now the production would be more of a performance, a big show involving large numbers of people from many stages of our lives who had gone to considerable expense to join us; with an exception or two, neither my spouse nor our families and associates were financially comfortable people. Other frustrations ensued. We had hoped to wed at an old African church meetinghouse in New England, but we shifted to a plantation-like home on the city's outskirts to accommodate the schedule of the Right Reverend Curry, then newly appointed as bishop of North Carolina, who was to take our vows. He canceled a month before the wedding, and now the symbolic associations of our choosing a plantation for the ceremony had become thin if not frightening. It turned out that the B&B I had chosen for the surprise honeymoon had been the birthplace of Robert Rhett, the architect of secession. The only close-up, black-and-white, unstaged photograph of the event, the sort one sees in a Pottery Barn catalog representing the type of material comfort I hoped to achieve, the kind my white professional colleagues have, was taken by my high school buddy, a cameraman. With that unfailing familiarity that old friends have, in perfect focus he shot me grimacing and my wife flashing a lovely, enameled, smile. He captured the day.

My wife was embarrassed by the photo and never made an approving comment about it. I framed it anyway, because it was the best one we had. Eventually I put it in my office at work.

At the altar I was seconded by my cousin, the person I respect most in the world for his integrity, a teacher and community activist in Baltimore. Our tie goes back to Alfred Smith and Mollie Baskerville and slavery in South Hill, Virginia. Since my own father had passed away, I wanted to send the signal that the wedding meant blood family, enduring love, loyalty, integrity and commitment. My ex-wife had a large extended family and her sister was her second. But the exchange of vows was more of a duel of misfires than an intimate tête-à-tête. Throughout the ceremony, I never once caught my fiancée's eye to reach a private, mutually shared sense of attachment, a kind of heartfelt moment of joyful innocent anticipation. At the precise moment of the ring exchange, she looked for me in a way that was the most authentic that it ever got, more than the look she used the night she accepted the diamond. Our moment draped in white-and-black fingering gold was a public time of flashing cameras—photographs that I have never seen—and a hundred other people's hopeful expectations. I shrank from sharing our dream of the future with them at that time, because I had wanted to secure our dual understanding first. But we missed each other. When she looked again, her eyes were narrow and distant.

As we loaded up the car to drive to the coast for a thirty-six-hour-honeymoon stint on Cape Cod and prepared to leave the little flower girl with her grandparents, which seemed appropriate to me at the time, the slender six-year-old said plaintively, unbidden, and on cue, "I guess I'll go live with my Dad now." The first of two articulated heartaches that day. When she learned that we were going to have a big ceremony celebrating our new lives together, she had asked if her father was going to be my best man. Her youthful dreams were important to me in my own way and, as I too fell in love, taught her to ride a bicycle and spell and tie her shoes, I couldn't avoid the dilemma of parental control, the need to shape the destiny of my child without interference. At the beginning of the romance, when I was reminded of this point a couple of times by family, I told them it was none of their goddamn business.

With the car door open and the engine running, we reassured her jointly, in fact, we beseeched her, but maybe there was more to it than that. The day's events had shown her something of the exclusive oxygen only for the couple. She felt left out, an afterthought, out of breath. An older person, almost certainly one who had been married before, might have made a different wedding show entirely, but my wife was winding down her twenties and I was thirty-three and still imagining the harbor of the absolute.

Our private world spun and unspun just as on that day, even as Nathaniel and Mitchell entered our lives in the first decade of the Gregorian millennium. It's funny what you remember. When we lived in Richmond before the boys were born I went to an academic conference somewhere for the weekend. In that brief interim, my wife had decided to organize a yard sale. The one thing she sold was the only thing in the house I had an interest in keeping, Maude Jones's rocking chair, which I had hoped to repair. In the process of putting up a sign, she had smeared Crazy Glue on the front of my windbreaker. It's funny to have so much of life reduced to a jacket and an antique.

My youngest son, born on Sunday like his older brother, retains no living memory of any event that his parents attended with him together, from dinner to church to a birthday party. When he asked me two years after the divorce if his family might live together again, I thought that his pain was coming later, comparatively, as he gathered from his brother and his other mates what he had been denied. As the old song used to say, "Sent for you yesterday, here you come today."

During communion a young woman darker complexioned than the bishop, and attired so that her navel is visible, plays violin from the sanctuary. While her exposed skin is unconventional, the skilled rendering of classical music finely accents the rare service, and gestures toward the church's early nineteenth-century history. My family takes communion, the three of us walking across our short pew and through the length of the longer one to get to the nave, and then receiving communion from the hands of the bishop. On my way back, I greet Mrs. Ada in the third pew, who is like my second mother, and who shares words of profound love, kindness, and beauty with me every Sunday. She had been absent last week. Mrs. Ada began, in my memory at least, to express her affection when I started bringing Nathaniel and Mitchell to church as babies, on a sojourn from Georgia, where so much love was receding. She could tell from the way they looked something about the kind of women I loved. When the offering has been taken up, my mother tells me that the woman accepting the collection is the daughter of Mr. and Mrs. Edemy, my parents' friends who have gone up yonder. I don't often have the chance to recall them. Mr. Edemy was a suave dresser, one of black men who had evolved a sartorial style in the 1940s and in distinction to the extravagance of the zoot suit. The last time I saw him, I was buying a graduation ensemble and he had counseled Hickey Freeman. Mrs. Edemy ever retained a flapper quality, and she ended her days in style, residing at an apartment on Charles Street in Homewood. To anyone in the city, black or white, this was a most enviable management of her affairs.

When the soloist rests her bow, the choir breaks into the 1719 Isaac Watts dirge I grew to love at St. Paul's in Atlanta. "I love the Lord, who heard my cry / and pitied ev'ry groan. / Long as I live and troubles rise / I'll hasten to his throne." I am one of only a few people familiar with the melody. Although I am not a singer, I belt out the tenor lyrics with the occasional moments of baritone. When the melancholy carol ends, we gather our wraps to leave. Years before I had torn the words of "I Love the Lord" out of a church program and folded them into my wallet. Even though this testament for my apotheosis is safeguarded, I whisper to my son, "This is my funeral song." He will know.

I dreamed, and behold I saw a man clothed with rags, standing in a certain place, with his face from his own house, a book in his hand, and a great burden upon his back.

—John Bunyan, *The Pilgrim's Progress* (1678)

All fine clothes I despised in comparison with my interest, and never kept but just what clothes were comfortable for common days. . . . As for superfluous finery I never thought it to be compared with a decent homespun dress, a good supply of money and prudence. Expensive gatherings of my mates I commonly shunned, and all kinds of luxuries I was perfectly a stranger to. . . . I never was at the expence of six-pence worth of spirits.

—Venture Smith, *A Narrative of the Life and Adventures of Venture, a Native of Africa* (1798)

Lent: Appraisement of Negroes
at the Folly, or Dinner

I dreamed of my father's father at home. The imaginary setting, an unpainted wooden frame house with a living room and
a gently sloping roof and veranda, was familiar, but yet un-
real. The house stood alongside railroad tracks. I take a seat
at the table with him and a woman and I ask about his recipes
and accept a plate of food from the stove. At some point in the
dream, the domestic scene with my kin isn't satisfying enough.
The elaborate theater dissolves and I step outside my body and
transform into a more singly channeled stream of desire. I am
beyond objects and sensations. My purpose is to be the source
of confided secrets, a remote and mysterious oracle. Despite our
differences in time and training, I fully understand my grandfather's golden tooth idiom. I know what he made out of the
years in the South on the farm and on the railroad. I am endowed myself by what he tells me. The emotion intensifies from
being the consulted legatee.

The modest wooden stage of the reverie is really my own private fantasy graduating him to the class between peasant and aristocrat. My grandfather grew up in a chinked cabin with ten siblings by Sandy Creek in Keeling in Pittsylvania County, Virginia. In life Grandpa Jackson worked often as a cook, a craft he learned in the 811th Pioneer Infantry, a Negro labor battalion, serving in France during the Great War. At the end of his days, he bunked in a two-room shingle house with his sister and brother-in-law near the CSX tracks in Blairs. They relieved themselves in an outhouse. A clapboard frame cottage is something my grandfather could have rented only during his laboring prime in the 1930s and 1940s, when he lived in the cities Danville or Roanoke or Norfolk. My dream stretches to fill the gaps of black meaning and belonging, and to acknowledge a natural, ineluctable love. It is also wanting a prideful legacy.

The dream recurs to me because most of my own family's past was buried to its heirs the very day we left the Virginia farm. The black past is one to be protected from. The rescinded, mortuaried heritage is a serial problem of all of our generations, the need to cut off our place and our time. We remain at liberty so long as we can outstep the bill, evade the contract. At seven years old I could think aloud that the American slave past was preferable to the present in Africa. This is indeed the majority view. But the price of that idea was also to reject another inquiry: who was my grandfather's father? I could not form the question before anyone who knew its answer was long gone. It is a shame, because that ineffable question had a twin in the deliberately erased and irrecoverable family skeins. The condition is one of neglecting the past that could be known in favor of retooling to recover the history that was already permanently effaced. Even when the lanes were clear it was a penury of memory.

But my grandfather's father was a ten-year-old orphan when the Civil War ended. For the entirety of Edward Jackson's long life, he grew tobacco in the fields of his white neighbors who had either survived Pickett's Charge at Gettysburg or were related to its dead. Briefly he labored in the fields of his wife's light-skinned black father. My ancestor inherited the uneasy position of the "shot free," those whose bondage was ended by force of arms. He was a freedperson cast upon his own feeble resources.

In their papers, the Perine family of Homeland have a picture that reminds me of the precarity of such boys as my ancestor during the 1860s. The portrait features two officers, former classmates from West Point, one Confederate, one Federal. The Union man is George Armstrong Custer, and the rebel was a cousin of the Perines. A sad-faced black boy with bandaged feet is nestling into the southerner's groin. That shameful obligation to seek favor like a dog is a personality trait of the most vulnerable of the enslaved.

The dish of liberty stews in that pot of sacrifice. My great-grandfather had known slavery, but he lived a nineteenth-century life of residential integration oddly foreign to his children and grandchildren. Grandpa Jackson's life of wage labor took him to Roanoke's Old Lick, Henry Street, and to Danville's Holbrook neighborhood on Union Street, the black parts of those big towns. My mother's parents went to the limit and wedged themselves onto a residential vestibule for twenty-five years. Then bulldozers cleared them away and into an even more profoundly all-black experience. My parents bought in as the blocks were busted out, and the whites had all gone by 1970. Nostalgia sometimes cast the segregated across-the-tracks neighborhood as a haven of united black committed effort, one that tends to overlook a feudalist church or predatorial petit bourgeoisie, to extoll a neverland where even the n'er-do-wells did well, the bootleggers and numbers runners, the jook joint owners and brothel madams, the drug dealers and the drugged, the razor scarred and razor scarring.

Cutting through this illusion of wholesome black neighborhood life becomes inevitably some kind of requiem for my seven-year-old self's standpoint, the heartiness of the pork and corn diet of the slave quarter when compared to the protein in the ngyam, the African antecedent. Access to public schools and accommodations, voting rights, and housing protections are the cornerstones of desegregation in the United States. "Integration" is always held out as another kind of ideal, a candyland almost, a free market, self-interested-choice world that fosters mutual satisfaction without sacrificing ethnic integrity or turning the world into a homogeneous gray. But the legal protections guaranteed by all three branches of government between 1954 and 1968 were really mainly interested in taking an unskilled workforce through enough school to sell labor on the open market and to purchase a home. That was the sought-for surety of a people for a century. After all, sizable percentages of blacks and whites, and presumably Asians and Latinos too, enjoy life with people of the same background, heritage, language, and fundamental assumptions, viewpoints, and shared rituals. But the desirable black ethnic colony in an American city, regardless of its precise social class composition, lives only in the imagination. The "thriving black community with excellent public schools, an attractive and growing tax base, low crime rates, a host of stores, restaurants, and recreational amenities, in short, something approximating the advantages of majority-white communities," does not exist in America. It makes me think that when Baltimoreans pontificate about the wonders of segregated Pennsylvania Avenue, or glory days on Druid Hill Avenue, even Martin Luther King Jr.'s "Sweet Auburn" Avenue in Georgia, they are reaching for a mirage.

King's Atlanta is the home of a great deal of contemporary black middle-class dreaming, and it has served as the urban beacon lighting the way south since the 1980s. DeKalb and Fulton Counties, Georgia, are home to the nation's largest cluster of college-educated, home-owning black Americans. My youngest son attends a private academy near the airport that requires for tuition what a minimum wage job pays annually. In the sixth grade at least, half of his classmates were black, and included the children of gaudy musical entertainers and high-ranking politicians. The presence in the same class of the children of both gangster rappers and the mayor suggested to me that the public education system made no claim to confidence in the neighborhoods where black people live. And even the seemingly lofty salaries in the City Too Busy to Hate do not permit black Americans to move from black enclaves in Lithonia, Stone Mountain, Camp Creek, and Cascade into upper-middle-class Candler Park or the city of Decatur. In the white city zones housing stock is sturdier and more valuable, closer to the downtown jobs, and features desirable commercial amenities and more consistently reliable schools. The joy of family, lovers, and friends in a black enclave combined with the transcendent markers of tangible financial success (new, big, new, big, new, big) have created the terms for a place that no one wants to leave, but no one could leave if they wanted to.

The miracle of the black middle class is one of a selective infrastructure that prioritizes the road over the school, the athletic field over the educator, and blends it with dollops of consumer consumption. It is easier to enroll children in gratuitously expensive, competitive preparatories and secure them in three-story suburban luxuries of stained concrete, drywall, hardiPlank, and pine straw and blast the air-conditioning and trap music in a Mercedes through the traffic while snacking on a meat and three. The airport and its vacations frame liberty and prosperity in terms of wanton delight that would be legible to both John Smith and Ian Smith. The sounding brass and tinkling cymbal of Atlanta aside, the city in Fulton County will always to me be the place of cigarette-dragging expectant mothers, randy men in hospital parking lots shouting at the top of their lungs to passersby about their sexual destinies with their nearby dowager mates, the complimentary Freedom Park concert engineered by

the migratory middle-class radio hosts to foist misogyny and violence onto a most unwilling public of the indigenous black poor,
inebriated men attempting to snake a hand into the stroller to
taste my son's pacifier, femme fatales in form-fitting red dresses
threatening felony violence when abrogating traffic laws, and
gentle-faced young busboys who carried firearms on their person at all times away from home.

But the illusory nature of its health is, in fact, even greater.
The true middle-class expansion in the "city" took place in the
conservative, northern white and Asian suburbs Sandy Springs,
Alpharetta, and John's Creek, and Cobb County's Marietta. In
sharp contrast, blacks are south of Interstate 20 and moving east
along that road to Fayetteville and Conyers, west to Villa Rica,
and south to Peachtree City and McDonough, zones largely not
served by public transportation or the dedicated highway corridors enjoyed by those to the north, where the blue ribbon schools
are. Without any extended family as a safety net, it was impossible to plow through traffic to work and live out the Ebony fantasy with school-age children. The combat for the middle-class
grail was perpetual: the two-bathroom house that would appreciate in value in a zone with a competitive elementary school
biking distance to work at the intersection of the Clifton and
North Decatur Roads. Starting from scratch, it took us fifteen
working years and eleven married years, and the stinting climb
destroyed my family life. The plateau I reached in Candler Park
had a handful of black families. John and Titus were inter-
racially married, and James and Angelou rented in two places
before they moved away. My photographer homeboy Rahmeek
lived for a short time down the street, married to an Ethiopian
woman. I never got to know the family who had built a brand-
new house, oozing with creature comforts. Those were the only
black residents in houses I noted, on either side of the park, all
the way to downtown Decatur. After that the Homeland house
in Baltimore, its homeowner's dues and agreement to only build

with stone, wood, brick, or copper, and to abide by the committee's ruling on the exterior colors of your house, felt to me like a cathedral of redemption.

Modern-day Homeland, roughly speaking, runs between Northern Parkway and Homeland Avenue, between Charles Street and Bellona Avenue as it blends into York Road, near where Perine's original gate once stood. The neighborhood is rather different from the 21212 zip code, a larger territory from Cold Spring Lane to Stevenson Road in Towson, between Charles Street and the Alameda. The York Road constitutes what seems to me the city's sharpest division of black and white homeowners. Of the 32,000 people in the village of postal zip code 21212, nearly half, 14,000, are African American. Black Americans occupy about a quarter of the 8,708 privately owned dwellings. If the new industries of the world are in finance, insurance, and real estate, the homeownership figure squares with the fact that 73 percent of whites in the district have a college degree or better, compared to 22 percent of blacks. That's the city average of college education by race, three to one, the same as the nation by and large.

Without any rowhouses and only a handful of duplexes, Homeland as a discrete neighborhood accounts for 2,328 households in the zip code's basket of 4,453 units of detached residences. The housing is old stock, created during the era of the Roland Park Company or even before; only 433 of those houses were not constructed before the Germans invaded Poland in 1939. But if black people own around two thousand houses total, that number of homes falls quite a bit in Homeland proper. Here we are 6 percent black, owning 140 houses total. After I neatly trim my front yard, my homeboy from the West Side compliments me by saying, "That's a white man's lawn." My sons and I are living a dream.

Honestly, even the 6 percent figure seems inflated. West of York Road I can't actually imagine where even that many black householders might conceivably live. Six percent seems like the number of blacks at the elite colleges, walking on the campus and in the library. Most of the schools think it good form to post on brochures and electronic media that 10 percent of the student body is African American, but at the Ivies and their wealthy peers, it usually feels like about half that. No one today recalls that black faculty entered white colleges and universities because one person, Edwin Embree of the Rosenwald Fund, wrote to about a hundred college presidents in 1947 and asked them point-blank if they would hire a Negro if qualified personnel could be found. White man to white man, he sent out black PhD personnel lists to the administrators and started getting results. But transforming the racial makeup of American universities always strikes me as an errand similar to returning Americans to church. Academic life is not so distant from monastic life. It is liturgical. As the monastery is the parent of the academy, the demands, poverties, rigors, and personality abasements of academic life make it roughly as attractive to blacks as Episcopalianism. Who wants to scribble alone in a frosty cubby, talk to themselves, and live like a hermit? Who wants the headache of maintaining a suburban house in a historic district?

The problem of the inadequate black professoriate appears in upbeat commercial magazines like the *New Yorker* as on par with integrating student bodies, with a caveat: "wait twenty years." It is far easier to produce an incoming frosh and graduate them than it is to mint a PhD and tenure her. The number of professors is usually half of that 6 percent. Hopkins faculty was barely 1 percent black for most of its twentieth- and twenty-first-century history, and in 2020 it had, in the arts and science college, fewer than 5 percent. That would be 17 out of 342. In our democracy when we get down to the brass tacks of the solidly middle class, there is an attrition from the black 12 percent of the population falling to 6 percent of the enrolled, dwindling to 3 percent of the credentialed functioning every time. The number is eerily similar to the percentages of black Americans married to whites.

Maybe for that reason finding the opaque black homeowners becomes a minor color storm building to a hurricane. One afternoon on foot I work my way north to Melrose Avenue, the official outerlimit of Homeland, and then east to Sycamore Road. Perhaps I will rescue a lost colony; or I might be rescued. The houses there are two-story frame Cape Cod bungalows with asbestos wood-grain siding, but the doo-dads in the yard and the Subaru wagons, alongside the appearance of the people walking in and out, suggest it is as solidly white as where I live. When I come back home I have the same sense of the neighborhood as before. Black Odysseus of Homeland has only observed six other African American families, and two families with one African American parent. None of them live on my street, nor do I see them walking the dogs, or run into them at my neighbor's annual holiday party. In our community magazine I have read about two other families that I have not met. The family most recently arrived has a son in high school with my boy, and they live in a three-car-garage palace with a massive wood carving out front. They are a happy smiling bunch, clambering in and out of German SUVs.

If I sometimes see myself as the odd guest at the party, I love walking the four square blocks around my place. Overall, I admire the decisions my neighbors make about the exterior adornment of their homes, the color schemes that tastefully restate the prime features of the natural world and inflect the history of the land. But the obsession with alarm systems, security cameras, and security patrols are ones I do not share. While they perceive surveillance more generally as a technological convenience and the lack of privacy as a small concession to modern living, I am opposed to it in another way. By and large, I have experienced a higher degree of crime, violence, and degradation than my white neighbors and am relieved to live here where it is such a negligible feature of life.

It's like being a board weathered by a century of seasons all at once: integrating the land's history of injustice with the principle of private property and a person's right to security from offense—whether loud music, a glare, an insult, or the two-legged hyena. Because they created the police force in American cities to control black people in particular, upper-middle-class whites tend to report property crime more frequently than anyone else. Declaring allegiance to this special burden of the privileged is one I am disinclined to take on. It would be necessary for me to think that police didn't deliberately harass black people. In fact, it would be necessary for me to have lived another life altogether. A white man in a militia, at a Trump rally, or a white supremacist cell meeting strikes me in nearly the same way as a black man who belongs to a deadly street gang or the Taliban. But I sometimes have the feeling that I am the only one bothered by the display of those commitments on cars driven into Homeland by the plumbers and masons servicing my neighbors, the diverging economic realities of the black and nonblack. Trump, after all, was president, not Farrakhan. In the same way that the emblems of white supremacy donned by the mechanic class of Homeland pass by without comment, no one is surprised that black men in their late teens and twenties, sometimes flairfully enscarved, routinely try every car door on all of the main streets in Homeland. Everyone knows their color because apps and websites circulate their photographs throughout the neighborhood and on to the police.

When I leave the door to the car unlocked and on the street, even on holidays and in front of the house, thieves ransack the glove compartment and console. Once, a mechanical genius repaired an inoperable garage door opener and stole Nathaniel's Christmas bicycle, leaving a tattered steel clunker behind. From time to time, four or five shirtless teenagers will trot through the alleyways with searching, cavernous eyes. I shout warnings to two boys on bicycles, because one of them is relentlessly menacing an elderly, slow-moving cyclist. The brigand shoots a volley of triumphant curses at me while the other boy responds childishly, sensibly, fearfully even. "Please sir," he wails back to me from up the street as the other child invents new expletives for parthenogenetic reproduction. "Don't call the police."

The cries for the police are the most vigorous from the southeastern corner of the neighborhood, which informally includes a cluster of condominiums and a gated townhouse unit, bordering the apartment dormitories of a Jesuit college. Perhaps the lost colony of the 6 Percenters is there? One morning when Homeland carts its children to school and parents to work, I walk east to the opposite side of the neighborhood, to the southern bottom, at the edge of York Road and Woodbourne and Tunbridge. There are 150 homes there that, relative to Homeland, are affordable and on smaller lots. If I had been shown a house in this part of the neighborhood it would have fallen to the lower half of my list because it lies just outside of the catchment zone for the area's noteworthy public school. I walk along Paddington and Broadmoor and Medfield Court and see exactly the same white people driving Subarus as in other sections of the neighborhood. I only notice that some people still have a bushel of leaves spotting their grass, probably because I am the one person on my block who does his own yard. Like some of the other neighbors who do that work, I am convinced that I am more attentive than any landscaper.

Heading north, I see a parade of cars zooming down Paddington toward Tunbridge Street. Ferrying across the river of York Road dividing the races and into Homeland are black strivers in secondhand automobiles taking their children to a charter school hosted by the Catholic Church. There are few more acute tales of two cities in the United States than the wonders of Homeland and the wiles of Govans. It is actually a distance of a few rods.

My Afro-Asiatic inheritance directs me to Govans proper. There are three Caribbean eateries, one of them Jamaican; a beauty supply store that sells the "cruddy brush" so that my children can massage their hair into a stylist's simulacrum of budding dreadlocks; a Chinese food market with affordably priced rice vinegar, dried black beans, chili oil, and varieties of jasmine rice in twenty-pound sacks. But the more typical stores are ghetto boutiques: a cash merchant, a Boost mobile shop, cheap tobacco specialists, booze, and fried salt-pepper-ketchup carryouts. The crown gem of the shopping district is a block-long mall built in 1940, anchored by Beauty Point beauty supply store, Corky's Liquors, and Pizza Boli's, a national chain. Although they have uniform brick store fronts, there is no interior plaza connecting the nine businesses, and then there is a weird duplication, two minor telephone service stores, and two corner groceries specializing in cigarettes. Everything caters to the most urgent transactional commercial and emotional need.

The first couple of times I test out the block alone, touts offer to sell the standard variety of urban pick-me-ups and put-me-downs. The evident open-air drug market and the legendary violence along McCabe Avenue make me wonder if the students occupying the Loyola University residential units west of York Road, which expanded when the school bloomed in the 1990s, aren't the commercial engine of the drug trade. The boutiques are owned by Tan Fu and Seo Soon, Tom Song and Song Ki Bong, Virk Singh and Daljit Singh, and Okojie Philip. Although these are mom-and-pop stores selling state lottery tickets, bagged fries, sodas, and grape-flavored cigars, their owners have little incentive to live in the neighborhood. The local schools won't benefit from cheerful, bright, high-achieving children of the Chinese, Korean, Indian, or Nigerian immigrants, the ones who achieved such miracles in Silicon Valley. Although David Perine seems to have unloaded a grape canister at the British at North Point, his road and entranceway to Job's Addition is today a visitation of calamity wrought by Clive's victory at Palashi, Elliot at Kowloon, Eyre and Morant Bay, Rawson's expedition to Benin City, and the Race to Fashoda.

The clash of bloody empire leaves its economy of violence with us still. In thirty-six months along a four-block strip between a Carroll gas station and a Crown gas station, seven people are killed, most of them shot, at 8:00 p.m. or 4:00 a.m., 4:00 p.m. or the ides of midnight. A young man named Deontay McKnight dies after a brief gun battle captured on closed-circuit TV. The epic tragedy of the film becomes surreal as you realize that the battle is being orchestrated by a commander in coveralls who ranges in and beyond the camera's eye, without himself ever toting a pistol. At Sheridan, the streets have the four canister klieg lights rigged to a generator set up by the police department so that nighttime is an absolutely hard fluorescent brilliance. Always there is an assortment of men from my age to the young blades dotting the corner. The younger men cluster in doorways peering into their telephones, their bicycles piled onto the sidewalk. The older men smoke with purpose, waiting for the Glenwood Life Counseling Center to dispense methadone. The men my age need to drag hard on their cigarettes. In Govans, men shot dead in the street are forty-one and forty-eight and fifty, and fifty-four, and even sixty.

I cannot quite call myself a stranger to Govans. I grew up with two brothers, David and Peter, and both dated girls from these streets, Beaumont and Benninghaus. I was regularly in the sputtering car with either of them to pick up or drop off their sweethearts on our way to a party, always in a state of or anticipating an intoxicating bliss, the dreams of twenty-year-olds. We thought that we came from a tougher part of the city, but we also never traveled alone when that could be helped. Naturally, I run into Peter, a connoisseur of the city's Jamaican eateries, lolling on the steps of Max's Caribbean and American restaurant place. He is destined to pass away at fifty-five, and I will read Sterling Brown's "Odyssey of Big Boy" over his casket at the funeral. Leslie Stansburry from elementary school lived on Winston Avenue, a little closer to the Alameda, and Harry from church grew up a rod or two farther south on St. Georges, a parallel street to York Road, but still on this half of the neighborhood, north of Cold Spring Lane. When my grandmother required assistance to go about some of her daily tasks, and benefited from a community nearby, she moved into a senior care facility called Epiphany House at the junction of York Road and Bellona, the head of the Perine gate. I have an old picture alongside that building. I am wearing our neighborhood standard ragwool fisherman's hat and I had just purchased my first pair of high-top Nike Air Force 1s. The high-tops had navy blue soles, slickhead shoes, the antithesis of a Subaru. My grandmother's oldest sister in Baltimore, Daisy Mitchell, lived in the last narrow frame house on hilly Ivanhoe Road, in a sort of country outpost in the city. She had a grape arbor.

By the time I get home, I feel sort of like a Govans Greek among Homeland Trojans, and the exterior of my house a gift horse concealing a messy black inside. Part of me longs to have the interior life of a true Homelander, able to combine a few tasteful antique pieces and some modern furniture, everything emphasizing utility. The decor I have been striving for is what I called, in another period of my life, "Afrocolonial," which meant homemade Shaker with African accents. I have a couple of dowel logs suspended by forked wooden brackets that feature the cloth of the Senufo or Baoulé. I appoint the rest of the walls with art collected at random and photographs of the children from the year we spent living in Côte D'Ivoire. Overtop of the fireplace is the silkscreen of the woman in blue wrap and blue gele. When I put up the commanding portrait of the woman, my mother asked, "Who is that man?" I have the solid irons my grandmother grew up using to press clothes that became doorstops, and a few of the crocks and ceramic jugs that my father always collected from Frederick, Maryland, that I now understand strongly resonated with his Roanoke childhood. Here and there are masks, but I bought all of them at once, from an Ivoirian dealer at a flea market in Cape Town. At the time, I had no idea if I would ever return to Africa, and I was attempting to harness a lifetime of longing into the mementos that a duffle bag might contain, already stretched by a djembe drum. My favorites are in a middle class between the Chinese, machine-made fakes and the danced masks. They are carved and painted but without eye sockets or mouth holes, only built for being mounted to remind one of spirits in contact with Europeans. Two of them are in my office at work, along with a caricature song sheet I pulled out of a bookshop on the backroads of Vermont one summer, near the border of New Hampshire.

I have four items from a furniture store of the sort that might have been bought over time: a sleigh bed wedding gift, which I was allowed to keep; a concrete sofa bed from a jejune furniture store in Little Five Points in Atlanta that proved so cumbersome it eventually broke me and I gave it away to graduate students; three interlocked leather electronic reclining chairs for the basement; and the bed I bought for my oldest son when I moved here, in 2016. The basement chairs replaced a mortally wounded loveseat. In the dark I had misjudged the distance between myself and the small blue couch, and leaned back to sit down. As I kept extending horizontally to catch the seat, I smashed through the center frame board with the back of my head, like a karate chop. The unassembled bed for Nathaniel's room was so heavy that to load it from the bay at the store, I had to stoop under it and fish it onto my back and then turtle-walk over to the trunk of the station wagon. At home I had to work it end-over-end down the path and I still thought I might be crushed finagling it up the steps. It took two years to position the leviathan correctly in his room. My entire life I have borne weighty objects like a snail or an ant, the same way I saw Ivoirians in Bouaké, towing a motorcycle to the shop on the back of another motorcycle.

When the house hasn't been cleaned or straightened it can all feel like so much debris, carted and molded by my own hands. Over the years I had scavenged my Atlanta neighbors' castoffs for wingbacks and wooden-arm accent chairs and sofas. I purchased brocade from Forsythe Fabrics and hired a craftsman to reupholster the neglected waifs. All of my stock has withstood some hard use. I even fractured the Duncan Phyfe sofa during a champagne-guzzling New Year's celebration, and, when it got to Homeland, mended it with tension straps, glue, and screws. Everything else in the house, the tables and shelves, I manufactured from pine and poplar sticks and boards. We mark and stain and spoil our belongings without strong guilt.

In the house of home-fashioned and salvage furniture, my son and I study on the ten-foot cherrywood table, handmade to fit the entire length of our dining room. My first holiday in Homeland, when the boys were visiting from Atlanta, I hosted a twelve-person Thanksgiving dinner. My idea was to build a welcome table from scratch. I went to a lumberyard in Cockeysville, the headright of Captain Ridgely but gained by his son-in-law Thomas Deye Cockey, and I splurged on plaintively beautiful boards and posts and skirting. At the time, I knew nothing of Perine's orchard, and had only worked on pine, poplar, and a little oak from the big box stores.

The very idea of the hard, majestic fruitwood inspires me to leave in all of the blemishes when I rig together the tabletop leaves. By the time Thursday arrived, with the friends and family due and greens aplenty to cook, I find that my twelve-volt drill lacks the power to drive through the posts and set the legs of the table. It is a recurring problem of mine: the equipment isn't heavy enough for the job.

Not until the following summer, and with an eighteen-volt

drill, am I able to drive in most of the screws, assemble the table, and walk it out of the garage and around to the front. Even with the legs somewhat secure, Nathaniel was not then quite able to lift an end of the table high enough to angle it through the doors and entryways into the house. The table had to sit on the front lawn for the afternoon until a Samaritan capable of jerking one hundred pounds overhead happened by. The spare cherry sideboard, finished with only Tung oil, has to wait for other seasons of feast.

Culinary preference is the pillar in the temple of my aggressive bigotry. My sister, who spent a lot of time on bivouac and outside of the Green Zone, always jokes with me about having acquired a taste for "fine food" and putting on airs. Even my mom and I descend into an ancient quarrel about the difference between intention and good works that erupts over ingredients, portion size, and taste. One Sunday before Mitchell heads off to the airport she invites us over for dinner. My grandmother's youngest brother, the final survivor of that family, is there with his daughter. After we have finished eating fettucine in white sauce, I ask about his mother and say, What did Maude Jones like to cook? I am curious about the family past in a fundamental sense that I don't completely divulge. What are the oldest memories of living human beings that we have seen?

I ask my grandmother's brother Harold the question not simply because he is past ninety-five, but also because he is a twice-wounded veteran, in Germany and in Korea. Excepting the college lads who became airmen at Tuskegee, I rarely see the labor and sacrifice of black veterans celebrated. My family's tendency to ignore the impact of racism and segregation in the lives of people born in the 1920s became obvious at a Christmas dinner a few years earlier. I asked my great-uncle about elements of his service that he might have been prone to discuss in the company of civilians like us. He had declined to see the movie *Saving Private Ryan* with me, I thought because he did not wish to relive the violence of the events. But I also suspect he was reluctant to talk openly because so few people care to listen, another of the lost arts. He opened up during dessert, and he told us a story about Thanksgiving leave in 1944, and the War Department's refusal to permit black troops combat training in Texas to return home before being shipped overseas. The reason? There weren't enough cattle cars to send the Negro soldiers home. As he reached the finale he broke into tears. His children and his niece had never seen him cry about anything. He always told wry jokes about losing a finger to an ax-wielding teenager on a dare. When his unit was heading out on a winter patrol in wartime Korea, a picture shows him mirthful. I placed my hand over his and he wept silently until the dinner table conversation noticed his tears.

Having held on to that wound so long there may be others that Uncle Harold is dearly hoping to pass through life without having to reveal at all. He says little about his own mother or her cooking. My mother can remember only her grandmother making bean soup. In a way, this makes sense. While my grandma grew up on a farm in Bracey, farm-to-table luxuries of garden vegetables and fresh cream and butter notwithstanding, she was not a joyous Virginia country cook. Ample portions went against her sense of well-being, too. My grandmother learned not only nourishing, simple food from her mother, if white bean soup with canned or preserved tomato with ham hock was the dish; she also learned its most frugal variety. That certainly reconciles with my memory of her culinary preferences, which relied greatly on chicken gizzards, necks, and backs, cooked translucent cabbage, paparikaed (late to the game, I realize this is ground cayenne pepper) chicken thighs, and instant mashed potatoes. She liked canned green peas and creamed onions, and, on the occasion when she could get it from the market, scrambled cow's brains. I can remember making the short walk with her to eat at the local McDonald's on Reisterstown Road. She never failed to marvel at the dollar meal of hamburger, small fries, and small coffee. She always called the food a "treat." I thought she meant that the meal was handy and neat and the wrappers easy to discard, but she might have meant that it just tasted good.

Wondering aloud about the inheritance from people born in the 1880s stirs resentment in my mother, who spends the next twenty minutes slyly ridiculing my question to my own children. She relegates my interest in the stories of kin to cheap accusations of infidelity. She treats the question as a threat to her own monopoly on intimate ancient sanctuaries. A recipe or an anecdote about the old days unlocks a door onto her privacy, and she suspects that I am either a clumsy or a heartless judge. I don't agree with her, but I know why she thinks that way.

When my forebears lived in the country, culinary wealth, perhaps real wealth, was almost certainly based on the amount of ham and chops and bacon that could be comfortably and regularly served. What I can remember of childhood is mostly after 1973, the onset of the catastrophic inflation and sharp cleavage between middle-class values and middle-class lifestyles. By then, meat for us was a rigorously rationed luxury and its consumption a source of friction and argument. Since my return to Baltimore, my mother has privately decreed to me, You were small boned. I can remember things my father said and one thing he did.

The memory of those times stirs a bilious resentment, the kind of gall of the person whose family insists he was a prince but who trusts the frog staring back from the mirror. But my own life as a father begs me to reconsider the innocence of childhood wounds. Children take the household belongings, including its heritage, as theirs to tinker with. They assemble and disassemble, discard and disdain as they see fit, to the everlasting frustration of the parent. The parent might want them to have the whole, not simply the part. My sister told me one of our grave family secrets when I was finishing high school, and

I used the tragedy as the spine of my college application essay. My mother, never a revelator of our hidden ignominies, shares another of these stories at Christmas about her own father and the difficulties of marriage and mental health. She sobbed as she told it. I think the information would have been valuable to me exactly a decade earlier. Even after I can afford the hide, I get the recipe to cure ham too late. I have given up pork.

The discord extends well beyond the bean soup. It turns out that my professional life is the tweedy notch of Sir Walter Scott's romantic hero Edward Waverley. He is a man fully satisfied "in the quiet circle of domestic happiness, lettered indolence, and elegant enjoyments." I show my main pleasures at refitting the library, sipping Old Line whiskey, and tottering about the landscape. My mom, as the survivor of the segregated world, is the Jacobite rebel Flora MacIvor to my Ed Waverley. She has endured consignment to the rear of the Virginia bus, has stood at the reflecting pool to listen to Martin Luther King Jr., and has raised a family and held a job in the world where prejudice toward black women was the rule of the land. She is the witness to the fact that "high and perilous enterprise," the feat necessary to become a "celebrated ancestor," is not my forte. Mom is counselor to the shameful parts of my humanity, the stories I would hide if I could. Her authority notches me in the category of the romantic "eulogist and poet" and, more so, keeps me there by supervising what I can possibly learn. I know it's pointless wanting to find out about the old woman's soup. I am just putting on airs.

My children are not yet my allies enough to ask my mother what she likes to eat. She prefers Mornay sauce, a lava of cream and cheese. She is also fond of blue cheese, sour cream, cottage cheese, yogurt, and mayonnaise. These are accoutrements added to an educated American's diet sometime between the rise of Nick Gatsby and the death of John Kennedy, from the ice box to the refrigerator. To mount the foray onto a briefly racially integrated street in spring 1960, my parents armed themselves with a *Betty Crocker Cookbook*, the segue to Camelot. Fried chicken, yams, and greens smacked of segregation, our world apart.

But the Christmas Day favorite in my house, Hyannis Bay Clam Chowder, never suited my taste. I cannot remember a time when mucus goo, hot or cold, salty or sweet, did not turn my stomach. Put mayonnaise even near my food and I won't touch it. My mother found a recipe for lasagna bursting with ricotta and cottage cheese about the time that my mouth watered at the sight of Polish sausages cooked with onions and peppers and served on submarine rolls at the open ranges at street fairs. Although no one remembers this now, pizza was an uncommon food in the early 1970s. After being introduced to it, I refused to eat it without pepperoni. I shunned vanilla ice cream. My mother and my sister adore this dairy food, the northern European culinary glue. They are also battered by mysterious gaseous ailments and nerve pain. When I turned twenty-five my Igbo really began to show in the form of congestion after consuming milk, ice cream, or soft cheese. The end of the wheel.

There was a force beyond my own petty preferences. My sister and I were manually chastised early on, and less than the other children we knew. But we were also sometimes reprimanded by short rations, an uncommon punishment in our circle. I would be sent off from the table for manners. And then there were not infrequent occasions when we children would go ten or fifteen hours without food, as a matter of course. Deliberate malnutrition was not our parents' intent. But there would be a misadventure, a car failing, a series of precisely timed appointments, and food—meat, really—was an inconsequence. We drove to Washington for the Tutankhamun exhibit at the National Gallery, waiting eight or ten hours in line to see it, with nothing to eat that day, and when it was over, a strong lesson in patience for us children, my mother visited a street vendor. There were four of us and we shared one sandwich.

Like the hero in a primitive fireside tale, I wandered in the desert for meat and drink. It was a joined adventure, shared by all of us lads. I would sit in next-door neighbor David's kitchen and salivate as he ate fifteen or even twenty slices of bacon or ten Parks sausages on toast in one sitting. He would share a portion, in the manner of a lord to a liege, Cedric to Gurth. My family did not consume that much meat in one week, and we never bought Parks, whose million-dollar business was in the fork of the three great boulevards. From junior high through college, I was in search of a more massive roast and fry. But my father passed away from a disease that began with colon cancer. Before he died, he had offered his chili with ground turkey, a request I scoffed at, likening the substitution of fowl for beef as similar to pledging allegiance to another flag. A year later I encountered black Muslims the same age my dad would have been who emphasized fish, yams, beans, and celery juice. In Northern California I began making basil pesto and fruit smoothies. For only a few coins I could munch fresh dim sum, steamed vegetable buns, burritos, and hummus shawarma. Frisco and Lakeshore begat a world of experimentation and recipe. And then, leaving the locusts and honey, I was baptized by my mother-in-law's home cooking.

I find that I am fundamentally a person suited to the southern side of the transition zone, Sahel to savanna. I am the man in his thirties reunited with rice and sauce. My mother-in-law was from Jacmel in Haiti, where, with some of the French advantages over the cooking of their vassals, the English, they have produced the main synthesis of West African cuisine in the New World. When I lived in West Africa, in Côte d'Ivoire, one of the two reasons that place had so much magic was the high-quality food, which I had access to through the pots of Haiti.

I can understand now that my father was the first African that I knew. My mom was a Negro, an outrider to "Gitchi gitchi ya ya da da!" But Patti Labelle and Nona Hendryx's urgent ministry didn't unwelcome my dad. He was from what we called "the country" in southside Virginia, or at least that was where he took us to visit his side of our family. There might have been one year that my Dad grew corn in the backyard, and everyone in Maryland that I knew planted tomatoes, but he was not a vigorous farmer by the standard of East Arlington, Baltimore City. He didn't grow collards, cook chitterlings in the house, or bring slaughtered hogs from Virginia to the freezer. He was just fond of journeying to the Lexington Market for pig heads and feet to season his beans. He hung up a string of dried red chili peppers near the heavy iron and porcelain stove. I would hide his favorite tassel loafers so he couldn't go off to work in the morning, wanting to keep him home, and to be near him while he claimed his joy.

I wish he had lived to eat my mother-in-law's Scotch bonnet-pepper-laced cuisine. But at some point toward the end of Jimmy Carter's term in office (the perpetual era of Baltimore mayor William Donald Schaefer for us), my father succumbed to a maddening desire for fried trout. No one wanted to fry fish at home in the 1970s and early 1980s. Our prewar rowhouses had not been updated since they were built, so the exhaust fans no longer spun, and the odor of fried fish could consume the entire first floor of a residence. The lingering scent could wilt the lilies and spoil the ambience created by the impressionist paintings and Ethan Allen furniture that my parents bought after they finished college. My dad also liked to use cornmeal as a breading, and the grit always left a stubborn deposit in the bottom of the pan. He was experimenting with a variety of cooking oils, as much a victim of the Suzanne Somers–led fitness craze as anybody, but you simply couldn't get a fine fry in a cast iron pan if you weren't willing to use Crisco. But what to do with the tainted leftover frying fat? There was something unbecoming about entering the era of the microwave oven with a battered coffee can of stale grease beside it.

Certainly there were several places to buy fried fish in our neighborhood, but I suppose the one restaurant acknowledged to have the superior catch was on Reisterstown Road, just beyond our post office and hardware store. It was called simply Lake Trout. Possibly in the 1960s it had had another name, maybe the Red Rooster or something like that, and later it did carry the name the Roost. For some reason I seem to recall someone jubilantly painting the "Lake Trout" sign in orange cursive letters the day it must have come to life in about 1978. Lake trout to me is not our ignoble whiting fish, "trout" delivered "late" from the day boats and linguistically eased over time into that homespun "lake trout," batter dipped and fried. No, it is sustenance from a single source that carries with it the experience of a particular place. But to call the eatery a restaurant is an exaggeration. For all of the time my dad served as acolyte to the delicacy, Lake Trout was a carryout joint on our side of town for the country folk, increasingly hungry and loudly impolite as the night wore on.

My father would go there whenever his fancy took hold of him: after work, lunchtime, and especially in the cool of a late summer evening after the Erol's video store had closed. If traveling from work he wore his signature sport coat and tie. At night he would brave Lake Trout prep style, in penny loafers, jeans, a windbreaker, and a straw hat, jockeying in the line of customers wearing house shoes, T-shirts, and pink hair curlers, smoking cigarettes while awaiting their orders. No one I ever saw in all my life treated my father with anything other than attentive respect.

When he returned, he would unwrap the foil and the steaming pieces of gummy white bread would fall away with little crunchy bits of the flour batter from the fish lodged in their pores. There would usually be four or five pieces of fish bound together in bread and hot sauce, and he would munch contentedly over one or two, and feast on the carcass over the next day or so. Not always but sometimes he would bring a Styrofoam side dish of collard greens or potato salad.

In my recollection Lake Trout was an extra-dinner snack, chow on the side, consumed in glorious, gluttonous private, quite different from the 6:30 p.m. fare that we all shared. From time to time he would invite me to a portion of the ration, but the idea of picking through the bones and even the texture of the meat itself was unsavory. For me, and when I had three dollars, there was a Korean sub shop two blocks away that sold grilled chopped meats. My fasts didn't bother him at all. I understood, in fact, his selfish philosophy of culinary delight. I had known it from my young boyhood when we were down to a single hot dog roll at our dinner for four—and I made quite well known my desire to enjoy the roll in solitary relief—and thus was prohibited from having any at all.

But he would bid me to accompany him to the carryout at Reisterstown and Hayward, two blocks from the Preakness racetrack, the way I bend Nathaniel and Mitchell into the car to Rogers Avenue and the Caribbean restaurants today. When I couldn't forestall the errand I would sit in the car and listen to music, hoping not to have to stand with him in the hot, brightly lit restaurant, the crowd's loud banter passing over me in waves. I was swimming along cautiously, and never felt particularly African, favoring steak over fish and greens, and the Rolling Stones over Ray Parker Jr., in spite of the unshaped bush haircut I always wore. I had in fact been roughly handled by two older boys on my way from the store with hotdog rolls shortly after that fateful dinner when I first appreciated my father's food philosophy. It didn't take much for me to imagine that the voluble and uninviting strangers in line were related to those boys. Because Lake Trout always struck me as a place on the verge of disorder, a contest land requiring you to hold position tenaciously in one line to order and pay for food. That hurdle and chore surpassed, you then needed the wisdom of Solomon to know when what you had purchased had found its way into a bulging, white paper bag.

There is a picture of the two of us from those years. We are sharing opposite ends of a parking lot curbstone on Harlem Avenue in West Baltimore. We were attending an outdoor jazz concert. The only musician I can recall from that hot late afternoon was a thin chain-smoking white guy who played the organ and wore sunglasses. I guess I remember him because he was the only white person around and at the time I was pretty impressed by the keyboardist of the Doors. My dad had coerced my presence, and I tried to show my displeasure by getting away from him and not letting him talk to me about jazz on Pennsylvania Avenue, a story he enjoyed. On the other hand, I wasn't all that comfortable in the neighborhood we call Sandtown, and I wanted the security of his company. So we looked away from each other, sitting on flanks of the cement block, him in his straw hat and me with a little afro, our precarious balance.

Living in our West African homeland, which used to be called the Tooth Coast on some maps, Negroland on others, and just a war zone on the most recent ones, I was reminded of my dad's pleasure. Two experiences with food brought me immediately to him. For dinner, my cook brought out peanut soup, pounded yam, stewed vegetables, and fried fish. I would do someone harm for good peanut soup, and the last time I had it that I didn't make it was at the Senegalese place in Philadelphia in 2000 with Greg Carr and my fiancée. It was Greg who brought us together so that Nathaniel could be born. But my cook Estelle's soup was the best I'd ever tasted. It had taken a week of negotiation across English, French, and Baoulé for me to convey to her that my preference lay in local, regional food. In Côte D'Ivoire, it is said that the western Bété people love sauce vert, made of palm leaves. The large central group, the Baoulé, the people exiled from Kumasi in neighboring Ghana eons ago, they are fond of gombo—okra to most Americans, and gumbo to Nawlinians. The Jula, the trading people of the north, are devoted to soupe arachide, the groundnut dish that tastes so good to me. Fascinatingly enough, the smidgen of DNA evidence that I have collected over the years points to Mali and Burkina Faso, a bit north, for my dad's family origins.

Later that week I was having dinner with about ten men. We ordered all kinds of specialties, chicken kedjenou and grilled fish and even something that was sort of like opossum, but the poisson braisé with attiéké, charbroiled lake fish and ground cassava, seemed everyone's favorite. Konan, my neighbor at one elbow, bragged several times that he was Adjoukrou, coastal stock, and that if he did not have the head of the fish, it was if he hadn't eaten. I had heard the same idea about eating soup that hadn't been prepared with enough peppers. Konan lectured me that eating with the hands was not only elegant but digestively necessary since important juices came out of the fingertips during the eating process. His plate was piled high with the cranial remains from three fish. I understood that while he could theoretically understand that the large majority of my ancestors had come from the same savanna land where we were relishing our meal, practically, on account of my skin color, it was a difficult conclusion to draw.

Ousmane, the less stentorian man on the other side, reached into the communal platter and put the final third of the fish on his plate. With his spoon in his left hand and his fork in his right, he picked up the tail, the crispiest part of the grilled fish, and cracked it over, I thought, to discard the bony fin on a small plate we had been using for waste. Instead, he lifted his fork and crunched that savory bit, his eyes dancing with succulent delight.

The Ivorians accept the grilled fish and the shredded cassava or attiéké as their national dish, the one that is void of ethnic origins. But for me the ethnic tastes were the beginning of the real story. I ate my Thursday afternoon Thieboudienne,

vegetables and the three relishes at Quatre Mangues off of rue
Ahougnansou. At home Mademoiselle Kofi and Aloa introduced
me to the world with Sauce Arachide, Sauce Graine, Sauce Da,
Sauce Verte, and Sauce Baoulé. But those pepper ragouts over
rice or ngyam didn't feel new because I was coming to them
from a temple of Diri Kolé, Diri Djon Djon, legumes, Sos Pwa,
Banane Peze, and Soup Joumou, or twice-cooked beans and
rice, dried mushroom rice, eggplant-based stew, ground bean
sauce, twice-fried pressed plantain, and pumpkin soup. Those
dishes on a single platter are what I would like to eat in the after-
life. There are traditions of women expressing love for men that
involve being served food and if you don't come from them and
you experience them you can glean the marvel easily. I have
photographed my mother-in-law cooking. My boys and I spent
the better part of our excursion to Montreal tracking down the
foodstores and restaurants of those children of Dessalines. Their
techniques led me to teach myself to make soul food that I enjoy,
collard greens with Scotch bonnet peppers and palm oil and
my black-eyed peas with garlic and the holy trinity, but Soup
Joumou and poisson frites were the inspiration. After learning about the techniques of the culinary smiths from the fer-
tile crescent, the Gulf of Guinea, I started looking differently at
Maryland's staple, crab soup. If you removed the water, and sub-
stituted okra, black-eyed peas, collards, eggplant, and ngyam
and added that spice, what would you have?

Like all good cuisine, African food takes time and work and
a place to do it. Making daily dinner can easily eat up three
hours. A good, not a fine, meal involves an inordinate amount of
thinking, selecting, prep, weight-training cooking, and aerobic
cleanup. The kitchen in my house is emblematic of Homeland
itself. It features a granite countertop I had long coveted, petite,
but plump enough that three people can gang around it on stools
and eat comfortably. In my first house I wanted a counter so bad
I built a poplar-wood breakfast bar and reversed the hinges and

frame of the back door to accommodate it. All of that has already been done by what seem at first glance to have been competent hands. My kitchen is cute, but I find that it is not really the site of meal construction. It was conceived of by the medical couple (or the banker before them?) as only a site of food warming. The magicians who redesigned the kitchen had their eye on decor to the neglect of practicality. They have set the stainless steel sink on top of the tile, making it impossible to sweep granular refuse completely into the sink, gliding crumbs over mortared joints notwithstanding. The exhaust fan has a hand-size remote that slips into disuse somewhere between the pots of collards and the rice and beans. The top-line double Thermador electric oven joins the party, chirping and flashing its error code. Rather than engage an electrician, whenever those birds start singing I just disconnect the circuit breaker for a week.

Sometimes I feel the fatigue of a person dragging that sled. When my son gets into the station wagon after school, a duty that, cutting the day as it does and requiring a confrontation with traffic, the human being at their least interesting and most deadly, tends to throw me in a sour mood, he says on cue, "I am starving." I don't even hear it as a misused metaphor. I have this craving all of the time, a desire to eat until I am satisfied, tired, and needing rest, like the satiety I experience from my own food at the holidays. It is like the last stand of the libido.

At the house ten minutes later, the short return circuit going against traffic, my son has taken all of the probable candidates for a meal out of the refrigerator and placed them on the counter. I have spent thirty minutes today vacuuming and cleaning the kitchen floor and counters. I am touched by his agreeability, at least partly. The meal ingredients consist of a half pound of frozen ground turkey, two uncooked crab cakes, and a container of leftover spaghetti, mushrooms, and marinara sauce. I decide to fry him a crab cake made from Venezuelan sea animals in olive oil, to tide him over. The lump meat tablet has been in the refrigerator for two days, and I am disinclined to eat the remaining one. The South American meat tastes to me like sea chicken, rubbery and bland. Crab, which Alexander Dumas described as the province of Africans from the beginning of time in *Le grand dictionnaire de cuisine*, are mainly of interest to me in claw meat, made into cakes. Apparently, in this lifetime, I will not outstrip my origins as a Maryland native from a flinty Baltimore house. I like my mother's crab cakes the best, and partly because she never used the top grade of crab and did not bury it in mayonnaise. I can't consume lobster, because the meat is too rich, too ample, and I can have the same feeling about the lump meat from larger crabs. But it is also a mistake to buy crabmeat outside of the Chesapeake Bay, which, unhappily I did, lured by the price that has surely been driven down by people being shot in the streets of Caracas, $12.99 a pound.

The occasion of the crab cake depresses me, and I forlornly reinsert the spinach and leftover halved onions back into the icebox, the remnants of the idea of a meal. There is nothing else to form the bedrock of dinner. At Giant's that week, I found myself unable to buy the meat. The fish always looks slick and unattractive in its freshly bleached cases. I ignored the chicken and ground turkey for Nathaniel. I am giving up. My "elegant despair" tells me that I can't bear to make dinner.

There is a food calculus between two people that is sometimes hard to shake. If we go to the supermarket, as in the larger regional chain store, Giant of 1967, the one whose brand connotes safety and wholesomeness and inspires my loyalty, we inevitably spend two hundred dollars. This is a fascinating number, because, if there were four of us it would be roughly the same, and if we ate beef or pork at every meal, it would be cheaper. I stock the cart in the vegetable and fruit aisle, fearing the carcinogens in the pesticides by the apple trays and the laced romaine lettuce. I buy a half gallon of the least pus-filled milk for my son, and some sort of alternative for myself, for smoothies.

My inner battle takes place with the Utz cotton seed oil potato chips and the Entenmann doughnuts, and usually I come out all right. Marinara sauce at $2.49 for a Mason jar always seems a steal to me, again, easily enough for four. Three containers of chicken stock. Taco shells, fifteen dollars worth of bread that neither molds nor goes stale, a chemical miracle. Week in and week out the salmon and the crab will get a pull from the salt-water Geechee. Frozen food means a pint of Häaagen Dazs and tasty frozen meatless sausage patties, another chemical wonder. Sometimes I get the frozen pizza from the brand with an Italian name. It simulates well the destruction that has happened to pizza since the decline of hand tossing and the creation of the delivery chains, which shifted the regular ingredients into a smaller package that could fit onto the seat of the economy cars that their deliverers drive. It's like eating pizza ingredients atop baked caulk.

But the dilemma is the hour prep and the cleanup. Chop the garlic and onion and get the cooking underway with two fry pans, one sauce pan, and two bowls. Another calculus makes it better to eat out. If you can discipline yourself and stay under $30 for two, that puts you at $210 for the week, $10,920 for the year against $10,400 eating at home. The problem is, what you cook at home tastes better. My usual comment to my sons about the restaurant meal is "It's not horrible," or, "Horrible." Occasionally food is "Good," the experience is "Pleasant," but more often not really worthy of being mentioned. I only enjoy my own food enough to say that it is "Tasty!" or another inanity, like I have made the perfect pancake. I long for the days of Estelle Kofi putting down a small plate of rice, sauce, and a pan-fried fish. My nutty children consider a spiceless meal from Chipotle good food.

Because it is nearby, we go to one of the two restaurants in Roland Park. I am pleased by the fact that an ordinary convenience exists, a mile and a half away and within the tree canopy.

This is the essence, really, of the old suburbs: proximity to the town, but unperturbed pastoral privacy at home. Even though now it is no longer a suburb. If I went the other way, east, to the old turnpike road that had been the formal entrance to the estate, I could have found American "fast food" establishments, with entirely black clienteles, as well as a gallery with different kinds of pub food, where some of the servers and a few of the customers are black. But not in Roland Park, like a little wedge of France but with English standards for bread.

The restaurant has two identities joined by a hostess table, a café and a restaurant both. When we get to the station at the entrance, I realize that I have had brunch and lunch at the café and dinner in the restaurant. The lunch menu, and the lunch menu price, would completely satisfy my needs right now. I do not really, on a whim of not wishing to spend the three hours to prepare and clean up something good to eat, desire to spend gourmet prices.

Now, what are American gourmet prices? Chez Panisse in Berkeley? I was considered for a literary award in New York City one November and my mom always wanted to go to Tavern on the Green, so I took her. Since we got beverages and soup, I bet it was nearly forty dollars a person all together, and it was only lunch, but my memory of the experience was fair grub at a place frequented by Russian women in heavy makeup and tight white pants. I know my son got a hamburger. I went to a town-house near Union Station in Washington, DC, that served food worthy of the pretty penny. I like a bit of range and piquancy, but starch and sauce and a fin are my mainstay. Is forty dollars for two people at a restaurant making a valid bid to serve food with a napkin and fork unreasonable?

As the server approaches, I ask if there is a difference in the menus between the two departments. He tells me, Not at all, and asks if I prefer being seated down steps and to the right, the elegant restaurant side, which I agree to. Nathaniel has on remnants of his school clothes, slacks and shirt with a pullover, the same way I am attired. Neither of us has on a blazer, and we both wear shoes with laces from the genre that have replaced penny loafers. He guides us down the grotto steps and takes us over to a booth in the warmest section of the restaurant, near the bathrooms, for which I am actually grateful, not perceiving it as the septic seat but the hearth perch. I find the plush decorated booth in some sort of gleaming coppery finished fabric, with a warm overhead light much nicer than the stiff chairs on the windy and frosty café side. Two well-dressed women in sweaters and silk scarves sit in the booth to our rear.

Our waiter, a tall woman with a streak of gray and a gentle tummy, comes over in welcome, telling us about the special. I hear the two women in the booth behind us making decisions about the merits of a second cocktail. "You'll have to call an ambulance," says one of them. The special is meatball sub, a choice of ground beef or turkey. The critics of the restaurant industry warn against Monday dining, because the kitchens unload all of the remaindered meat from the previous week before it spoils. Especially they warn against eating the fish, which rots quickest. My son is obviously going to order the special; which meat he will choose, I can't be sure. I want to order the rockfish, but the thirty-dollar price deters me; pushing the bill towards fifty dollars because I don't want to eat frozen pizza is insane. I choose shrimp tacos, for twenty-one dollars, knowing that my son has bested me for economy, even if I am not sure precisely how much the special costs. The outer limit of a wintertime meatball sub can only be fifteen dollars, about double the chain store price. We are grazing on the menu's budget end, but the affair is yet an extravagance.

The well-dressed women behind me order wine in lieu of more sugared hooch, which reminds me of something a similarly smartly dressed, fashionably short-haired white woman said the Sunday we felt like walking and attended Redeemer Church.

It was chilly in the nave and during the Peace a man said, "We should have soup with our snacks," and the woman whipped around in her pew and remarked in earnest, "No, cocktails." That day I felt so good about walking to church. I was both preserving the environment and exercising, important to an overweight person like myself, closer to being obese than to what the physician would declare normal. The doctors conceive a healthy range for me that begins at 108 pounds, which is what I weighed entering high school, eating the diet of a hunter-gatherer. I understand the purpose of their pointless, unattainable metric. On any given day I can feel the arteries closing down, the blood thickening, the nerve endings exhaustedly firing from the tiniest hint of glucose that can't be processed, the growths bristling through my skin, the retina throbbing. I have a shirtless picture from my last summer in Atlanta, and the five-year contrast indicates I have totally reversed course away from the Celestial City. The stresses of work and the Baltimore foodways may be a cause for despair.

The grub soon arrives and we set our hands and forks to it. Nathaniel's meatballs look like ground beef turned into a sausage. But he has a plate smothered in incredibly tasty fried little potato bits, what seem to have been the ends of a large batch of French fries imprisoned at the bottom of the hopper. Despite the fact that they look like remains, they are enchanting, and I help myself to several of them, the width of a pencil, the length of a quarter. He bolts it all and remarks, "It was good. It wasn't cold."

On my dish the first thing I look for is the black beans, which I expect to be married to the rice, but which are actually pureed and squirted illiberally on the tortilla shell with a similar paste of avocado. The two grilled shrimp on each of the three tacos are large, and the pieces of pineapple in the salsa taste like mango. Even though the dish arrives within minutes of our seating, it is already room temperature, and will be chilly before I finish eat-

ing. The starch dish, Spanish rice with tomato, has no perceptible flavor. An aggressively salty taste would certainly be bad,
but the Spanish technique is to fry onion and garlic, add tomato
paste and the rice and chicken broth, which what I am eating is
certainly not. Roland Park and Homeland are English neighborhoods, with covenants and restrictions dating back one hundred
years meant to keep them so, but whatever might have been exclusive about the English palate is mystery to me. The restaurant entrance is a dugout facing south, but the western face of
the mall on Roland Avenue features a French restaurant, Petit
Louis, that I visit on special occasions. I would call it pricey,
but it is not unreasonable for a local, reliably decent, specialty
café. The basement restaurant is American fusion. I feel like
we should have supported the Senegalese bistro on York Road,
where the service is slower and the food is good, but expensive.

The server and then the shift manager, dressed in informal
clothes of good taste, come over and ask how our meal is. I feel
a wretched burden in these situations, as if the weight of my clan
is upon me. I have been delivered of a portion that I can certainly
finish but could neither recommend nor bring myself to reorder
without a serious investment in spirits. There is chatter from
my parents in the back of my mind about the dawn of desegregation and black couples going to downtown restaurants for the
first time and sending a lot of food back to show that they were
familiar with quality service and knew what properly prepared
food tasted like. While this is indeed a necessary tactic, commensurate with the goal of "getting what you pay for," my parents had noticed that it became a persona all by itself. Sending
back the food was a source of recognition and satisfaction quite
apart from the way it tasted or how quickly it came, and some
of their crowd became insufferable. It wasn't fun to go out with
them because they would always make a scene; being unsatis-
fied was part of the satisfaction. In a way, I have already failed
that measure by agreeing to sit near the bathroom, which my

father never would have allowed, and I have also accepted warm food. I smile at the shift manager, concealing my disappointment. I know that my efforts at subterfuge are imperfect—my son enjoys telling me when they are—but my inadequate mask only imitates the behavior I regularly receive. It is in fact the mirror of a restaurant drama I face habitually at a sit-down establishment of the second class. There, the hostess greets me with a bright smile and suggests, "Take out?" When I answer, "I'd like to dine in," I can see the clouds form on her face.

I too sometimes frown at Baltimore dining. I used to know a boutique sandwich shop in Bolton Hill. That means that, although black people work in the kitchen and white people wear clean clothes and pocket the dollar, the white people are assumed to be proponents of civil rights. They are not working for the monopoly chain restaurants on the beltway ring; they are walking to their cars on the street and needing the same umbrella of goodwill to safeguard them on their journey as anyone else. I liked going there, it reminded me of what I had read about in books. You could sit on the sidewalk under an umbrella and drink coffee and read while looking at rowhouses that were more than a century old. I always find that to be some enjoyable daily relish. Black people didn't really live in the neighborhood per se, but there was a state office building nearby and occasionally the workers would come up for lunch. Two prosperous clerks came, used to heavy meals, hungry and seeking service. They rejected the restaurant's nuanced menu choices. One woman wanted to add bacon and tomato and mushroom to a sandwich, which also should have come with fried potatoes but did not. She spoke in a noisy, declarative manner that was impossible to misunderstand. Nonetheless, the waiter repeatedly clarified her requests and bemusedly added the additions and bantered, in an overfriendly manner, that the women resented. I knew because they discussed his behavior when he was absent. When the bill came the woman adamantly refused to pay for any of the extras. Her bill was being padded, and, had she known of the additional charges, she would never have incurred them. The two women did not call the waiter a racist when the manager came out, but they did become loudly belligerent, which eventually won them a free lunch and the waiter sitting on the curbstone smoking with his apron over his shoulder in disbelief. The restaurant closed not so long after. I could not genuinely wonder any longer why restaurant menus that cater to multiracial crowds typically have a clause that no substitutions whatsoever can be added to the dishes on the menu. It's better than dress codes and having to pay the bill in advance.

I am afraid of adding things to the menu that I am unprepared to pay for. When the waitress brings the bill over after I decline the desserts (on a slate in chalked writing they are advertising a six-cookie "bargain" for $17.50), she offers, "First time here?" I wonder if she is consciously mocking politesse or if this is just as good as it gets.

In my mind, I blame all of this on Nathaniel for not combing his hair enough. It's like the day years ago when I was visiting a judge's grandson on our part of town and rode with him to the post office in Walbrook Junction. The fashion at the time was black knit hats, although in Baltimore, black knit hats are always in fashion. As we left the federal station we were surrounded by patrol cars and a half dozen officers. They held us frozen in place. One officer, missing a name tag on his uniform, stood somewhat bashfully in front of the car in the ready position, which is shoulders square, knees bent, hand on gun, but not drawn. My friend and I remained obediently motionless. After a long while, the sergeant came over. "Report of Puerto Rican looking guys. Robbed a store," he rambled as he handed back the driver's license. After the squadron drove off on some other escapade, my homeboy turned to me and said, "They stopped us because you are wearing that hat."

It is a frosty day so Nathaniel and I return home and I visit the bourbon-filled decanter on the butler's tray. The cultural mores that wince at the medicinal demijohn are familiar but rejected nonetheless. I am old enough now to see the utility of that barrel on the mule cart in my great-grandfather's time, working its way down the lane to give winter sustenance and remedy to the workers of the field. I have been to Johnny's one time for a beer, but I prefer to drink in the York Road bars down the street. Drinking after work in the wintertime is connected for me to marriage and children. I had an evening class that ended about 9:00 p.m., a class that took place in the fall of the year that my youngest was born. When the seminar ended, I would have a nightcap at the Brickstore in downtown Decatur, and it was there that I learned about the fineness of Belgian ales. Oddly enough, the bartender was African American and he patiently worked with me to find the taste I was looking for. Franziskaner Hefeweizen is my session beer; Saison Dupont farmhouse ale is my prestige brand. This is not to malign saisons or wheat beers like La Fin du Monde's Blanche de Chambly, La Chouffe Blond, Piraat, Ayinger Braüweisse, the pricy favorite Fântome, or that rare thing of beauty, the St. Bernardus Tokyo Christmas batch. But, the person so crude as to consider a Trappistes Rochefort 10 a taste of Guiness and Champagne, I found in Tourpes's "Vieille Provision" exactly the potion I had always been looking for.

Homeland has no public house, though it supports a Tudor-style "olde" wine shop that carries Belgian ales. But to be with people and raise a glass, I have to seek the permission of another clientele. Within a mile is a restaurant with a bar, but I hesitate to fully commit myself. It is like falling in again with my old friends, and our memories of life when we thought we would live forever. The preferable neighborhood place of recourse is called Flight and it is half restaurant, half tavern, a smaller version of the Roland Park double, split over two buildings that have been connected. The restaurant is in a brick storefront that extends mainly easterly down the street and they serve ample portions of pub food. The bar side is in an older frame structure, built in 1920 and painted a sad white on the exterior, and they even feature a kind of restrained sidewalk patio, a real novelty for a neighborhood place. In another era it would have offered dancing and an upstairs room.

I like Flight because of another kind of nostalgia. The Baltimore I grew up in had sort of an ecological sadness, in that, for a city of small rowhouses crowded with people, the bars and fried chicken corner stores offered only carryout service. Whether it was the expense of licensing and operating or the recognition of the desperation of the population, the city was devoid of black clientele lounges. We had the 5 Mile House and, farther west, the Half Mile Track, but I associated them with older people. We had Wesley's Bar on Baker Street, the Oxford Tavern on Fulton Street, the Walbrook Lounge, and Roots on Smallwood and Vine, if we were feeling quite brave. But a local tavern, quaint and reliable, we had not.

Flight seems like a neighborhood place, but, hard as it might try, York Road does not fall into the same class of turpitude as Reisterstown Road. The first time I had a beer there, a group of men sat around and recounted the neighborhood lore, the contests in the street, the brushes and run-ins and outright failures, the fistfights and long disputes, the sentences to prison. The scene had an Arthurian feeling, adhering to the same heraldic recounting that I do with my own bunch in our places of leisure and comfort, wherever they might be. We take stock of the departed and memorialize them and recount their derring-do. The conversation is also off-putting, or at least designed to be so to strangers, and that term can be taken many different ways. I can't quite recall what I said to enter into the conversation. I probably laughed at an appropriate moment, but when I said where I had grown up I was welcomed to participate or to dwell haplessly on the periphery of the circle of intimacy, mewling over my own beer.

Just before Christmas, I sat at the bar at Flight with my date from senior prom. A recently divorced mother, she and I occasionally exercise together or share a link to a jazz song. We wound up there for last call after I succeeded in convincing her that the afterhours place at Carey and Franklin was too "wide open," our term for anything goes, for things that happen in a shocking manner. Flight was a fitting rendezvous because we had started our high school romance at a house party on Cold Spring Lane a block or so east of York Road thirty years before. Besides, I always am fond of the guy who not only makes himself at home in the world but who can extend that courtesy to the center of his love life. But that has not been my fate.

One of the worst nights of my life, when my aspirations fell so brutally short of reality, went awry when I was leaving the San Francisco club Nikki's Haight Street Barbecue with a charming cosmopolite. A project hustler counting money was leaning up against my car. I walked directly to the vehicle and opened the passenger door. Wordlessly, he began moving off, and I returned to the street to the driver's side. The city had its spots on Fillmore and in Potrero Hill and the Mission with the vatos, even if I wouldn't have compared what happened there to home. Having never before regarded a man counting money as a foe, I didn't register a threatening situation. But I did not usher my date into the car, an impoliteness connected to the distance I'd felt from her when we were dancing earlier. She said immediately once I was inside that she could have been abducted and raped, a suggestion about her vulnerability that I wouldn't have guessed. I was too surprised for words, which made it worse.

My companion at Flight grew up in a neighborhood known for its corner and she could handle herself even if she has lived in the county for a long time. The night of our holiday breakfast there were several lean young women at the bar. I find them really dangerous. They can turn you out wide open. I fear connection to them, too, because I suspect that they can add shimmer to real emptiness. The women also fear it, I can sense, like the time I spent with a lithe girl and found the green and white and green perineum piercing and she said, *Don't go that far.* Too much closeness, too much openness is the one guarantee of emptying it all out. The bar closed and we went to Albion Road for a nightcap. My prom date got tired and slept over. That night she wore marvelous underclothes, silkily elegant, and I realized it had been many years since I had enjoyed a woman's fine lingerie. After a while, she allowed me a simple favor. The dream of the house is the dream of shelter, a vessel for life on the barren rock.

I looked, and saw him open the book, and read therein; and as he read, he wept and trembled: and not being able longer to contain, he brake out with a lamentable cry; saying, "What shall I do?"
　　　—John Bunyan, *The Pilgrim's Progress* (1678)

[A] wonder I had not given up the ghost.
　　　—George F. Bragg, *A Bond-Slave of Christ* (1912)

In the garden. Where we used to play.
　　　—Blake Baxter, "When We Used to Play" (1987)

Eostre in Lafayette Square

An apparition began to form in my mind. Homemade wooden easels held foam-core posterboards, all of them propped up in the naves of the four churches around Lafayette Square. The posters would be three feet by two feet, and feature an attractive picture of Billie Holiday with her signature gardenia and the logo "Jazz in the Square." The message simple and succulent: a free concert, a jazz holy day. The parishioners of the churches, some of whom live in the rowhouses flanking the square, some coming from the outskirts of Washington, DC, most living in Woodlawn and Randallstown, would comprise the core. Then people from the neighborhoods, Harlem Park, Sandtown, Upton, Marble Hill, and Druid Heights. Then people from Johns Hopkins.

As a child, Eleanora Fagan would walk around the Lafayette Square neighborhood and lived on both Fremont Street and Argyle Avenue. On Christmas Eve in 1926, when she was eleven, she was statutorily raped by two men in a cathouse on Riggs Avenue. The assault was shocking enough to be front-page news, and the girl soon changed her name to Billie Holiday. A truant, abused, and institutionalized, Eleanora was the sort of child whom Father Bragg of St. James tried to rescue in his orphanage, and hers was precisely the kind of bawdy, vernacular art that women and men of his ilk wished to erase. I thought a public concert not two blocks from the crossroads of her suffering might honor her resurrection and art. Her story of childhood tragedy, adult wantonness, and skilled creativity chorus through the decades for black Baltimoreans and into the present. The same qualities had marked the time of Frederick Douglass, then Frederick Bailey, who knew Dallas Street the century before Holiday hung around there. A free concert would be the method of proper memorial and the means of coalescing a new group of citizens. Sandtown would be the perfect place to renew jazz.

The idea had special magic because, in the same way that Holiday and Frederick Douglass were scooped out from the city, so too was Baltimore's contribution to the foundation of the art form. Like my friend Keith Gilyard, I think early jazz was a polygenesis affair. Far from the Mississippi's deltas, bays, bayous, and basins was a style of black musical playing that emerged from the estuary culture of the Chesapeake, the Patapsco, Susquehanna, and Potomac. It bellowed out from the decks of Captain Brown's boat as they approached Gibson's Island and Brown's Cove. It was shouted, blared, banged, and pounded by the likes of Joe Rochester, Eubie Blake, Ernest Purviance, Reggie Haymer, and teenage Elmer Snowden. The good Baltimore sound they created in the 1910s was next door, literally, to ten-year-old Cab Calloway on Druid Hill Avenue in 1920, and it was the belt of the shafts driving the four-stroke power engine of the drummer on Broadway Chick Webb. As Duke Ellington said, gushing over Joe Rochester's sideman Elmer Snowden, "the No. 1 Banjorine Player," who would pluck Ellington from his obscurity as a young DC squire and take him to the Kentucky Club of New York for rebranding as a Duke, "he had something extra going on that really upset everybody in Washington—musicians and audience. He had a flair for soul, plus ragtime, and a jumping thing that tore us all up." Billie Holiday's father, Clarence, a talented enough musician to shift from a bugler in the army to a guitarist for Fletcher Henderson (Benny Goodman's ghost writer), lived for many years two blocks away from Rochester. Snowden, born in 1899 and who was almost certainly beguiled into the banjo by the riverboat excursions and fairgrounds along the Patapsco's branches, grew up on Whatcoat Street, about four little blocks west of Arlington and Lafayette. Baltimore old-timers adore "The Avenue," meaning Pennsylvania Avenue, which blossomed with the Douglass Theater in 1921, but there was a more ancient sound from nearby that doesn't even yet have a name.

That nameless sound reappears in new forms. Older Baltimoreans enjoy a breezy jazz that preserves an open seam between rhythm and blues and straight-ahead jazz and the Baby Boomers' elegant doo-wop harmony groups from the nightclub circuit, a place where Sarah Vaughn and Nancy Wilson and hometown favorite Ethel Ennis overlap. Unlike our considerably wealthier cousins in the District and in Prince George's County, who kept the band structure as vital to their music, the generation I belong to was both richer and a lot poorer than the Boomers, creating an electronic dance music whose name never evolved beyond the nest of its origin, "Club Music." It is brash and repetitive and its elegance comes from the eclectic borrowing of transmuted Africanisms, from Michael Jackson bleating "Mama se mama sa mamakousa" to George Kranz odling "Din Da Da." It blares from the stoop and radio, and everyone living in the city knows the loops and mixes from the early 1990s heyday when the clubs flourished. But to hear the sound of the city as it is communally agreed upon, old and young, working or not, scrambling or not, one must attend a holy-day event.

The year of the first Jazz in the Square concert, my third full year back in the city, sickness struck us on the final day of my youngest son's even-year visit from Atlanta to celebrate the King Holiday. After a financial and legal ordeal, I "won" custody of his older brother, but not the little boy, and on no odd year until he is eighteen should I ever plan to spend three days in January with him. His parents exchange about two hundred terse words of email per year, and his life is fully mediated by the state of Georgia. Watching him clamber over the pedestrian rail at the airport to make it to our rendezvous point, I can't believe how big he is getting. He's old enough now to travel unescorted, and having gone through the airport so many dozens of times, no longer wants my help to exit.

By the end of the weekend reunion, Nathaniel is showing the symptoms of a hearty cold. Unwilling to risk his coughing and sneezing turning into fever and nausea, I will only be able to subject him to King's "Why I am Against the War in Vietnam" at full volume as his homage for the day. Although this speech isn't a staple on scholastic playlists, the boys don't ask any questions about the antiwar exposé. They have been hearing it their entire lives.

I lightly coerce Mitchell into roughly straightening his room. I hate the ravages of the pigsty, and Mitchell has taken so many liberties with discarded morsels of food that he has previously attracted mice. I hoped that Mitchell, the younger, Sunday-born male child, Kwame Kakraba, will remain in a coopera-tive, sunny mood. The comings and goings between Baltimore and Atlanta are, for me at least, wrenching. I know he has his own pains and discomforts. Mitchell is losing the last bit of baby fat, and, petulant and willful, he can be unreasonably stubborn. While I don't think he gets obduracy from me, I can remember dragging my book bag a mile in a crying fury from the no. 58 bus stop tearing a hole in my US Army surplus pouch. I had to give it up to two big boys to duck getting banked.

Those mishaps are a world apart from my sons's encounters,

but I regularly stimulate their wariness. My favorite picture in the world is of my two boys walking out from the gate of our house before school in Bouaké in Côte d'Ivoire. Unsmiling and hair cropped close, they are in the uniform of khaki shirts and shorts, Nathaniel staring south and Mitchell staring north. My junior men reconnoitering the day.

My sometimes irritable Northman also has a deeply rooted sense of compassionate empathy. When he was about eleven or twelve months old, when he could communicate with us but could not exactly do for himself, I would burp him to help his digestion, and, after I patted his back gently, he would raise himself off my shoulder and look at me and return the gesture, patting me on the back with one little hand. I always thought he was pretty unique for doing that. I also think both boys are spoiled, but as the absent parent I find it difficult not to cater to Mitchell, the assault trench in the everlasting battle to win his affection. Even though I hate all so-called rap music created within the last twenty years, I banter with him about his favorites, in a way that I am more disinclined to do with his older brother. (Jesus save me from Thug Life!) I ask Mitchell if he wants to put on long underwear, like I am wearing. From time to time he still likes to wear his footies all day. I love those days. At other time he insists on coordinated sweatpants and sneakers like the Migos. I bite my tongue, usually. I strove to create security and permanence for him, but I have moved six times and his mother has moved four times since he was born, and his memories bubble around points of trauma, falling off the bunk bed or putting the stick into the beehive. My favorite part of the days we spend together is when I tackle him and tickle him until he is out of breath.

I built him a boy cave underneath his bed with a bean bag chair, toy chest, and a light, and it quickly became his choice place of retreat. He swaps out the first-grade, coach-player basketball team picture of me with my hand on his shoulder in favor of the stock photo that came with the frame, a frog riding a skateboard. I coached his brother's YMCA team twice to winning seasons, but Mitchell would only now and then give himself over to the game that year. When we are together I try to encourage his sense of adventure, and when he's had enough he bounds up the stairs to his room with its handwritten "Do Not Disturb" sign and shuts the door. He prefers his own company.

Before his 3:00 p.m. flight back to Atlanta, I decide to take Mitchell solo over to the MLK parade on Preston Street. Our service will be to hand out some flyers, a task I had intended to pay the squeegee boys to do. Sometimes I try to involve those guys in a light business conversation, to see if I can get them thinking beyond the immediacy of the street. Baltimore's poverty has apparently revisited the highs of 1983 when boys first began pouring out to intersections to wash car windows. The corners, at North Avenue and Hilton and Mount Royal and North Avenue, are as full as they were more than twenty-five years ago, when in 1985 the city council imposed a ban on the activity. The difference today is that now on occasion I see women and girls there. Such gender equality is duplicated in homicide statistics; more than 10 percent of the murder victims in 2019 are female, a record.

We park at Bolton and Dolphin near the Fifth Regiment Armory and hike across Dolphin Street, where I notice the numbers of parked cars and can hear the booming drums of a marching band. Mitchell and I test a series of tall fences at the main entrance to the subway at Eutaw Street. When I was young, there was a ten-foot fence separating the most powerful swings from the rest of the playground, swings with chains and hard, vulcanized black rubber seats, that the most daring of the boys would actually loop-de-loop. Sometimes they leapt from the swings straight into those chain link fences. Sometimes they just climbed over and leaped to the asphalt like mighty black squirrels, impervious to gravity and fear. I was too tame to try such hazardous feats, but I did get the principle of the adroit stomach flip to full pike at a run over the four-foot fences. Shorter barriers were simply to be hurtled. Though I can't remember mastering the tallest fence, the children of today don't seem to climb as we did in the past.

The Baltimore subway was a landmark of my childhood, a promise that the city any day would be like New York or Philadelphia or Boston. But our subway is not even the diamond cross that DC has. Our spoon-shaped spur only takes people from the prestige suburb of Owings Mills in northwest Baltimore County to the state's largest private employer, Johns Hopkins Hospital in East Baltimore. There was a giant station visible from my boyhood home, just before the train gets to Mondawmin, the name of an old plantation. If a line going from the northeast to the southwest were created, making the system into an X, from say White Marsh to Halethorpe, maybe the areas in between would prosper and development might bind the communities together. Even though the racial dynamics of the state are such that since 2003 both Democrat and Republican governors have had African American running mates, large-scale public works and transportation projects connected to job growth in the city have been squashed.

The parade is forming on Eutaw Street, and the marchers are clustered in their camps along the sidewalk and street. As we get closer to MLK Boulevard, I see the members of Kappa Alpha Psi, my father's and my fraternity, bunched together on the western side of the street, blazoned in the clan's colors of crimson and cream. I walk over, wishing that I was a more heartily gregarious person. I rely on mood to dictate my social connections, which is a terrible arrogance on my part. Sometimes I can't suffer enough to brook much human interaction. I typically feel a bit over-Whitmanesque, like I have too many multitudes, and at the same time I keep widening and opening up more inroads. What a contradiction! But I try to masquerade for the children's sake. I don't want them to be squirrelly, afraid of people or their own desires and needs.

I spot Donald, a fireplug of a man, in the center. He was number one on his line, a distinction because for the six or ten weeks that the pledges, called Scrollers, march in unison wherever they go, number one sets the cadence. "My Brothers!," he shouts, before we all lift a boot and march off to a doom-filled session with the older initiates. The pledge process, during which we learned lore and arcana about the old gathering of black collegians and sang blues songs, seemed mainly designed to encapsulate the bonding experience of a Middle Passage, or an initial planting season on a farm, or a stretch on the chain gang. Both my dad and I were number two, though my dad had a zero number on his line, which I did not. Donald and I have only known each other since I returned to Baltimore, but he is precisely the kind of brother I love, the one I strive to be. He is a comfortable black person who accepts himself and is not pretentious, but is ambitious and competent. While he is shorter and lighter colored than I am, he exudes a kind of Nikita Khrushchev–like masculinity and physical presence. He is intellectual and curious, but whenever he opens his mouth, he infuses his speech with the rhythms and twangs of the old neighborhood; it is impossible to uncouple him from his indigeneity. When we first encountered each other at a presidential debate happy hour, we hadn't been conversing for five minutes before we were talking about jail, selling drugs, and gunplay on Bloomingdale Avenue: the coded reverie of urban struggle that grounds us, like the conversation with the men at Flight. A week later, he invited me to a meeting with the state officials who administer the federal government's small business grants, a local banker, and two clothing shop owners. I presented my idea about investing in central business arteries on the city's west side, and the black banker said he liked a lot better the idea of sustaining a business community with some blacks and some whites.

Donald invites me to march and I just sort of set the question aside. I am not sure how much Mitchell will get a kick out of being a part of the show, I don't have on our colors or paraphernalia, and I don't want to commit to marching the full route. But I do exchange greetings with some of the younger guys, just feeling spirited to see them in their regalia and twirling canes. Having once performed at an event with the hip-hop group the Jungle Brothers, I can recall the joy of the step show. Between their inception in the early 1900s and when I became aware of them in the 1970s, the black fraternities seem to have created multiple syncretisms derived from West African initiation dances. (Numbers of initiates in the oldest black fraternities' early years at the single letter chapters came from Nigeria, Ghana, and Liberia.) Each group has a root dance that etches a foundational percussive rhythm. The Alphas step with a high hop and a lot of arm signifying; the Omegas jump vigorously from side to side, spin kick, and drum their fists on their chests; and we Kappas work the ground in place, accenting the beat with the staccato cane. Our side-to-side bop seems to honor the coveted Bantu agrarian rite: dig a hole with the toe, drop the seed, and cover it up. This could be done by just stomping with feet and clapping and slapping our thighs, but we are taught that we added the canes to accommodate injured veterans after the wars. Canes were also a symbol of gentlemen's dignity until the advent of the automobile. We all believe in the rituals of singed flesh. Many initiates routinely brand a single Greek letter onto their arms and chests with a hot iron. The choice Kappa brand is the capital letter K inside a diamond.

A few months ago, the highlight of my introductory African American studies course occurred after I texted one of the brothers in the Hopkins KAPsi chapter, asking to borrow a cane, our step show performance prop. Years earlier, I had given away my stepping cane to a recently crossed neophyte. I bring the cane to class to demonstrate the connection to one of the earliest known

examples of African Americans dancing a cakewalk in an early
Edison film. I was lecturing about the cultural continuity and
the transmissibility of African expressive forms. Using the borrowed cane, I executed a couple of wrist rolls and some flips
and a hand pass I learned from a Jamaican who exclusively
wore suede Bally boots and silk shirts. I was embarrassed, a
little, and I did all of the step show twirling tricks pretty fast.
When I asked if there were questions, Lucie Afko, a tall Togo
American said, "I just want to see you do that thing with the
cane again." I declined to do more, but her asking was the highlight of the year.

Mitchell and I eased up to MLK and Eutaw, where the presiding would begin, past the top-down Cadillac with the day's
prince of blackness, the soul singer Raheem DeVaughn, who sits
atop the convertible bundled up in furs. We worm our way to the
edge of the sidewalk, the cold bringing unusual brightness and
serenity to the day. We stand between a white couple and a slender young woman with a nose ring and three tiny children.

Dressed in clothes and boots that emphasize comfort and
warmth, I look a little old-timey. I was recently mistaken for my
older son's grandfather. I inhabit a complex fate on understating
blackness. I have a view that proposes that black people are encouraged to be the tip of the spear of consumer consumption,
thus associating disposables and new clothes and new cars with
us. I hate that presumption, and sometimes I go to great lengths
to deny it. If I am right about that, I know the way I dress informally and even formally strikes a discordant note, like I am an
Uncle Tom, though I think of myself as an Uncle Tom in reverse.

I like to go to MLK events to meet other black people that
I would rarely encounter in Homeland or Homewood, not to be
that person for white people seeking the same thing. At the same
time, I have lived long enough to know now that any white person I encounter anywhere on planet earth has such a huge store
of advantages over me, both material and epistemological, that

I am foolish to spurn an opportunity for even the most casual association. But the fact of it all irks me and makes me snooty.

I am also pretty firm in my belief of the primal nature of complexion and color in America. When I go out to dance clubs, my one occasion when I wear trendy T-shirts with my boots or sneakers, I notice the white people looking for each other, hoping to stand near one another. Sometimes they will even stand near a light-skinned black person. I have never noticed an American or African or Caribbean black person of any hue do that. So the white woman at the parade starts to be a little chatty, which I discourage, since I have only a few more hours with my boy.

That's when I notice the pile of manure in the middle of MLK at Eutaw. Probably the police horses had been standing there; the Arabbers have diapers for their ponies and mules. The mound looks like three large brown wads of potatoes triangled on the yellow line. Obviously the marchers will either head through it or around it. It is a kind of train wreck happening, though one with devilish symbolism. For the sake of Martin Luther King Jr. and the artwork that Mitchell made at church in his honor when he was four, I look for a piece of cardboard or wood detritus to scrape the manure pile over to the median. I talk to Mitchell about the way typhoid is spread and look in vain for an implement, a primitive tool, a lever.

A female barker calls the groups into line over a loudspeaker and the parade gets underway. The cars notice and avoid the dung, and the first sorority on the march, the Deltas, designate an ensign to stand in front of the foul impediment and bend the line around the obstacle. I notice a man strutting forward in all black golfing attire and sneakers, who holds himself with some perceptible air of import. "Are you, sir, a parade marshall?" I ask in the most stilted manner I am capable of, tugging his sleeve. He smiles with affirmation. "Can you contact a representative from the sanitation department to speed a shoveler here to remove the manure pile from the center of Martin Luther King Boulevard?

All he need do is scrape over to the side of the street, so that, on this important day, our race won't have to walk through feces to celebrate this civil rights holiday." I said it in as officious a manner as I could muster, in the hearing of the white woman, who had already begun sniping at every delay and miscue that was taking place, and the thin young woman with the children. The marshall, however, alertly grasped the significance of the problem. He hurried away and before two more organizations had rounded the corner, a tall man with orange traffic cones had cordoned the spot, vaulting back swiftly with a large snow shovel. The Department of Public Works employee enjoys his newly pertinent value to the parade, in the dead-up middle, where he had perhaps not expected to be, and he somewhat efficiently, somewhat disgustingly, scraped the manure pile ten feet to the median strip. I have run metal shovels and push brooms up and down Arlington, Pimlico, Lafayette, and Sumter Avenue and I have encountered it all, the feces and needles and broken glass and Styrofoam, chicken boxes, diaper and cigarette wrappers, all of the human being in the street. I would have tried to execute the maneuver more cleanly. However, I am gleeful and unabashed talking to Mitchell about such a huge victory on King's celebratory day. We have saved propriety with our probity! We have also addressed the spread of disease. I am not sure it is possible to have been more useful to justice. When Mitchell turns to me I offer him a celebratory Swedish jellyfish.

Kweisi Mfume walks past, waving to the crowd. He has returned to the public scene to try to win a special election to resume his seat in Congress after the death of Elijah Cummings, whose body has lain in state at the US Capitol. I first learned about Mfume when I was about eight, and I had always presumed he was a Japanese man and pronounced his name with a silent *e*: Kwhy Sy Ma-foom. But this renamed Ashanti is a self-made man, up from the block, and the shift he made during the Reagan years to win the congressional seat invokes the image making and remaking vacuousness of electoral politics. It seems to me that when the odds were against us, like in the voting scandals leading to recounts in 1970 and 1980, the politicians were more sincere. When I was a child we would canvass for the people my parents believed in, Norman Reeves, Howard Rawlings, and Parren Mitchell, slapping handbills into the palms of voters on their way to the polling places. Mfume left Congress to take over the NAACP, more than moribund at the time, similarly moribund today. When Mfume is sworn in, in Congress, he will console the audience that black bigotry is as reprehensible as white bigotry. As he walks by, a kind of local African patriarch now entering his eighth decade, I notice his jet black hair.

The Kappas swing along, and I am elated to see a new group among them, including undergraduates who have taken my classes and also helped to landscape the Arlington Avenue memorial garden for slain black children. They are happy to see me, and it is curious to shake hands with the young neophytes, born in Houston of parents from Kumasi or Nairobi, stepping along in their ancient hightop fades, painted in crimson and cream, twirling their canes. The marching bands and the women and girls in white patent leather boots and wide heels come next, accompanied and sometimes led by middle-aged pom-pom men in tights. I suppose they are the gel that keeps the community together, and for every girl who has recently become a woman and whose tights and boots can't hold her back, there is a bearded, middle-aged 250-pounder high-stepping to lead her out.

On battered equipment the Dream Nation plays a rhythm that describes for me precisely the day and time that the drum was recovered after slavery had ended. I used to be so troubled that African Americans had been stripped of the drum, forced to develop the banjo and play out the essence of our humanity on cow ribs, a fiddle, and a washboard with a straw. Probably this was connected to reading. In his novel *The Sound and the Fury*, William Faulkner smugly disparages Luster, who hits the Compsons' saw with a hammer, trying to reproduce the sound made by a traveling minstrel. But the marchers and drummers of the Nation had helped me know why Dilsey came out of the cabin first wearing the maroon velvet dress.

In our part of the Chesapeake—Igbo, Mandingo, Bambara enclave that it was—the veterans from numerous conflicts used military drums to keep the African sound alive. After the War of 1812, the war that happened here, the black drummers re- vived that sound riotously. Today's marching band musical in- gredients, the bass and the triple-hatted tympanum, closely echo the ancient rhythms of Guinea's djembe and dundun. There is a flexible drum stick used on the tympanum that reproduces the tone, slap, and "ghost note" of the djembe, while the bass drum contributes its booming accent. More than a glorified marimba, the xylophone provides the missing steel note. And it was this sound in the back of Chuck Brown's mind in 1969 when he heard the Puerto Ricans grooving and led him to invent Go-Go, the DMV music. In Baltimore, when our public music programs ended, the sound was just concatenated with the heavy machin- ery of the Sparrows Point steel mill, then modified into Club Music. In America, the African American marching bands and their inimitable arrangers are our return to the source.

The musical reverie is followed by the Black Nationalist vi- sion of the rapture: one hundred lean black male saints dressed all in black, joyfully singing out our deliverance. The black men in black seem giants sent from above to return us to the mysti- cal plateau of our nativity along the Futa Jallon. They tide for- ward, a bounce to their step, an incredible, electric élan, and their assertive cries capture the afternoon. They are confidently jogging and chanting a call-and-response chorus in unison, "We all we got! We all we need! . . . We all we got! We all we need!" Mitchell and I leave the parade spellbound, inspired. We plaster the cars up and down Dolphin Street with flyers for my upcoming speakers' series.

Even as devoted acolytes of the chanting Abyssinian princes we have a sore task at hand. A few years before, nearby Sandtown had erupted in the largest-scale street disturbances since the nationwide riots of 1968. A man from the Gilmore Street public housing complex named Freddie Gray had his spine severed during the course of a police detention that was as brutal as it was pathetically unnecessary. A guy I knew had coached him in Pop Warner football, and shared a funny story about Freddie's hapless ways. His death and the police department's unwillingness to admit any wrongdoing precipitated a citywide conflagration, called in some quarters an "uprising," an ancient term familiar to Perine for the revolt of the enslaved. During the Uprising, more than 380 businesses were damaged or burned. About one hundred were Korean merchants, including dozens of liquor stores, many of them operating on the fringe of the law, emended in the 1970s to curtail alcohol distribution in residential neighborhoods. The weight of the federal government falls on a young man in a gas mask on a bicycle, charged for using a steak knife to puncture a fire hose while the CVS pharmacy burned that April. Greg Butler had been a basketball star at one of the leading public schools, but because he tried his hand in honors and AP classes, his total grade point average made him uncompetitive for NCAA scholarships. Baltimore public schools in his time did not believe in a weighted GPA.

Politicians of every stripe habitually condemn Baltimore's black citizenry. In 2015 the first black president faulted "criminals and thugs" for the disturbances. Four years later, a president who comes closer to avowed racism than any resident of the White House since Andrew Johnson, flips off Sandtown and part of the black-represented city as a "rat and rodent infested mess" where "no human being would want to live." The neighborhood takes its name from the sand that escaped the Patrick Flanigan

asphalt Company's trucks as they wound through the city from
their depot at Monroe Street and Laurens. There is a kernel of
truth in the political screeds about domestic life in our town,
but it obfuscates more than clarifies. There are 708 abandoned
houses in the seventy-four square blocks of the neighborhood,
surrounded by Upton, Druid Heights, Edmondson, Harlem
Park, and Easterwood Park, which also have a high number
of vacant, dilapidated, uninhabitable homes. The city reports
nearly seventeen thoushand derelict abodes, but some estimates
put the number beyond thirty thousand. The hovels were owned
by landlords living abroad who rented them out, neglected repairs, and never surrendered to the changes in the housing code,
such as regulations outlawing the use of ungrounded electric
sockets, leaded paint, or asbestos insulation. The city fines the
properties, placing liens on their potential sale; the most deso-
late of the Sandtown beauties are in the millions of dollars. At
a removal cost of $20,000 a piece, the city government couldn't
afford to eradicate the abandoned housing blight if it wanted to.

What the government has offered to the working poor is no
better. At Freddie Gray's Gilmore Homes, built in 1942, the
queue for basic repairs had become so long that the city housing
department's overworked maintenance staff were accused of demanding sexual favors from the residents to get a faucet tight-
ened. Speculators scour the neighborhood and flip houses back
onto the market after shoddy cosmetic repairs. Teetering on the
edge of collapse, the Italianate-style rowhouses in Lafayette
Square, with marble steps, scroll-sawn deep bracket modillions
supporting the window and roof cornices, and full-height French
parlor windows, are replaced by ninety-day wonders of particle
board and vinyl siding. The new houses might survive a single
generation. The nineteenth-century rowhouses in repair and disrepair, the public housing from World War II, the empty spaces,
and the shrink-wrapped PVC and vinyl Generation Xers from

the first Opportunity Zone go-round, all collide in a stew of after-thought, postponement, and desertion.

For most of my life I probably thought that there was a riot unfolding at Pennsylvania and North Avenue. The intersection was a deliberate tipping point of black life, loud, chaotic, intoxi-cated, opinionated, that invited plunder and conflagration, and regularly wrestled with state force. Older people, who recog-nize their relatives, neighbors, and blood descendants, would be more inclined to see it as a place of the rich carnival of human life described by Mikhail Bakhtin, where the poor speak with-out reservation their criticisms of the rich, where the utterance and performance of word and sound add rich depth to mean-ing, and where speaking is braided to resonances from the past and insists upon future responses. I thought of the entire ave-nue as an adult place. The toughest kids at my school were from Whitelock, but we all flailed when it came time to battle the Huns of Booker T from McCulloh, Druid Hill, Division, and Fremont. The everyday acts of public violence that I witnessed, at school, on the playground, and in my neighborhood, at the track meets, at AFRAM, at the City Fair, the cussings and the slappings and scratchings, the being stolen, the bankings, and the bottle-over-the head breakings, belonged to an unruliness that peaked for me at places on the avenue. How could I be sur-prised when I was in Atlanta making dinner for the children in April of 2015, four days after Freddie Gray's murder and CNN cameras showed two high-school friends, Darryl Green and Cordell Hunter, in the middle of North Avenue at Baker Street? Flames could be seen in the background and the two men were shouting, wielding bats. Not far away, another old friend, Stephanie Rawlings-Blake, the mayor of the city, was uttering the now-infamous words misconstrued by the press that "those who wished to destroy space" could gather without fear of arrest. Because the mayor of a majority-black and poor city expressed concern about overpolicing the citizens whose welfare she was sworn to safeguard, against the profits of multinationals specifically and the sanctity of private property in general, she ended her political career. She was five years ahead of her time.

Two weeks later I flew to visit Baltimore. I met a friend on Pennsylvania Avenue and stumbled into an impromptu session featuring Congressman Cummings at Penn-North, a subway stop that is also a gigantic open-air drug bazaar. Sometimes the police simply set a patrol car on the north side of Pennsylvania Avenue, attempting to push the traffic south, between the library and the Arch Social Club. It was stopgap policing. Schools are run the same way. Before reaching the epic crossroads, I visited the family at Everyone's Place Cultural Center, where I had bought my first books. Cummings, who held on to his parents' South Carolina dialect in a pearl-clutching kind of way, was addressing television news cameras, making every effort to be framed inside the ruins of the CVS pharmacy.

Cummings was a true pioneer of the palliating tropes of blackness in the post–civil rights era. His pearls were sharecroppisms, verbal cues that called forth a rural experience of enslavement and debt peonage that had been by now fully obliterated by urbanization and deindustrialization. In the manner of a pretender, the dialect linked him to civil rights figures like John Lewis who had led righteously under strenuous duress and at great personal sacrifice, and whose later congressional career seemed to create a compelling arc between the advocacy of voting rights and the management of government. But Cummings had less of a right to that legacy than even DC's Marion Barry. Cummings was more a legal careerist of the 1980s than a Freedom Rider of 1961. But his pearls narrowed the distance between a student of the segregated southern 1950s and an urban one of the early 1970s. The folksy lingo that seemed to embed him so completely with his downtrodden people was a slender sign of fidelity to a legislative agenda addressing Sandtown's needs. His breakthrough program for the highest-achieving students in the district was to take them on summer tours to Israel.

I struggle with these performances, which strike me as compelling and absurd. I shared a podium with a minister who was about ten years older than I was, and she resolutely and passionately grounded her authority on the experience of having endured rural peonage. I responded with the dismay of a person watching someone attempt to pilot a helicopter on the basis of their expertise at riding a bicycle. The recourse to the agrarian past is the move of the person convinced we are still living in a nation-state that is designed to serve the social welfare of its people. We are not. We are indeed living in a market state, maximizing the capacity for individual opportunity. Cummings knows this because he oversaw the transition. He was at the first, nearly impromptu, congressional hearing exploring the CIA's Nicaraguan drug running that fueled, if it did not indeed create, the crack cocaine firestorm. He was so effective in his performances that with few legislative victories and only his seniority, he was later eulogized as a fallen "civil rights" icon and his casket left to lie in state at the US Capitol. Referring to him that way seemed to me a fabulous anachronism, more so because it obviated what he did do. Cummings was actually at the helm for the main catastrophes: the purging of remedial affirmative action in education and employment and the floodgates of mass incarceration. Recapture the majesty of the cotton row perhaps, what he said at Penn-North was meaningful to people who would later watch on television.

A few yards down the battered sidewalk stood a tall, dark-skinned man. He was mesmerizing a cluster of passersby with an unscripted, urgent homily, the kind of political sermon that only the grass roots could hear, a conversation that demanded belonging. The art of streetcorner speaking is sort of like picking a side at a crowded city basketball court. The right of speech roughly follows the contours of democracy, but the players gravitate toward the person who has juice, an attribute of skill and charisma joined to appearance and appreciable ease. When the clarifications of the rules become necessary, or when deadly participants must be either mollified or vanquished, these captains of the yard are the arbiters. Moreover, every group, every tribe of people has its own indigenous intelligentsia, and it was easy to see this was a man of that priesthood. He combined without effort the idiom of the local neighborhood, quite distinct from the cotton row patois of Cummings, with an understanding of the political history and personal failings lynching Sandtown's modern development. It was a rare occasion for me to hear an authentic leader speaking up and gathering his legion.

Motivated, I returned to Atlanta and redesigned my entire Introduction to African American studies syllabus, turning it into "Introduction to African American Studies: Baltimore Riots." I added books from sociologists who had taken Sandtown apart, and found the problem in government programs that undercut parental authority, and health care treatises showing that before heroin, crack, mass incarceration, and AIDS, tuberculosis, rum, eugenics, and syphilis had dug the narrowest of channels for black Americans in the city. But these shibboleth busters were just to get us started. Rejecting both the "container" model of education, which considers students empty vessels that need to be filled with content, and the internal dialogue/monologue model, which insists that the classroom and paper read by the professor are the satisfying terminus of student work, I decided to treat the students like collegians in other parts of the globe. What would they do if they saw themselves as the intellectual leaders of their communities with the capacity to articulate their preference for particular democratic and social ideals? The class would use its skills as researchers and journalists to engage beyond the university and directly impact the conditions on the still-smoldering Sandtown ground.

The new course began with Module One, a three-week tra-ditional classroom experience looking at racial segregation, urban migration, deindustrialization, urban spatial restructur-ing, political representation, health care disparity, mass incar-ceration, urban violence, and grassroots political organization, but with an emphasis on team teaching and collaborative pre-sentations. Next, students developed research projects in con-junction with groups active in education, housing, health care, and incarceration reform in Baltimore. We Skyped everybody, including *Democracy Now*. Because I was taking students from a majority white environment to a black one that would be foreign to even most of the black students, I wanted them off the Emory plantation as soon as I could forge a pass. I arranged for them to sit on collaborative panels at the A3C Hip Hop Festival and the Atlanta Public Library's Hammonds House Museum in the West End with counterparts from Spelman and Morehouse Colleges, where my friends were teaching. The forums would give the stu-dents a chance to work collectively, get to know academic peers from another context with different assumptions, and present their ideas in public. My goal was to reorient the place where they delivered the findings of their coursework, beyond the white, hygienic bubble of Emory's campus in Druid Hills. The awfully suburban students at Emory would need to hone their skills in preparation for Module Three, their research work presentations to grassroots partners in Baltimore. One cluster of students supervised a website for a doctor working with children and nutrition; another group created an annotated bibliography and booklists for an alternative high school; some coordinated with a local think tank, Leaders of a Beautiful Struggle, to expand their work in criminal justice reform; another lent their efforts to a city housing advocacy cadre. The course culminated with an active learning and public presentation during a seventy-two-hour critical assessment visit to Baltimore in December. Twelve students, a third of the class, traveled from Atlanta to Baltimore,

met with teachers, elected officials, city bureau commissioners, and community activists. My students gave panel presentations wherever they went, including one to the congregation at
St. James. We went to the Gilmore Homes housing projects to the
see mural devoted to Gray (torn down now), and listened to a man
on Baker Street describing Gray's fatal injury.

Later that year I visited an alternative school, housed in the
building where my mother had gone to junior high. I went to
the Clarence Mitchell Courthouse to attend the trial of the officers charged with Freddie Gray's death. I sat behind his family;
one classmate from elementary school and another from church
were the sheriff's deputies. The next year I wrote about the uprising and the police trial. I described the city mood and history as the trial of the police officer for Gray's wrongful death
got underway. In the article I tried to convey in an unadulter-
ated, direct form the misuse of terms like "riot" and "violence,"
within the frame of my own history in the black world of the
city. I argued that the rioters, victims of a long history of regi-
mented inadequacy, expressed themselves in the only way that
made sense. Within days of the article reaching newsstands,
two black men quoting Malcolm X ambushed policemen in
Texas and Louisiana in bloody shootouts. In the middle of it
all, I found myself nominated to return to Baltimore to teach at
Johns Hopkins University, an opportunity that had never before
seemed likely. Hopkins's prowess on the lacrosse field was like
its mighty reputation in the English seminar room: snooty, successful, and racially exclusive.

Even stranger, I was interviewing for a position funded by a
billionaire graduate of the school. To make my appointment, he
had to revise the strictures of the gift, designed to foster cross-
divisional appointments in the sciences, to cross disciplinary appointments within a single college. I would work across English,
history, creative writing, and Africana studies and contribute to
the work of the Sheridan and Peabody Libraries. Considering

the degree to which academics had found my professional work unoptimistic regarding elite stewardship, racial integration, or the idea of black progress, I found it astounding that so many units were able to reach consensus on the appointment.

I had not expected the negotiations to go well. I had been a professor for twenty years when I presented my work in progress in Baltimore. The English Department's Donovan Room was the whitest academic space I had ever been in, white like Salzburg, Austria. Excepting one person, the black people in the room that day were all related to me, and the room was so crowded that my mother had to sit next door. The walls featured not merely people who had owned slaves but portraits of people like Caroline Donovan, who funded the university from the profits of commercial slave trading in Baltimore in the 1860s. It appeared to me, to some degree, that the endowed chair I was being offered, would be more aptly named after the person who had to give up his life to inspire the moment of the exigency, Freddie Gray.

Founded in 1876, the school owed its original bequest to the will of a Quaker, whose given name came from his mother's family, Johns, but which most black Baltimoreans correct to "John Hopkins" when they refer to the school. A Baltimore and Ohio railroad magnate and business tycoon, Hopkins was remembered in public as a very different kind of nineteenth-century American than David Perine. A slaveholder, he believed that, for whatever reason, the wealth he earned shipping grain was bound to the sorry national condition of black people after the Civil War, one that he contributed to by slaveholding, a condition that he sought to remediate. He was apparently moved by the triumphs of black soldiers who joined the Union war effort, like Baltimore's Medal of Honor winner Christian Fleetwood, and he took seriously the obligation to provide for the orphaned children of the black soldiers who did not return. Alongside the bequest he left to found the university, Hopkins had apportioned deposits to address the immediate aftermath of that chaotic era. Scores of impoverished, homeless black children were a sad feature of postwar Baltimore, which hosted a number of Catholic orphanages for destitute African American youth. Hopkins designated two pots of money for a "colored orphans asylum" and a school for training black girls to become nurses. With Galloway Cheston, he founded an institution for the children at 519 West Biddle Street, with a plan from an architect named John Niernsee to build a twenty-six-acre campus beyond Mt. Olivet cemetery. Nine months before his death, Johns Hopkins had added a codicil to his will to specify that the asylum accommodate three hundred to four hundred black children, and he designated annual money, up to a quarter of the medical school budget, to make sure the plan worked. The trustees in 1875 thought Hopkins overgenerous and restructured the gift from an annual $20,000 down to $3,000. The Society of Friends orphanage agreed to change its name, take the small stipend, and admit only girls, about two dozen. In 1894 the Biddle Street operation went to the two-acre site of former Maryland governor William Whyte's brick Remington Avenue and West Thirty-First Street home at the edge of the modern Homewood campus.

The Remington Avenue mansion was larger than the Biddle Street rowhouse and could house up to seventy-five girls, trained as cooks and laundresses. At any one time about fifty girls boarded, seated at table according to their degree of tractability and implanting a hierarchy of three social class stations: the tables either had fresh flowers and linen, oilcloth, or the girls messed on bare board. At the age of eighteen, they were outfitted in a smock and apron and sent to work as domestics. But somehow even the manual education institution modeled after Hampton and Tuskegee could not survive the vigorous and deadly apartheid of the Progressive Era and the medical scientists coming out of Hopkins. John Whitridge Williams's

1903 *Obstetrics* textbook charged black women with biological indecency. Then in 1904 a fire swept through Baltimore's downtown from the Inner Harbor to Fayette Street, devastating the purses of the local grandees, and even the endowment at Hopkins. Before 1915 the orphanage work was curtailed, and the school was redesignated the Johns Hopkins Convalescent Home for Crippled Colored Children, serving only the most acutely needy, as a rehabilitation center for youth recovering from surgeries conducted at the hospital. When the European war drove up the cost of basic supplies in 1916, the trustees began to tinker again with the bequest, eyeing the convalescent home as a place of retrenchment; it would now need subscriptions to keep it afloat. By then both the city and the state were contributing resources to Hopkins's efforts. Baltimore City had provided a teacher so that the children could "keep up with their studies during hospital treatment." But the next year hospital superintendent Dr. Winford Smith declared the school unable to offer the luxury of the black convalescent home at all, and on June 1, 1917, the trustees ended their support. There was little handwringing over the fate of the young women at the time. During the Woodrow Wilson presidency, Popenoe and Johnson's authoritative *Applied Eugenics* had become a kind of bible at Johns Hopkins. "When tested by the requirements of modern civilization and progress," the doctors asserted, "the Negro race . . . may be said to be inferior."

Johns Hopkins's radical reconstruction plan to improve the quality of life of the city's black poor lasted, in fits and starts, for fifty years. Apparently, the last orphan aged out of the asylum five years later and the home closed its doors in 1923. For several years after, black Baltimoreans like Father Bragg, who knew the contents of Johns Hopkins's famous will and had taken communion to the orphans on Remington Street, wondered in the press, "Why was the Johns Hopkins Colored Orphan Asylum discontinued, and the property of the orphanage given over to a department of Johns Hopkins University, or Hospital?" Others, like physician Nima Garfield, more disconcerted than Bragg by the university's work shaping the field of medicine (even as it was practiced by black doctors), condemned Hopkins and its medical research as "the one factor in American life and influence that contributes most toward hindering the progress of the Negro."

The university did not degree an African American undergraduate until 1950, and the nationally dominant medical school graduated its first black American doctor in 1967, after enrolling a Kenyan and an African American from DC in 1963. Dr. Robert Gamble, thought a genius by some, finished in four years and converted to Islam, changing his name to Abdur-Rahman Yusuf Ibn-Tamas. It wouldn't be surprising if Dr. Ibn-Tamas became politically as well as spiritually transformed during his time on Broadway at the medical school; the hospital wards there remained segregated until 1973. Despite a sterling international reputation, Hopkins did not prioritize black enrollment until roughly fifteen years ago, when it created the Center for Africana Studies and launched a program to provide scholarships to incoming first-year students who had graduated from Baltimore's public schools. Today the university claims to register more than six hundred undergraduates who identify themselves as African American. But if you ask the undergraduates if they have more than 11 percent of the student body, they will look at you quizzically and say it feels more like one in twenty.

Occasionally my Baltimore relatives will ask me about the university. What they want to know is whether or not the elite whiteness threatens me in some unusual way, or, if there is some scandalous exercise of power that has not yet reached the press. I always disappoint everybody with how little I am immersed in the shenanigans. But sometimes questions arise from other black quarters. Kramoko, a Fulbright colleague who had come to the United States from Alassane Ouattara University in Côte d'Ivoire, where I had taught in 2014, asked me at the end of a meal, "What do you do?" He wanted to know what measures I was personally undertaking to remedy the condition of the black people engulfed by the world of narcotics and prostitution along the road just south of his apartment near the university. A clean-shaven, youthful-appearing Ouan man, his ungentle inquiry was completely rhetorical. It was a Signifying Monkey, Brer Rabbit, Brer Anansi jibe.

Kramoko didn't mean to conjure the undergraduate tutor at the Traverse Square public housing project in Middletown; the D.A.R.E. program mentor in Ohio; the teacher bike riding to the Shule Mandela Academy in East Palo Alto; the adult literacy professor at the Maryland Department of Parole and Probation; the Black Bard poetry workshopper at Skyline and McClymonds High Schools in Oakland; the full-time faculty member at Howard University earning the custodian's wage. He knew the answer to the question. And though it was not true, I felt like I was doing the same thing he was doing to uncover the cure for malaria. Would extending my work into the world of the politician, policeman, social worker, drug counselor, and employment specialist make my biographies of black literary figures any more compelling or trenchant? My own mother had spent her working years in precisely these occupations, as had my father and their generation of college-educated black people. Were their career achievements without value? Kramoko, whose own mother had given her best years to stir a pot suspended by three clay kpo over a log, had shared multiple holiday meals with my mom. But he would not have asked her about what she had done or how she, living alone, could sustain herself. For Africans like me, this is the "Big Man" problem, where we are unable to change the world because we can't glean the significance of what the "Little Women" directly in front of us are doing. (Of course, these are metaphors and not gendered full stops.) And it is also an African prerogative, the insistence on the right to be indecorous.

One Saturday morning I dragged him to St. James to work on the street and when he asked to walk around, I toured with him a little bit on Mosher, where there is more hustling than on Lafayette. When I am fully sober and people ask me if I want to buy drugs I feel put upon, though the narcotics are offered in a kind of singsong way that is possible for an outsider to misrecognize. Speaking English as a third language, Kramoko discarded anything that wasn't said directly to his face. I was reminded of the uncomplaining way that the autobiographer Venture Smith described his parents' death, his abduction, and enslavement. All he wanted was to see his own children work hard and sacrifice and forgo the pleasure of silver shoe buckles. Torn, true, but I feel embarrassment and guilt at the sight of the black poor, selling narcotics or begging for money to buy them. Did Kramoko feel that way watching people bathe and launder clothes in the canal off the northern autoroute on the way in to Adjamé?

Was I being weak minded because I was absolutely hounded by his impertinent question? When you arrive at the lake of resource, what recourse do you take? I could imagine some of what I wanted to do. I wanted to test out a new body politic and foster the conditions for mutual interaction in the city's most historic black neighborhood and with the city's most affluent public group. Obviously, I thought the resources of the university needed to be bent into a more equitable relationship with the black communities whose labor and land they had appropriated as a headright for a century and a half, telling anyone who asked that they were lucky to get that. Black people in the city had unique, remarkable talent, but resources to cultivate it were few. The historic example of the orphanage, the distance between the intent of Hopkins's original purpose and how quickly it was

discarded was a conservative tragedy. And the standing brokerage model, represented in an outstanding way by the politicians,
whereby a few blacks with access rewarded cronies, needed dis-
rupting. I wouldn't be the first person trying to ensure greater
reciprocity, insisting that life improved for everyone with the
obvious realization of value and mutuality between Sandtown's
Harlem Avenue and Homewood.

I liked Billie Holiday for having transcendent artistic value,
but she was also a politically disruptive figure. A statue of
Holiday with a pedestal course motif of aborted fetuses sits at
Pennsylvania and Lafayette Avenue, across from the location of
where the Royal Theater once stood, where she was playing in
1946 when her mother died. Holiday's real tragedy and legend
began the day she had the temerity to record a song that opposed
the ritualistic killings of black people. I began to use her life and
her art as the source for graduate research seminars into topics like the Harlem Renaissance or Baltimore jazz. The coursework became occasions to investigate the Baltimore City and
Maryland State Archives, and examine documents like police
ledgers to learn about the city's neighborhoods and people in her
formative years, and to shed light on the political history of race
and musical culture. Her energetic struggle against the odds and
her deliberate cultivation of a distinct local idiom made her an
obvious symbol for commemoration.

I had known early on that a career at Johns Hopkins that
was valuable on my own terms needed to go beyond a personal homecoming; I wanted to help stimulate a renewal of the
university's contract with Baltimore City. My line of thinking
went back decades to my godfather, Victor Dates, the second or
third black person to endure Hopkins enough to graduate, who
wrote about the shortfalls of professionals in the year I was born.
He thought the remedy lay in a "deliberate investment" in the
"wasted talent of Negro Americans." In the months before I graduated from college my father passed away and my good friend

Donald Bentley was murdered on the city streets. It felt then to me like the world was coming apart. A few weeks after graduation, I had a conversation with a member of the hip-hop group Public Enemy, describing some of my writings and my ambition to host a summer peace conference in Baltimore to ease the bloody tensions on the street. That fall I went to graduate school in Columbus and shortly discovered the African American studies extension center on Long Street on the city's East Side, where some of my dad's cousins lived. In college we had tried to push the association between the college and the needs of nearby black people, but it had always seemed either improbable or patronizingly fleeting. But the extension center, which had been struggled for by the citizens who had known of Ohio State's debts to black Columbus, was tangible and real. What intrigued me about the extension center was the rearrangement of the center–periphery and intellectual–community dichotomy models of scholarship, a key imperative of the Black studies movement. While nothing is perfect, the value of what they hoped to achieve stayed with me over the years. I wanted my Holiday project to modernize the college's reparative social justice efforts by creating a mechanism to bring faculty and students into reciprocal engagement with communities outside of the Homewood neighborhood. In the process, the project could help to revise the city's racial demographic polarity, the so-called Black Butterfly of African American neighborhoods in the east and west portions of the city.

Since the university already had a significant buildup and footprint in East Baltimore, it made sense to direct my efforts west. To drive through the southern tip of the city along Interstate 95 is to witness the difference between a modern, waterside, near-luxurious cityscape and a terrain lacking any visible sign of enhancement to the built environment in almost a century. The eastern areas showcase Hopkins's anchor investments and the subsequent downstream development, but once beyond the Ravens football stadium on the western edge of Martin Luther King Boulevard, a fallow West Baltimore unfolds, home to the majority of the black population and the black political base. What stands out is the old Montgomery Ward building on Monroe Street, a couple of hundred yards from the plantation manor of Charles Carroll, Baltimore's largest slave owner and the builder of the old manor that sits on the Hopkins college campus today. I hoped to establish a more durable passageway between racially and economically calcified territories in the city, with the idea that by opening a circuit of sharing, of reciprocity, of mutual regard, and an appreciative exchange of talent, we might amplify the dynamism of both Homewood and Lafayette Square.

In what seemed to me like early successes, I negotiated a budget, three postdoctoral lines, and some dissertation fellowships. Two years later, I raised funds from the provost's and president's offices to hire an associate director. A Washington, DC, native who had lived in Africa and run radio programs, my new appointee was uniquely qualified to bring the vision to practical life. The project began with a twin mission: to preserve the African American print material archival record in the city and surroundings, and to create opportunities to share the research efforts of Hopkins students and faculty in the city.

The archival objective grew directly from a job application I once sent to Hopkins, encouraging the collection and safeguarding of local African American archives. I had worked patiently through the scraps of Ralph Ellison's materials from the 1940s, and in the case of Chester Himes, only half of the writer's manuscripts, papers, and letters had been preserved. Black writers' effects were traditionally undervalued and frequently discarded. When I got to Baltimore, I had several collections in mind that were in peril and might be appropriate for university acquisition, including photographs, politicians' libraries, and literary materials. But instead of treating the endeavor as merely a win for the individuals and the university, I wanted to build a larger collectivity that would share information and acquisition methods and have a broader impact on the preservation of Baltimore's black history. With the help of library staff, I hosted about five dozen external participants at a 2017 symposium that included the local HBCUs, private and state-run archival repositories, and black churches, museums, and social clubs. The open forum, which brought together historically white institutions and their black counterparts to discuss the problems of unequal resources and ethically engaged collecting, was one of kind, and the attendees, many of whom had had their shoulder to the wheel for quite a while, were enthusiastic about what we might do in community.

My childhood relationships were another place to start. After a dispiriting football game back in high school, my teammate's uncle John took us home. An irascible man, our coach Haswell Franklin had not said a word to me since the season began. He lived in a pretentious Homeland mansion, and he bragged to us that he graduated from an expensive prep school named after the first president of Johns Hopkins. One day four of us were late getting to practice after a Black Student Union meeting and the coach rained spittle and dragged us around the field by the face masks of our helmets. He never culled the best of our efforts, and we played haphazardly and ineffectively. We were at the age when blackness becomes real, and the unity among the boys in the high school was necessary to me at least. My friend and I were fifteen, the same age and stage as James Baldwin's nephew from *The Fire Next Time*. The serious epoch was upon us. The next year a classmate from my middle school graduating class was shot dead walking on Franklin Street; we had been the two boys who had gone to rival parochial high schools, Loyola and Calvert Hall.

We stopped to pick up a sandwich at a deli on St. Paul Street, an unusual surprise. When the young woman, only a little older than my teammate and I, asked my friend's uncle, What would you like? he said knowingly to her, "Your smile will be sufficient." His comment elicited real pleasure in the face of the woman behind the counter. You could see the saffron rising up from her cocoa cheeks. It was one of my earliest lessons in the nearly imperceptible shaded and layered intimacies of black beauty.

My friend's uncle John Mayden had survived the blocks and the corners, in a sense, with a camera. He was a significantly built dark-skinned man and he talked intimately of athletics, coaching us and building us up, despite our lackluster tackling. I had known him as a board member at the Druid Hill YMCA where my dad was the director, and he lived on Linden Avenue near Whitelock Street in a rehabilitated rowhouse that had its brick interior exposed, something I had never seen before. It seemed as odd to me that John lived on Linden Avenue as it did that he sometimes carried a 35mm camera and was the first person I knew with a video camera. He was intrigued by people randomly sitting at bus stops, or blurred figures in the snow. What could possibly be special about that old neighborhood, Whitelock, where I had been at the mercy of the no. 28 bus, or Druid Hill Avenue, or Upton, where my dad had insisted that I listen to that jazz band on a curbstone on Harlem Avenue? Though my mother had grown up across the street from the Linden Avenue house, a stone's throw from North Avenue, it was to her almost from another country, another time, like the 1900 block of McCulloh Street, where my great-grandmother had lived in the 1940s. For me the distance was considerably farther than that.

When I started my job at Hopkins I went over to Ten Hills, where John lived, and talked to him about preserving some of his prints. He took me out to his backyard studio, and I could see him warming to the idea as he turned over the yellowed edges of the heavy stock. In rusted drawers he had dozens of versions of single images, achingly printed with variations in the developing chemicals to accent minute portions of the background or subject, grain, and texture. He had photographs of me and my father, from around the time of the football game. I let him know that archiving in the library could indefinitely preserve cherished portions of the collection. He showed me the catalogs they had issued from shows he had participated in with Gordon Parks in the 1970s, in which James Baldwin had flattered him for the depth and revelatory power of his art. When he agreed to bring the collection in, we raised some money so that the press would publish a book. He called it *Baltimore Lives.*

I was hungry to do more than just collect and preserve. Even though I went to a Catholic high school, my social experience was among the children at the city public schools. During our holidays when the city high schools were open, I would go with my friends to hang out at the coeducational cafeteria at Poly, City, Walbrook, and Carver. Thirty-five years later I return to the schools that I knew by proxy. I visit my cousin Charlie's class at Edmondson. I take my students to several classes at Baltimore City College. I visit the AP English class one afternoon at Carver, and return on another occasion to be with the first-year students.

On the morning that the ninth graders finally pour into the impromptu lecture at Carver, we are thirty minutes behind schedule. From the time the security guards at the entrance wand me down and I meet with vice principals of the floor, trades, grades, and divisions, heaven and earth are indeed being moved to accommodate me. But meanwhile, the children's daily lesson has been derailed, and the technology at no school I am familiar with, certainly not in the Hopkins classrooms, works on demand. One mouthy, rambunctious fourteen-year-old girl, as in a single student, reclines splay legged in a way to gather and atomize the attention of the entire class. Is she a brigand? No, she has reached a developmental milestone that her peers have not yet encountered. Perhaps it is true that the most successful child in any city high school class, in terms of their future capacity to maintain a consistent household, raise to adulthood children they have conceived, and earn a living wage that will enable them to enjoy life without the necessity of government assistance, is the child who reaches those milestones somewhat later and is open the most to the best of what takes place in the classroom. That is the wager. But for the children who are to grapple first with an adult body and have to confront the adult world without the hiatus of childhood, should there not be obvious pathways to information that might be immediately useful?

The high school students present the looming world of the soon to be adult, but the elementary schools can be enjoyed with almost complete delight. A couple of weeks earlier my running partner David Miller invited me to the elementary school three blocks up the street from our childhood homes. His brother and father and my mother still live on the same block. While the public school has been renamed, we know it by its number, 58. Because he has a national reputation for creating innovative remedies to inspire urban young people, administrators have contacted him to engage their "troubled" students and are anxious about having enough adult male "role models." My dad would take my sister and me sleigh riding in the alley at No. 58 when the cement iced over. I would play speed pitch and stickball on the asphalt there with my guys, David and Arnold, Gerrod, Reggie Alexander, Rondy, Gary, and Tumas. The playground was the stepping-off point for us to go through a hole in the fence and across the tracks to the basketball courts at Towanda, the home of the Shirley Avenue boys. Chuck Green was the Wabash Avenue hothead who held up our side of the tracks' end in those summer evening contests of basketball and humanity's fiery edges. While I was annoyed that they tore the courts down, I was relieved not to be so young and vulnerable there anymore.

Four of us are there to preach to the boys. David planned to have the afternoon catered with chicken and hamburgers and pretzel sticks and fruit. I'm the odd one who is not a graduate of the school. Arnold is a veteran and correctional officer. Richard is a professional singer and talent manager, and I am a professor. The tallest of us is five foot eight, helping us to connect easily with the children, and since I have two sons who have only recently left this same stage, I know well the way to connect to the still innocent boys. Talking to the room of fourth and fifth graders who are the youngest children of people we grew up with is unbelievable fun. Even though it takes awhile to get all of the plates set up and for the boys to be seated on the library floor, it is beautiful, in spite of the ugly moments that I usually dwell on, like the small, light-skinned boy who is having real emotional distress and is attired like he is in foster care, and the one black man that I do see working in the school, who wears long braids and has a lot of tattoos and is using hardened street profanity in a conversation with eighth graders in the doorway of the cafeteria.

The boys are bubbly and curious, genuine and tiny, like children, not remotely like adults. They aren't embarrassed by being smart or enthusiastic and they even know a few Motown hits. I relish telling them about how to get over childhood spats, insisting that they be prepared to get over small slights and envision big success.

David startles me by asking the nine-year-old boys if they have seen *The Wire*. While I know that part of his manner includes a kind of calculated abrasiveness, the reminder of the burden on these boys for no other reason than race is unhappy. I am always depressed by the themes of children's books for black kids that discuss the weight of slavery, racial segregation, and inner-city decline to "reach" the kids. I am saddened by approaches that build a bridge by trampling innocence. These bridges, in fact, are predicated upon the end of innocence and insist that the children have rights only if they are obedient. I remember the boys talking about *Penitentiary* when I was in grade school, but an adult would never have asked us about an R-rated movie or the popular documentary *Scared Straight*, which purported to deter juvenile crime by detailing the reality of prison rape. The mythical book I remember best didn't talk about the ghetto or the broken home at all. But the way I identified with Willie and that damn snowball or trying to whistle has remained with me my entire life. Of course, Ezra Jack Keats was white.

Despite his gruff parts, David has hit a long ball with the children, from the tasty treats he subvented to the free copies of a book he has written about a smart boy from the inner city who has food allergies and is trying to cope with neighborhood bullies. As the guys filed off to class, we make them all shake hands with us. Every single boy tries his best to exchange greetings and look us in the eye in a way that I have never seen captured by a newspaper or broadcast. It is as difficult for me to understand a father rejecting this duty with a son as it is to accept people who stand in the way of that relationship. A father playing with his sons is magical.

A week after our visit a political website reports that the mayor of the city has received from the medical system of the state university, whose board she sits on, hundreds of thousands of dollars for writing a children's book series called Healthy Holly. Thousands of copies of the books are reported to have been donated to the school system for the benefit of the children. The short books purport to be African American themed, but the characters have skin colors and facial features of South Asians, the ethnicity of the subcontractors from overseas who actually designed and illustrated the volumes. Healthy Holly's grammatical errors are so hideous that the school system declines to distribute the gift. It is revealed that assorted vendors seeking contracts with the city have also bought the standard package of two thousand copies of these worthless books. The mayor had lived in Ashburton, the city's only black neighborhood of tree-lined streets and grassy yards unmarked by abandoned homes. The public mess of her downfall exposes the cut-rate quality of the political imagination, and the failure of the brokers.

Regular visits to city high schools have motivated me to launch a new sort of partnership between my end of the university and the schools. The Hopkins Pathways program began with presentations by four English Department graduate students. The students offered their digital seminar papers uncovering the historical life of Marylander Frederick Douglass and field questions at Baltimore City College, the Maryland Historical Society, and Morgan State University. A week later, a more senior graduate student returned to City College and gave a presentation on her dissertation research, using examples of poetry written during the 1960s that reflect the black consciousness movement. We finally achieved a partnership with an experimental high school on Dukeland Avenue that was graduating students with two years of college credit, something that most public school naysayers thought couldn't be done. I know the area well. I had fallen off my bicycle there, and still have the grapefruit scar on my hip today; I had had a head-on car collision there; I lost my virginity there. A professor from the Sociology Department who specializes in public health and a South African filmmaker who had worked in the city years before go over to talk to the high schoolers. Two black Bluejay seniors, one a defrocked engineer who transferred his allegiance to film, and the valedictorian from Dunbar High School who has majored in creative writing, peddle their wares. The principal of the school and the students seem pleased. I was invited to deliver their commencement address at the Hippodrome, a famous theater on Howard Street.

The last time I had been in the Hippodrome was with my father and sister to see *Superman*, starring Christopher Reeves, Gene Hackman, and Margot Kidder. While we dressed up to see the film during that Christmas holiday showing, the theater was on its last legs, and Baltimore's favorite pets were scurrying in the trash up front. I couldn't recognize the fully renovated showcase theater of today; I just wondered who it was for. The high school had successfully gotten the powers that be to participate in the formal recognition of their educational miracle, graduating forty or fifty mostly black children with maximum college credit in four secondary years. Two of the graduates won full scholarships to Hopkins, and others were going to Ivy League colleges. The lieutenant governor, the city council president, and half a dozen other officials gave rhapsodic five-minute addresses. While I was seated in the center of the dais, I didn't make it to the podium until well into the third hour of the program. I should have cut my remarks out completely, but I was the main event and don't have the gift of a brilliant extemporaneity. But mainly, I wanted to try out a line that kept percolating in my mind from childhood, "Ain't gonna be no bank." The slogan in the Baltimore of my youth was kind of a Robin Hood war cry, a willingness to defy the odds and to seek fairness and justice. I am hoping to inspire the graduates and connect with their family members by using the native tongue of our homegrown democratic practices.

As fate would have it, about fifteen minutes into my remarks a fight broke out among the ample and stentorian women in the fixed seats of the auditorium. There might indeed be a bank from the seats below. I offered some consoling words from the microphone, but the combatants kept the ruckus going. The fray became hot enough for faculty to rush down from the podium and out into the first circle of the balcony. The security detail of the lieutenant governor, an African American and conservative party member, approached the stage. It was like the battle royal scene from the novel *Invisible Man*, but with the symbolism rearranged. A middle-aged black person in full career addressed the crowd, not a young boy on the verge of college. The audience was mainly of black Truebloods, becoming the uninhibited veterans of the Golden Day. The officials in a position to extend brokerage trinkets, by and large, were black. Adding to the lather of the hot afternoon, I had walked several blocks with a heavy box of my books on my shoulder, a biography of a black writer named Chester Himes, an ex-convict a bit more critical of the United States than his peers Ralph Ellison or James Baldwin. The books were prizes for the graduates, who danced elaborately as they received their degrees (and as I myself had done when I completed my PhD), but I had neglected to create some form of ceremony for their receipt. Ceremonies make the world memorable. Ceremonies can salve our yearnings for violence.

Ritualistic perhaps, fighting that doesn't involve firearms is hardly newsworthy. Throughout 2019, the city's deadliest per capita year and very nearly its deadliest year regardless of the population, Fox News hosted a series of "City in Crisis" town hall meetings, several of them in neighborhoods that had rarely seen news cameras asking residents their opinion on critical matters of governance. The station arranged a panel filled with prosecuting attorneys and police administrators, and political aspirants, and invited the most powerful city elected officials, who confirmed then withdrew from the event. I took my fourteen-year-old high school freshman, because I thought it was important for him to see the part of the city his father identified with, and in the same way that my own father habitually exposed me to the world when I was my son's age. We cross the campus of a teachers' college that had recently built a new ten-thousand seat gymnasium in the place where the funeral home once stood that prepared my dad's body for burial. We walk around a bit until we find the auditorium, where buff policemen with assault rifles and flak vests scanned the crowds. As is our pattern, my son sat in the back and buried his head in his textbook and I sat closer to the stage to supplement my weakened vision.

Wretchedly, my hearing is still quite good. The panelists never had the opportunity to justify their own work buttressing the police state because they were shouted down by audience members who lined up to perform soliloquies. The audience of concerned citizens abounded with organizational leaders, petit entrepreneurs who had overcome drug addiction, prison, failing school systems, and poverty and are now deeply invested in solving the problems of the city. The audience overwhelmingly backed governmental solutions to eradicate poverty, especially Christian organizations brokering with the state to hire and pension ex-felons. Jesus of Nazareth, the founder of socialism.

A lone elected official, born and bred in the city, braves the public meeting and tries to address the audience from the floor. Attempting to propose government solutions to crime, he will be drawn into a ritual rhetorical combat. The sere white moderator puts her microphone to the councilman with the $64,000 question, How can we stop city murder? Having waited his turn in the long line of Christian pensioners, the elected official starts off in a friendly, sincere manner. I have heard him before and know that he is a poet of the language. A thin man in a rhinestone jacket must have heard him before too. He risks his liberty in a primed denunciation of the councilman. "BUT WHAT ARE YOU GOING TO DEW?," the rhinestone-jacketed man cries, easily booming over the councilman using the public address system. "WHAT ARE YOU GOING TO DEW!" No longer a question, but an imperative. When uttered again it is an exclamation turning into a profanation. And again. And again.

The jacketed man becomes intoxicated by this new power and keeps testing the volume limits of the human voice. He is a disrupter, and male, and might become the focus of the appointed guardians of physical restraint. But silencing the councilman is enough. He does not leap over the seat to face his enemy but manages to content himself with his place in the seventh row of the seats on the opposite side of the auditorium. The heavily armed policemen in bulletproof vests walk down to his aisle, but decide to leave him be. The mechanical microphone is no match for him. Whenever Councilman Pinkett attempts to approach the problem of street violence, as soon as he begins to speak comes "WHAT are YOU going to DEW!" Shamefaced, Pinkett withdraws in frustration after having attempted to brook the ungovernable.

The event was a magisterial example of the burning heat known to accompany light. I had a point or two to make, but know that the line is long and the ferocity of the heckling suggestive of the result. A woman in the front row in a red dress jumps to her feet to loudly mourn her deceased sister. A community activist who holds sidewalk prayer vigils whenever violent death occurs declares Hopkins both the source of the problem and, through its scientific community and public health resources, the only possible solution. The red dress woman returns to her feet, this time shouting out the street address and names of the parents of the man she has accused of her sister's murder. Her outrage is raw and shrill and she teeters wildly from the edge of emotional collapse to outraged fury. As the meeting fully unravels, a small woman in sweat clothes rushes the stage and attacks the microphone, reeling off a litany of conspiracies before the heavily armed guards drag her off, either committed to securing the proscenium or having identified a mark they can reach.

Somehow I took these signs and wonders as an invitation to insert the tradition of the abstract thinker. The Episcopalian committed to his orderly liturgy thought palaver of the professors was the ingredient missing from the restive black public sphere. I thought the extrascholastic community would benefit by exposure to the professors more than the politician and preacher. At a school like Hopkins, the world comes to its auditorium. My colleagues in creative writing and French and Italian and political science, as well as assorted student groups, invited, week in and week out, writers and thinkers whose ideas were on the cutting edge and in great demand, people fawned over by the national newspapers and glossy weekly magazines. Sometimes I would race the four miles up to Nathaniel's school, fetch him, prepare dinner, and run back to hear the Marxist geographers, the literary surrealists, the jazz innovators, the writers who had won the Pulitzer Prize and the National Book Award in the same year, or twice in five years, the poet read by the nation, and the Nigerian photography critic. The audience was almost always lily-white, and heavy with people from the nearby neighborhoods. While universities today are, like my friend François Furstenberg says, a "tax shelter for the endowment." To retain their tax-exempt standing even the private ones are compelled to make educational efforts publicly available. But black Baltimoreans always think they will be charged a fee or tested in some way to prove their right to tread Hopkins's rarified grounds; there are uniformed guards at every entrance. Once, when the bike-riding duo of Mitchell and I attempted to leave one of my books on slavery and memory on the steps of the president's house, the guards become quite vigorous. The new digital registration formats are a kind of quiet apartheid mechanism, whereby private information must be exchanged in place of cash. Registration requires the latest computer equipment with the latest software and the leisure to fill out forms and to know your schedule in advance. The eradication of spontaneity and subordination to central planning is the primary control feature of the digital world.

So I picked veteran researchers to present their work in the Helena Hicks Speakers' Series, named after the black woman who led Baltimore college students to desegregate Read's Drug Store lunch counter in 1955, five years before the sit-ins began in Greensboro, North Carolina. The series takes Hopkins faculty to prominent westside churches, like Union Baptist Church on Druid Hill Avenue, the home of the Rev. Dr. Harvey Johnson's famous United Mutual Brotherhood of Liberty (a forerunner of the NAACP), and Sharp Street United Methodist, a church that goes back to 1787 in the city and whose founders were present at the creation of the African Methodist Episcopal religious denomination. But it was a bit of a gamble to take the Hopkins intellectuals away from the universities and upper-middle-class audiences to speak out at the schools and churches of West Baltimore. None of the people I raced to see could be described as particularly charismatic. With audiences outside of the academic bubble, it is important to make a human connection, in a way that is less necessary with students because they are being graded for their performance and the incentive is with them to achieve mastery. With black audiences, the connective work is even more important. The history of separate and unequal education and the "miseducation" that Carter G. Woodson decried has also had a hand in creating skepticism about the existence of unbiased sources of information. I kick the speakers' series off with a talk at St. James on Douglass's youth in Baltimore, and I also speak to the three women's literary societies, the Pierrians, the Du Bois Circle, and the Philomatheans. The lectures continue at Sharp Street by Hopkins's newly recruited black staff, including Haitian French professor Daniel Desormeaux, political scientist and Londoner Robbie Shilliam, a practicing Rastafarian, and historian Nathan Connolly, who reminds me of Frederick Douglass.

Pairing archives and speeches, even when they are rich and sincere, still forsook an important democratic ideal. Something about art in public and the dynamism it brings, the unity and joining of multitudes. And that's how I knew that we wanted to open the project's working year with a concert in Lafayette Square. It would be an event, using the philosopher Alain Badiou's phrase, to entail "a rupture in the normal order of bodies and languages," an occasion to imagine "the possibility of possibilities." We decided on the Saturday after Labor Day, and it turned out to be a magical day of perfect weather. My mother, who lived out a dream of hers and became a prominent sorority and clubwoman in her sixties, sent handwritten and hand-photocopied notes to her AKA friends and the St. Francis church guild and her club, the Pierrians. We would host a musical performance of the nation's true classical music in the beleaguered portion of the city where jazz had been created but was mainly now in hibernation.

My undergraduate fraternity brothers, including two that I had taught, one whose parents hailed from Nigeria, the other's family from Ghana, met me early to help set up the tables in the square and distribute water and trashbags. I had gone over to Morgan and bought fraternity T-shirts for all the undergraduates who had been working on the garden. Another fraternity brother, the dean of my line from college, drove over from Washington to provide the DJ interlude. We paid for a local security team, and they were men and women who were unobtrusive and blended in. The city had cut the grass and removed some tree debris and set up a portable stage. To me the square looks pretty good in general, but on that day it looked impeccable.

I opened the event by welcoming to the stage the Harlem Park neighborhood president. She began by noticing many people in the crowd who had grown up in Lafayette Square. "Welcome back!" she said to them. It was our first time meeting and she had the initial impression that I was parachuting in, a notion that made me a little peevish. Nonetheless, I asked her permission to speak to acknowledge her community leadership and to recognize her as my elder.

A crowd of a couple of hundred people had fanned across the grassy square from the stage at the intersection of Lafayette and Carrollton. Students drove and Ubered there; church members, faculty, and staff set out picnic baskets and blankets and played with their children; my homeboy flew up from Atlanta. The ambience was extraordinary. Dressed in a light-blue African shirt, I greeted the crowd and called the park "sacred ground." I told everyone how I had grown up at St. James on the other side of the square, and how my parents had married there and I had hunted Easter eggs on the greens. I praised jazz music as a crossroads form, both sacred and secular, both high art and vernacular, and then turned to Luke 14:8–11 to recommend an ethos for the day. It was all about being invited to share and not presuming. "When you are invited to the wedding feast, take the lowest place, so that when your host comes, he will say to you, 'Friend, move up to a better place.' Then you will be honored in the presence of all the other guests. For all those who exalt themselves will be humbled, and those who humble themselves will be exalted." I meant every word. When I finished the introduction the Harlem Park president told me that if she had known I had so many connections to the neighborhood she wouldn't have made any address at all.

A spoken word artist who works with a local black think tank that advocates police reform took over the microphone as the mistress of ceremonies. Lady Brion wore a turquoise-and-navy dress with the shapes of half suns, kernels, pickets, and herringbones, and turquoise lipstick to complement her blond-dyed locks. "Baltimore be on the brink" she intoned, invoking the concept of a sovereign "Baltimore State." "So don't that make us on the rise?" Confident and stately, she brought on the bands and added the spirit of the local youth to the day.

The musical performances abounded in love, sharing, and the tradition. A local reed player named Jamal Moore baptized the opening with his trio. Jamal wrapped his hair in guinea brocade, wore the copper and amber, and played the music in the way that indicated his belief in the divinity of John Coltrane. He played an opening baptism in the blues, which set the stage for all of us. The headliners were two of Peabody's extraordinary faculty, the slick drummer Nasar Abadey, who came on stage so clean I didn't want to be anywhere near him, and Sean Jones, the down-to-earth trumpeter who is an heir to Miles Davis. The diva in Holiday's tradition was our local legend Sheila Ford, who had grown up singing in Macedonia Baptist on Fremont and Lafayette. Learning about her heritage in the square and as a recording artist for Quantize studio made the choice enchanting. What was funny about hearing a woman who was from Baltimore, but conservatory trained, and who made a living singing uptempo soul music, was that she mainly connected to Holiday on the basis of her position as a jazz classic, the virtuoso peer to Sarah Vaughn. When she listened to Holiday, she didn't hear the vernacular Baltimore pronunciation that wrangles a *y* in front of every *o* or *u* so that "What are you going to do?" becomes "What are you going to dew?" as in *dyu*. But it was no matter. The performance was crisp, inimitable, professional, black, and brilliant.

My favorite testimony to the affair was signaled by two older sharpies from the neighborhood who had posted their lawn chairs cattercorner to the stage and did not budge for four hours. A student of mine from Southie in Boston had found such inner peace that she walked contentedly the five miles back to campus. My mom and her cousins, schoolmates, and friends from church flitted around and chatted and listened, feeling comfortable and good. After the jazz serenaders had wooed the crowd, my Kappa brother DJ Marc ED broke out the house music. I joined hands with a barefoot lass in consecration. I hoped that planting Freddie Gray in the earth had yielded a worthy harvest. But I knew that on one afternoon in the public square, the people of the city ate the new grain at the banquet.

A son considers it as incumbent on him, from a just sense of filial obligation, to become the avenger of his deceased father's wrongs. If a man loses his life in one of those sudden quarrels, which perpetually occur at their feasts, when the whole party is intoxicated with mead, his son, or the eldest of his sons (if he has more than one), endeavours to procure his father's sandals, which he wears *once a year*, on the anniversary of his father's death, until a fit opportunity offers of revenging his fate.

—Mungo Park, *Travels in the Interior of Africa* (1799)

As if an invasion of African Negroes . . . were armed, to change the fate, and alter the dynasty, of the British kingdoms.

—Walter Scott, *Waverley* (1814)

White Sunday: "An Invasion of African Negroes"

In my first year teaching at Homewood, I would fish for a parking spot on the southwestern campus edge. At the northern end of the Wyman Park dell, before gaining the school, I would encounter a statue with lingering words. Their repetition was a sound that became a medium, like a diaphanous gauze, which filtered and reoriented meaning. While the entire pedestal was home to a long quote, the face of it contained a starred summary, a quotient: "Purpose *** So Great." It is a lyrical refrain, much like Marlon Brando's movie line "The horror," from *Apocalypse Now*, the first R-rated film I ever saw, Francis Ford Coppola's homage to Conrad's *Heart of Darkness*. The chorus "purpose so great" will become a haunting refrain during my interludes on the campus, a chiding Kurtzian epistrophe as I pad the lawns and bricked paths.

In my second year, the mayor of Baltimore orders the statue and another, older monument on the northside of Homewood removed. It is feared that riots will break out among the citizens, after platoons of armed men, some pranksters and some lunatics, have staged a huge white pride rally in Charlottesville, a preserve of America's colonial past. For an undisclosed sum the mayor hires a construction company to tackle the bronze horseman with cranes. The statues went up in 1948, when the father of Congresswoman Nancy Pelosi was mayor, a public cenotaph undoubtedly appeasing the Democratic voters tempted to bolt over to Dixiecrat presidential candidate, the raunchy Strom Thurmond. The president of the United States publicly laments "the beauty that is being taken out of our cities." The horsemen are Robert E. Lee and Stonewall Jackson, in their final counsel on the battlefield at Chancellorsville, where Lee executed one of military history's most daring feats, dividing his army and sending the stern schoolmaster Jackson to flank the Union army and win the battle that was the predicate of their hubris and greatest defeat at Gettysburg. Purpose so great.

To a city native, there are oracular benefits to bona fide membership in the campus community. Fittingly, the experience of these benefits is structural. The school plays a role in the revival of the built environment along Charles and St. Paul Streets. The university has handsomely refitted a film and media studies building directly across the street from what was once a historic nightclub called Odell's, a place of love's fantasy, legendary music, wanton inebriation, and, naturally, since it's Baltimore, deep sadness, that catered to the needs of a generation during the final quarter of the twentieth century. While no one who came of age between the second half of the 1970s through the end of the twentieth century will reflect upon Pennsylvania Avenue as the cornerstone of what the city had to offer in nighttime conviviality, tens of thousands of true-blue Baltimoreans will happily recall Odell's and the bundle of nightclubs near the intersection of North Avenue and Charles Street. The club's motto, etched on a checkerboard black-and-white awning over the main entrance, which can even be seen on throwback tee-shirts was "Odell's. You Know if You Belong." Besides one eventful New Year's when Flint's Ready for the World performed, my homeboys and I did most of our belonging on the street outside the club. Shootings and narcotics trafficking and other scandals closed Odell's before I finished college. So I am impressed to see the sacred geography somewhat revived with a new cornerstone that includes other local colleges. The shuttle stops on either side of Odell's boulevard.

Permission to ride the shuttle itself is a choice tangible pleasure from belonging to this community. The bus runs every fifteen minutes from the Homewood campus downtown to Mount Vernon, or Washington Square, where stands the oldest American monument to George Washington, recounting the episode that made him genuinely significant: his resigning his generalship in Annapolis, a scene replicated in a painting at the Annapolis State House and in a mural in the cupola of the US Capitol. Purportedly that moment embodies the principle of American democracy, which would be disinterest, putting the community above the individual. The shuttle takes students from Homewood to the Peabody Conservatory and then over to the medical school and hospital, all distinct neighborhoods in Baltimore. Whenever I get on the shuttle, I find a seat and open a book and enjoy the unharried bliss.

On the upper route the Hopkins shuttles pass two theaters that have been reconditioned with university, public, and philanthropic dollars and are made available to the academic communities. To my mind the theaters had been moribund eyesores for forty years. Obviously, it is gentrification, but one that has been so expertly half-hearted and taking so many decades to unfold that it is hard to argue with. Nonetheless, gentrification has an invariable logic in a city like mine where, as Fanon once wrote, to be rich is to be white and to be poor is to be black. The criminalized black poor are removed and the rich white citizens move in.

The university I joined is already conscious of the ugliest of these dichotomies and has taken steps to revise its relationship to what's left of the black city. While there is an obvious doctrinaire, formulaic residue that seems about as nuanced as Mao's Great Leaps Forward, the initiatives underway extend far beyond the schemes of the other universities I have worked for and attended. On their best days, these institutions operated as titleholders whose obligation to their serfs, relative to their larger economic footprint in their territories, was simply a full board at the annual pageant. I can not recall the largest private universities in Palo Alto, California, or Atlanta, Georgia, doing even that much. The new day at Hopkins includes not infrequent conversations with the top administrators on matters of social and economic equity and the university's proposal to address the serious legacy of racism in the city. When one of my books was published, the president sent me a bottle of champagne. I preserve it in a corner cupboard for satisfaction at the right moment.

Usually I disembark from the shuttle at the Mount Vernon stop, home to the Peabody campus. Built up during the 1820s and untouched by the 1904 fire, it is one of Baltimore's oldest existing neighborhoods. Mount Vernon boasts distinctive Federal-style rowhouses and a square of Victorian neo-Gothic churches, an art gallery, a music conservatory, and mansions spoked along a cobblestone esplanade. There are four gardens in the roundabout, and while I don't frequent them, I daydream in the vicinity whenever I have the chance. A new bike lane, beginning in Roland Park and constructed because an inebriated Episcopal bishop ran down a cyclist there, takes riders straight down Maryland Avenue to Mount Vernon with few stops, a swift downhill jaunt descending a rider four hundred feet from the heights of Homeland to sea level. In high school there were people my age who already recognized the similarities between this part of the city and an elegant bohemia. But I was then far more enchanted by the new-to-me suburbs and their bike paths, their fertilized lawns for leisurely ball games, and the shopping malls filled with polo shirts. I suppose my happiness with the conveyance has something to do with finding a new neighborhood pleasure later in life. I can sip a coffee on a sidewalk in Mount Vernon and enter a reverie of memory of the European cities I have visited and the books I have read and the films I have seen about them.

Although bus access is restricted to students and staff, the drivers, all of them black, are directed never to ask for identification. A plausibly free bus running on a regular schedule is a strong civic joy to me, though to avail oneself of the privilege rests upon either insider knowledge or unusual boldness. But once on board, the bus is very nearly a mobile sanctuary through the urban landscape, a place of refuge affording an opportunity for serene repose. What's more, driving and parking have always signaled consumption for me. Because my father always selected inconvenience over fee when I was a child, my instinct is to regard parking garages and metered spaces as wasteful luxuries. To avoid the parking woes of any location in the central city, I ditch the car and take my lads to the shuttle.

Nathaniel has taken the bus to summertime athletic practice in Towson, and Mitchell takes the subway from College Park to Decatur in Atlanta, but neither have been with me long enough in the busy city to become competent traffic dodgers or double-yellow-line idlers. Sometimes either boy will sourly refer to a textbook rule about a crosswalk or a light while I am trying to usher them through the fluid, risky street maze. Once, when a street festival closed down the regular shuttle stop, a wild driver opened her doors in the middle of moving traffic so that Mitchell and I could weave through rush hour and board. Shazam, the double doors opened for us in the middle of North Avenue and St. Paul!

After generations of industrialists, urban designers, and politicians eviscerated mass transportation to empower the automobile, new city planners have organized a system that caters to people coming from the northern boroughs into the old town with books in their laps. In Baltimore there is free transportation if you use certain city corridors, and also a hassle-free, ten-mile-straight light rail from Hunt Valley, the town with few blacks north of Cockeysville, to the airport south of the city, that also has a station at the athletic arenas. Payment aboard the light rail, incredibly, is done according to the honor system. Charm City Circulator and Light RailLink together are examples of efficient low-cost transportation designed to reward suburban consumers making their way along the city's oldest commercial precincts. In the year before I returned to Baltimore, the Governor Larry Hogan canceled a "Red Line" subway projected to connect the black suburb Woodlawn and the rest of the city's sizable black western population with the region's best opportunities for career growth, Johns Hopkins's sprawling new Bay View medical facility at Baltimore's eastern edge. The state squandered $450 million of planning dollars and left on the table $2 billion offered by the federal government.

The bus is like a transition zone between the precarious and the secure, and I have seen its thresholds bending in both directions. In high school I remember watching a boy racing to get aboard the bus to escape a resolute gang. Either the traffic light or the driver were against him. The ruffians pried his fingers from the door and pulled him down to the sidewalk and administered a thorough beating. If only he made it beyond the coin-drop box. The free shuttle affords me mental elasticity, releasing me from the rigidity of the clock, and the burdens of the automobile. I ride whenever I can and I try to connect my classes to Peabody and the nearby Maryland Historical Society, less of a favored destination because it requires an entrance fee, but only two blocks away. The students and their world of a transferable, ubiquitous, digitally swiped ledger of credits and debits prefer Uber and Lyft and the newfangled electric scooters, but I hold on to my ancient ways.

Though I grew up in the city's black belt, I am one of the few people in my extended family and from my neighborhood to have been enrolled at integrated schools my entire life. My love affair with the bus system and the built environment is partly owed to school desegregation. My experience in schools with either a few whites and many blacks or a few blacks and many whites is an oddity, in a way. I have a younger cousin and many neighborhood friends who attended all-black schools from elementary school through college, just like our parents, though, of course, the laws had changed. While segregated schooling was indeed the way education still operated in the 1970s and 1980s and beyond, in the 1960s such a future was not then thought desirable. Still making adjustments and amends, Baltimore's school system entered into an arrangement with the Maryland transit authority in 1972 to provide free public bus service to any student traveling one mile, then a mile and a half, then two and a half miles, from home to school. Rather than purchase a fleet of yellow school buses (which we city scholars derided as "cheesebuses" ridden by county puffs), the city offered a monthly coupon book to students to adhere to desegregation orders. Theoretically, this complied with court-ordered mandates to desegregate schools and allowed families some choice in where their kids would go. The coupons were also premised on an idea about reliable mass transit and an osmosis process whereby civic ideals of punctuality, work, and thrift might be transmuted to younger people joining the flow of the city's workforce.

I seem to recall us all being handed bus tickets, whether we needed them or not. From 1977 to 1982 I boarded a smoke-belching MTA General Motors New Look special to school. I lived at Wabash and Cold Spring, five miles away from my "inner-city school," at McMechen Street, in a white neighborhood called Bolton Hill, on the exact edge of where my grandparents had originally purchased their home. When my sister started going to PS 66 around 1969, our reverse migration had begun.

On the 1940 census, my grandfather, grandmother, and mother have a curious sequence of notations in the box marking their race. They all have a "W," which means White, with a line struck through it and small "c" in the upper corner of the square. Their house on the south side of Robert Street, eighty-five feet east of Linden Avenue, was the only colored household on the block that year when my mom wasn't quite two years old, well east of the racial dividing line of Eutaw Street. Skin color and geography combined to fluster the census taker, before they adjusted their bearings to record a black homeowning family on a block where a white person might have lived. Another eighty-five feet would have put my mom and grandparents at Bolton Street, and in another neighborhood altogether.

I wonder how they managed that $1,500 purchase of a house built in 1885 from a landlord named Wylie and a seller named Hack, and if the census taker's initial confusion about their racial identity had anything to do with either amassing the nest egg or making the contract. My grandfather had only finished the fifth grade, so I am inclined to believe that deep chicanery would have unnerved him. My grandmother Christine had completed four years of high school at Lawrenceville in the 1910s. She took the train from her town of Bracey to do so, and then bought land from her mother's father in 1933, so perhaps she was experienced and nervy. In my memory of them, their educational level of achievement was reflected by their speech, though they had both been raised in the rural tobacco-growing farmlands and my grandmother used words like "heish" for "hush," or even as an exclamation. My grandfather did present himself as other than Negro to use some of the exclusive stores on North Avenue, though even that masquerade must have been dodgy if it required any speech or took place during the summer. His siblings and children dared not accompany him on those raids into enemy territory.

Following the 1954 *Brown v. Board of Education* Supreme Court decision, Baltimore integrated its schools more rapidly than any other city below the Mason-Dixon line. Virginia massively resisted the federal law, adding a spur for black migration to industrial centers like Baltimore with open schooling. Before the decade had ended, the majority of the school population was black, concentrated in the elementary schools and depriving the school system of examples of facilities with fewer than 90 percent of one race predominating. During the 1960s, the school system expanded even more, enrolling close to two hundred thousand students, and opening new facilities in the northwest section where I grew up. All of the Northwest's urban-riot-era schools—Greenspring Junior High, Walbrook Senior High, Northwestern Senior High, and MLK Elementary—seem designed by a paranoid architect to double as prisons or defendable redoubts. Certainly, their morbid resemblance to the Baltimore City Central Intake facility or jail, built decades later, bears out the Nixon-Agnew paranoia theory. One proposal to resolve the racial imbalance was to create a larger metropolitan school district, taking city children to Baltimore County and county children to the city. When I started school for half a day in 1972, we were approaching 70 percent black, while the public school system of Baltimore County was about 95 percent white. In 1973, my first year of kindergarten, the superintendent feared "the city is moving toward an almost totally black [school] system." Twenty years later that goal was fully achieved.

The original aspiration for a racially integrated public school system was not only a question of students but of teachers. While students may or may not have been perceived as value-neutral vessels who could be filled up with improvements that might countermand deficiencies at home, like, say, racial bigotry, or, conduct and beliefs that would consign them to poverty, white teachers were understood as essential contributors to the morality undergirding the middle-class value of academic excellence. Those of us black people who position ourselves professionally as examples of moral virtue, that is, as miners' canaries with a valuable message, might be surprised to learn that morality was then thought the main purchase of the whites. They had acclimated themselves to city life, unlike the blacks who were migrating to it. Whites were presumed to be more advanced in terms of touchstones of domestic life, like sobriety, chastity outside wedlock, frugal economy, general restraint, and conservative planning ahead. Although few black people who worked in white households as domestics would have agreed with such an assessment, the black people connected to the oldest churches and their leaders and the uplift organizations all extolled dignified manners as a key to segregation's lock.

A small number of these heralds of probity remained prominently in a leadership role through the 1960s. The elite model of behavior would be displaced, in a decadal process, when patient black suffering became delinked from the democratic ideal of disinterest and altruism, especially by way of the later works of James Baldwin and the public assassination of Martin Luther King Jr. But the model from the 1960s thought little of the organic elements black people brought to the laboratory of integration. Rather, retraining practices were proposed for whites to "assist teachers to develop courage to work around their middle-class values and to work with the values of . . . those from the lower economic groups." At the collegiate level today, the working assumption is that the intellectual and economic resources managed by the white majority are premier, and black students or faculty with the opportunity to avail themselves of such resources are fortunate. By at least one measure, this distinction is unquestionably true. As a faculty member at a historically black college from 1997 to 2002, I learned this firsthand through the chief mechanism of salary disparity; faculty at the HBCUs earn two-thirds the salary of their counterparts at historically white universities.

During the later 1960s and early 1970s, the assumptions were rather more succinct and included the field of morality. More than having an overlordship merely tolerated, "White teachers must feel that they are wanted in the inner city," mused Baltimore's school superintendent, concerned about waning black spiritual enthusiasm for this key metric of an integrated society. He believed that the education and moral efforts of the faculty needed to "be understood and appreciated by the majority of Negroes." This philosophy about black thanklessness, improvidence, and immorality in need of white supervision goes back a long way and had frequently been immortalized on equestrian statues. After gorging on a "lavish" and "bountiful" feast with his sons in the months after the war, Robert E. Lee advised his cousin Thomas Carter "to get rid of the negroes left on [his] farm—some ninety-odd in number, principally women and children, with a few old men." Turning out people to starve was not his concern; economy was, and good farm sense for Lee meant white labor. "'I have always observed that wherever you find the negro, everything is going down around him, and wherever you find a white man, you see everything around him improving." The two basic ideas, that black people exist due to white benevolence and that whites are natural engines of economic improvement, are the same idea.

In my life, my own parents have been the most ethically and morally exemplary people I have known. I suppose they chose PS 66 for my sister and me on account of the open enrollment programs during the desegregation era that allowed them to compete for "Model Schools" like Mount Royal, called by our local newspaper "the most intellectual of all public schools in the city at the elementary level." Mount Royal certainly did yield a group of writers from my time there, like David Matthews, a mixed-race guy who only kept white friends; Janet Sarbanes, whose politically moderate father represented Maryland in the US Senate; and Tracy Hopkins, who lived a few houses up the street from me and whose mother taught kindergarten at No. 66. At any of the city's three Model Schools, classroom size was capped at twenty-four. Built in the least imaginative brick-box style common at the end of the 1950s, No. 66 was the lone public school clinging to a white, upper-middle-class, single-family-home neighborhood built in the nineteenth-century city.

Bolton Hill had sustained its exclusivity by forming a corporation in 1960 to keep houses off the market so that black people wouldn't move in. My grandparents left the fringe of Bolton Hill in September of 1965 after a phase one federal urban renewal project called Mount Royal-Fremont demolished eighty-two acres on either side of Linden Avenue. The project was led by the Mount Royal Improvement Association. Most of the six thousand people displaced during the $10 million renewal program were black. If I was a professor at a place like Stanford, Georgetown, or Harvard, and I owned a three-bedroom, two-and-a-half bathroom house walking distance to campus, $10 million would not buy ten of them, and it might not buy five. But in 1965 ten million dollars was enough to upend the world.

A Facebook picture reminds me that there were eight white children in my twenty-four-person homeroom from the seventh grade at No. 66. My academically high-achieving class had the largest number of white students, one-third, and the other homerooms had one or two. But in terms of the combination of grades and test scores, the class was dominated by three white girls, conscientious scholars who made perfect marks, and who scored at the testable limit on all of the standard exams. I was their peer, but I was neither disciplined in the way that they were, nor was I socially isolated from the rest of the students, all of us ganging onto the bus or playing at the rec center after school. But it seemed to me like there was a decided gap between us and the next group of No. 66 learners.

While we sang "Lift Every Voice and Sing" as often as the national anthem, the majority of my teachers between 1972 and 1982 were white: Mrs. Liss in kindergarten; Ms. Smith in second grade; Mrs. Ballard and Mrs. Eberhart in third, fourth, and fifth grades; and Mr. Blair and Ms. Myerstol in fifth and sixth grades. My black teachers were Mrs. Jackson in kindergarten, Ms. Kelly in first grade, and Mrs. Richardson and Mrs. Kyler in fifth grade. In middle school Mrs. Fuller, Mrs. Tolliver, and Mrs. Robbins were black; Mrs. Kandel and Mrs. Smith from Australia were white. The black teachers I had in elementary believed in discipline first and scholarship after. They all spanked and Mrs. Tolliver pulverized, even in middle school. The music teacher, Delores Jones, a conservatory-trained contralto, was in a class by herself when it came to rapping knuckles and smacking desks with a yard-long wooden ruler. I tried mightily to avoid the swift palms of my neighbor Mrs. Hopkins and Mrs. Jackson who taught me to read and for whom I felt genuine affection. Mrs. Kelly was young and wore an Afro and did not spank, but from her room I remember being sat beside the boy who ate crayons at his desk and ultimately drove a no. 2 pencil through his tongue. That was the year Marvin Simpson urinated on me from his stall in the bathroom. He became a state policeman.

Mrs. Richardson based her sixth-grade science class semester on a dissection project. When the butcher delivered the cattle organs to the class and our group had obviously been handed a lung, the teacher, who wore a long wig like Donna Summer, insisted throughout the fifty-minute period that it was a heart. I remember being somewhat shaken that she had refused to correct such an obvious mistake. She also favored the girls, which only seemed to me like the prejudice that everyone universally decried. Mrs. Fuller was my favorite teacher in my favorite subject, social studies, and Mrs. Tolliver was a valuable disciplinarian but an uninspired mathematics teacher. Mrs. Robbins and Mrs. Kyler had had careers as teachers in the high schools and were finishing their years of service with the younger children, whether as a reward or a punishment, I was uncertain. I knew them all, and my conveyance to them was the bus.

The experience of bus riding, which made it possible for me to observe people and the built environment of the city, matured me and made me appreciate some chaotic intangible about urban life. The earliest ride I can still remember had all of the conjunctions of turmoil and surcease. My mother had removed me early from school, and on the bus home I was feverish and vomiting. If today I were relegated to the wiles of two public buses to retrieve a violently ill child from school in winter, I would think of it as a minor tragedy that might sustain everlasting injury to my youngster. But my memory of that trip, clad in galoshes and some thin garment that all children wore to brave the snow then, was that it was so soothing being with my mother, who was confident and caressing. And that vomiting into a cup with my head on her lap as she stroked my steaming forehead while chatting with another woman nearby meant that everything would soothingly be all right.

By the time I entered fifth grade, I was on my own. The agility, volume, discernment, and heft needed to board and ride the public bus contained the seed of the skills required to operate in a democracy. I learned how to weave in and out of swiftly moving car traffic and reach the stop as the bus sped toward me on Liberty Heights. I attained the patience of watchful waiting, bunched together with my classmates in the cold as we anticipated the advent of the Encoline Special. Often during those years I lugged a weighty trumpet case, large enough to straddle during the ride when the aisles were crowded, and that I slung into adult ankles and shins with abandon when we jammed aboard a teeming Special to Redwood Street. At times so many shivering children would force themselves upon the bus that we bunched on the steps and braved serious injury when the mechanical door opened or closed.

Attire mattered. On my no. 51 bus stop in the morning, three nattily dressed sports who went to Douglass Senior High School would groove to their anthem "Funkytown" on the ample-watt radio cassette player. Older boys and girls draped themselves in complimenting ensembles of Italian leather loafers, pleated skirts, colored boots, sweaters, pressed pants, and starched shirts. They all wore a herringbone chain the thickness of fettucine, pulled out through the collar and draping over the Adam's apple. My parents clung to the belief that only poor children wore canvas-and-rubber shoes to school or dungaree jeans, which wounded me as American style became more informal. I was also de-shoed and remanded to my stocking feet during after-school recreation, even though Buster Browns and Docksiders wouldn't scuff the floor.

The mostly male bus drivers wore the same caps as policemen, standard gray pants, and blue shirts with vests and sometimes gloves. The only feature that distinguished them was whether or not they used a specialized seat cushion and back-rest. They displayed inimitable sangfroid as they plowed the twenty-ton behemoths into the rapid flow of traffic on Druid Hill Avenue before making the daring left turn at Cloverdale basketball court, all the while we passengers were showcased rarities, like the rotating carousel of pork loins in the window of Leon's Pig Pen. Or the day of the riot on the bus, when the driver surrendered the cockpit, explaining to an adult rider, "Shit, it's Baltimore, man," as he jumped off the step. I don't think I had ever heard an adult's unguarded profanity before. The furious passengers ripped away all of the transfers and kicked out every emergency window. The days after a damp snowfall, it was perilous to sit too close to a window. Big boys all over town accurately sprayed the slow-moving buses as they climbed hills. A well-thrown wet snowball had both the sonic and kinetic impact of a rock or brick, and seemed able to stun the wounded bus, like an elephant kneeling before the hunter's rifle.

I eventually developed the courage to begin moving away from the parental authority of the bus driver and to make my way to the row of five seats at the very back of the bus. Beyond the backdoor irreverent riders boarded without paying, sometimes smoked cigarettes, and etched profanities with permanent markers, glue, or knives onto the plastic seats. By the time the high school boys at Mondawmin captured the no. 28 by the back door and passed the marijuana jay around me, I didn't even occur to me to call out to the bus driver. I could keep my cool. While it was a bit far for me to get the bus to high school in Towson, something about riding through the city got in my blood.

On a bright and blowy spring afternoon at the shuttle stop by the campus bookstore, a boy is splayed out on a bench. His arms and legs are draped over seemingly the entirety of the convenience, in an elaborately stylized statement of complete ease. I am immediately aware of him, first because so few black men stroll the paths of Homewood and second because I observe all black teens and young adults systematically, a survival skill I mastered as a child. I also habitually verbally acknowledge the black men I encounter on the street, some version of "What's up, man," "What's up, brother," "Hey, man," "Hey now," or a simple head-nod signal. The acknowledgment "A yo" and just "What's up" are fluidly ambiguous greetings and can also be considered threatening challenges. My reflexive recognition on the basis of race and gender stands to reason because I have sustained and been proximate to violent physical struggles with two categories of people, black males and the police, and from the time I have been on my own in public, I have kept meticulous track of where both groups were and where they were likely to be.

It turns out that these are the same preoccupations of the society at large. The university conspicuously supplies the information with electronic messages. Since the murder of Jeanne Clery at Lehigh University in 1986 and the subsequent 1990 act named after her, colleges are required to report serious crime. They fulfill the obligation with campus-wide email bulletins. Urban universities like Columbia, the University of Pennsylvania, and Johns Hopkins border working-class black neighborhoods, and they have an interest in keeping real estate prices low so that students and new employees can afford to live there, and also so that they can draw a workforce for the myriad unskilled labor jobs that ensure their campuses retain an understated elegance. Every person with a Homewood email address receives a "Public Safety Advisory" bulletin of the street crimes reported within a mile of the campus boundaries. Sometimes twice a week an email PSA alerts probably ten thousand people to robberies of anything from a cell phone to an automobile occurring to students, faculty, staff, and "non affiliates." The description of the assailant varies little: "male, early twenties, black hoodie, silver handgun."

In the Homewood section of Baltimore it is generally understood that the highwaymen are black men and boys from the Barclay neighborhood preying upon people between Thirty-Third and Twenty-Eighth Streets at any time, day or night. After completing the felony, the villains are always last seen in swift flight east toward Barclay Avenue, the last street before Greenmount Boulevard, which comes to stand as the briar patch of mayhem in this section of the city. Greenmount and Twenty-Ninth Street is the home turf of the Black Guerilla Family, a prison organization with roots reaching to black revolutionary martyr George Jackson. Whole stretches of Monument Street and Gay Street and Preston Street, and Frederick Road, and Monroe Street, Belvedere Avenue and Reisterstown Road, and Edmondson Avenue and Bloomingdale Avenue and North Avenue and many, many more, are just the same, some also controlled by BGF. But to me, the typical gang of highwaymen are fifteen-year-olds targeting a backpack or a cell phone, ostensibly of a white person who seems unlikely to resist. From time to time, a handgun will be used or a car violently stolen. A Dravidian student in my class was struck, maced, and robbed, having to limp into the CVS for help, pressing her hands into her burning eyes. She is politically mature and refuses to let the incident reverse her understanding of the ancient structures that have manufactured the wretchedly predictable crime and victim.

Moments before reaching the Thirty-Third Street university shuttle stop, I witnessed a thin, bearded black man wearing glasses begin a loud argument while walking through the intersection of Thirty-Third and St. Paul Street. A white van was cornering the pedestrians in the crosswalk. "Muhfucka, come back here!" the man kept shouting, his voice breaking and his thin arms flailing as he dramatized his anger. Yellow-jacketed security personnel hired by the university observe and report all of the deeds here, and there are so many other witnesses to the encounter that I can't imagine it will become genuinely dangerous. Nonetheless, the tenacity of the one-sided dispute is surprising, as the man kept shouting to the driver. His first retort made him seem pridefully civic-minded, but the second and third outbursts made the aggrieved pedestrian appear imbalanced, pursuing his principle of injury to the point where he was capable of inviting his own doom. The van nosed slowly down the block, presumably ignoring him. Of course, it might have been plotting to take him unaware on another occasion.

A few months before, a young man fleeing from police in a stolen car crashed the vehicle and spurted out onto the campus, where, after a "shelter in place" order was issued, he was arrested. But the brazen assaults, seemingly tied to the black neighborhood alongside campus thoroughfares, provided easy opportunities for sensational remedies. The climate of threat, fear, and accusation reached a crescendo that summer, and university officials began to suggest in public that the narcotics commerce killings and deadly vendettas connected to the city's most ancient drug bazaars and the mass shootings at secondary schools in Florida and music festivals in Las Vegas were a direct threat to the students. In October the faculty received an email that the campus would soon be patrolled by a "special response unit" of "highly trained former police officers whose mandate and location will be targeted to current or evolving threats."

While under most circumstances, like a car accident, a botched medical procedure, or a plain old heart attack, I am utterly responsible for my living or dying, these notes of jeopardy from a central command have enlisted me in a cause. The campus is mystified, however, about the source of our specialty gendarmes. The city's police department is under a Department of Justice decree to report all of its arrests and stops because it has confessed to systematic illegal harassment of black people. More controversially, a detective slated to provide testimony against a group of Gun Task Force officers indicted on bribery, racketeering, and drug-dealing charges, has died under mysterious circumstances. To some, the detective is the victim of a contract killing by his police department colleagues. Before the special response unit can be deployed, the university makes a more startling and comprehensive pronouncement. Hopkins will pursue an amendment to Maryland state law to authorize the creation of an independent university police that can detain suspects and wield deadly force. The scales of justice are shifting.

Without consulting its faculty, providing statistical evidence of an increase in crime, or any obvious examples of criminal acts other than sexual assault among the students themselves on campus, the university is pursuing a long-lasting change that will redefine the school's relationship with the city. The symbolism of the move is painful and glaring. The campus police force will become the raised banner of an unabashed colonial model of resource concentration, extraction, and exploitation. Having access to a police force does at first allow the concept of hermetically sealing the campus, protecting us from them, escorting the sub-urbanites to the parking garage and out onto the interstate. But, boundaries secured, the force inevitably shifts into a troop capable of its own adventures. It seems more like the readying of a pacification mission by the Belgians in the Congo.

A well-heeled university in a city like Baltimore, where the average student doesn't complete the public school system, is an odd beast. It aggressively preserves the past, its traditions and styles, and modernizes this antiquity, digitizing and updating it, bringing it online, keeping it in fresh paint and pointed mortar. A university also blends into the space of tradition the more daring of the modern innovations. The antiquity of the built environment or the litter-free, spotlessly clean landscapes and sterilized interiors and painstakingly maintained exteriors of the buildings and the uncomplicated access to the colonial foundations it affords are among the many otherworldly advantages of proximity or ingress upon private university grounds. Yet it is an odd partner, which allows some access but with the notion that its black guests understand that instant repudiation and chastisement, if not banishment, are not far off. It is the contradictory symbolism of the lovingly preserved slave plantation manor Homewood, sitting on the hill, to evoke the timeless, great purpose of the college.

The university's ethical responsibility to provide safety is less clear than it might seem. Can it reasonably charge its undergraduates nearly double the average annual income of the majority of families in the country, and then focus a police force on juvenile wrongdoers from two neighborhoods with incomes less than half of the national average? The police force makes new properties attractive investments in ways that they were not before. The university acquires more cheap property, raising the median home prices in its orbit, and files lawsuits against the poor unable to pay their bills. Real estate investment is where true power is levied. The face of the policeman's opponent tends to be black, youthful, and male, but the victim of gentrification is the black woman a bit older than I, which means educated before the marvels of integration, standing behind the cafeteria steam tray. The city's history of slavery and the exploitation of even the people who were free is inseparable from this fact.

The blue-blood institutions of the South don't go out of their way to foster a black upper class that might even embarrass, much less oppose it. Thus, Hopkins's first instincts are always to secure a conversation with people whose motive and orientation are exactly like its own. When the school fosters ties to neighborhood groups like the Baltimore Redevelopment Action Coalition for Empowerment in East Baltimore, it insists on property requirements for participation. The institution goes out of its way to protect undocumented migrants from other countries, but requires extensive citizenship tests from the poor within its orbit of control who might seek the use of any of its facilities. It also enables the creation of services and economic relations that primarily benefit the professional community of the university and rejects and obliterates the historical past and contributions of non-elite black communities. And thus enters a new generation of well-positioned investors to "improve" the built structure, the businesses, and services of the surrounding communities after securing bank loans that previously had been unavailable to longtime residents. There are multiple national scandals regarding the treatment of black citizens by the banking industry, such as the difficulty of gainfully employed black homeowners living alongside the University of Pennsylvania campus to obtain home improvement loans. These roadblocks prevent black families who have lived on the outskirts a long time from enjoying the benefit of the services that accompany rising real estate prices.

The most dramatic example of redevelopment and displacement in my lifetime was in Washington, DC, between two neighborhoods, Columbia Heights and Shaw-Howard. Massive gentrification has brought tens of thousands of white, college-educated Americans into a portion of the district that had seemed an extension of Howard University. But Ben's Chili Bowl and the Florida Avenue Grill are relics; Republican Gardens and the State of the Union bar are gone. The gentrificaiton reached a climax when Howard University's president, no foe of neoliberalism, had to issue an open letter to the area's new migrants. They had turned the school's campus yard into a dog run Saturday and Sunday afternoons, coming into conflict with the tuition-paying students. The students' ideal of a black college experience had run into the wall of Labradors and Boston Red Sox caps.

As soon as the Hopkins administration announced plans to create a private police force, a frantic group of the college's full-time black faculty scrambled over to the president's office to register their objections at this stunning proclamation. About a dozen of us have independently reached the conclusion that the police will embody all of the contradictions of "strange liberators," Martin Luther King Jr.'s term for American servicemen supposed to guarantee democracy in Vietnam. Despite the range of our social class, ethnic affiliations, and national origins, the black faculty's immediate objection to this proposal was instructive.

As we walked into the meeting, I bumped into my cousin, serving as a representative of the administration. The president, a Canadian in office for ten years, and the provost, the chief academic officer, a South Asian man who joined the university the same year I arrived, had defended their flanks. On their side of the table would be a black person from Baltimore and, what's more, a native-born American.

My cousin Jeanne was a long-standing city attorney and politico who grew up in the Sharp Street Church, the home of Frederick Douglass's mentor William Watkins. When I was thirteen, I spent a precocious week with her then-husband, also

an attorney, circuit court judge Robert Bell, and Legal Aid public defender Michael Middleton at the Clarence M. Mitchell Jr.
Courthouse. While my tutorial with lawyers, defendants, and
courtrooms was intriguing, I could not get over being allowed
to order what I wanted for lunch at the cafeteria on Lexington
Street. Jeanne's beautiful daughters were a couple of years
ahead and behind me at No. 66, and they lived near school on
Madison Avenue. Unlike my own parents, my cousin's professional career belonged to the 1980s and beyond. From time to
time I would see them all at church with my grandmother's sister and brother-in-law, her aunt and uncle, or at a party. Cousin
Jeanne's mother, Dorothy, was the historian of their church, the
oldest black church in the city, one of the oldest black churches
in the United States. My relative doesn't need to say anything
during the meeting.

The president made the case that the university itself was
precarious. Students had recently been massacred at a Florida
high school. He feared having to call parents to tell them their
children were dead. The school was hemorrhaging millions toward its public safety budget, which had doubled every year
since the 2015 uprising following the death of Freddie Gray. He
had a thousand contracted security employees working twenty-
four hours per day. He admitted that the horse had already left
the barn: plainclothes, off-duty police in unmarked cars were
already patrolling the campus around the clock. To render an
even higher and more transparent level of safety, he felt duty-
bound to the campus to create a police force, like the other universities of twelve thousand students in cities with large, poor,
black populations, like Philadelphia and Chicago. The private
universities in those cities were also our keenest competitors for
students. Parents deserved assurances that their children would
be safe from deadly assault.

The complex balance of the president's role was obvious. It
is unfortunate that ours in the meeting is less so. As was the

case with school integration in the 1960s, the idea that black
staff with job security and independence might have access to a
ethical and prescient grasp of this situation had not occurred to
anyone making a decision. Perhaps we were thought to coddle
criminals, or to have been flirting mildly with anarchists' chaos,
or fully in bed with a liberal guilt complex spiced by a sexual fascination with black men reverting to primitivism? And
of course, we may be seen as parading an oversumptuous morality. Which was too bad because our initial objections were
quite mild and could have been resolved using the same tool
kit already on the administration's desk. We were not opposed
to the idea of police philosophically, but insisted that the police connected to the university conduct their interactions with
Baltimoreans at a level above the standard used by the city police. One professor who had worked on the campus for ten years
asked plaintively that the school envision public safety as an
organic totality, a whole world, with law enforcement as one
component among many markers of community health. The
university should decline the opportunity of the desparate news
headlines as an occasion to show "strength" by permanently
arming the praetorians. We begged for things that would all
eventually come to pass, like review boards with representatives
from the local neighborhoods and student body. We wanted the
officers to take courses in Africana studies, the name of the academic discipline specializing in people from around the globe
of African descent and recognizing the historic weight of the
slave trade in the origins of the modern world.

Cautious and conservative, we sought, at the outset, to work
inside the grooves already hewed by our guild. We took the administration's response at face value when we were told that
there was no preconceived plan of action, no hidden driver behind these efforts, no opportunistic timing with economic forces
moving capital across the globe and making citizenship rights
the privilege of the rich. Our efforts didn't occur in isolation.

A coalition of campus organizations called Students Against Private Police went on to collect twenty-four hundred signatures, and held rallies and demonstrations, and finally marched on the Maryland General Assembly in Annapolis to provide alternative testimony against the doxy of black, male, elected officials in favor of the police force. Two vibrant black female state delegates and a few ministers in committed partnerships with the university voice their concerned opposition as well. The state legislature enforced a clause in its legislative protocols requiring Hopkins to hold public hearings about the police measures, and the university withdraws the bill from consideration for that term.

As both a university employee and a citizen who has experienced police brutality and harassment, I feel obliged to participate in the public negotiations concerning the important issue. I believe in a person's right to the safety of their body, an ideal frequently jeopardized by the contest in the streets that can have us at one another's throats. So, I agreed to host one of the mandatory public forums some ten months later. I moderated a panel of four professionally experienced police commissioners of university forces. Finding it an odd signal to begin the first of four public conversations about a university's responses to crime with a panel of law enforcement experts, I opened the session, attended by about three hundred people, with a preamble sketching the points of my opposition. The police chief from our Ivy League counterpart told me that I want "European" policing. Public safety without deadly force.

I learned another lesson from the public forum. I had strategized slightly with the minister of an influential megachurch, down the street from one of the proposed police patrol zones. In a sense, the young people living in the neighborhood of his parish will be the ones who have the most regular contact with the police force. Like Hopkins' president, he would get the midnight telephone call when a young person had been hurt or killed. I knew that his alarmed response to the announcement had been exactly the same as my own. I arranged to give him the floor after the panel concluded. When the time came, the minister opened his remarks by telling the crowd, including the school's administrators, "Before I say anything else, I want the university to know that whatever they decide, I support that decision 100 percent." He then delicately backed the consensus of the policemen. While I was initially shocked at the expression of public fealty to Hopkins, proving that, as the single economic engine in town, everyone saw their interest as alertly clambering aboard, I reflected a bit differently over time. I was advocating an idealized concept of full natural rights, but the pragmatic rights under law are quite different. Often enough, to enjoy the rights granted by legislation, you need powerful friends.

Well, it was good green corn before the harvest. In other words, the laws of the natural world are real, but that world responds to a seasonal rhythm that has perceptible and imperceptible modes. That's the reason why Ralph Ellison described making the blues and its child jazz as the birth of a good thing out of a foul-smelling room. The funk that created the music was "good green corn before the harvest." Before it was meal. Before it was cornbread. Before it slaked hunger. Before it was gas. Before it was shit. Bet be happy not no drought.

Seasonal rhythm and forgetfulness make it awkward to determine a permissible level of crime. Between the ages of sixteen and twenty-two I found myself in situations again and again with a deadly outcome at worst and humiliating outcome at best, and on the other side of the gun was usually a black peer or a white officer. And what is the gap between the citizen's duty to guard their property and the state's onus to punish the violators of its laws? Whatever happened to me outside my lawful address I always understood as mainly the result of a series of my own choices—my fault, my bad. But how do you know when the laws have turned against the interest of the citizen? Students at colleges tend to be brand-new, fully endowed adults and citizens, and the colleges cement a niche by offering families mild guarantees of protections as the young citizens step into adult responsibility.

I went to college in a town on the Connecticut River and it was the first place I had ever seen the narcotics laws of Reagan-era America openly flouted, and the defiance was done by white bluebloods. We had an unarmed campus safety unit that was led by a tall black man named William Heckstall whose wife, Shirley, worked as an administrative assistant in the dean's office. I spent a semester there as a work-study student. I liked them both and spoke with them in the same way that I would have spoken to an aunt or uncle and they were firm and guiding us, though they did not pretend to share the social class trajectory that we would be on if we graduated from the college. But I suspect Officer Heckstall gained our respect and friendship because he worked hard at doing it, and, without a lethal weapon as recourse, he had to rely on his mind more than his 9mm. He probably knew by name all of the black males attending the school, and he did his fatherly best to protect us. When I went to my twenty-fifth anniversary, the familiar face on campus who remembered me was William Heckstall. By then, the two main black male teachers I had there, both of them Heckstall's age, were dead.

The necessary protections were not quite abstract. One afternoon during spring break, when my line brother and I were working on the campus grounds crew to save money to pay school fees, we were shooting around at an outdoor basketball court by my dormitory. Two men in jeans and tennis shoes walked up the street. One guy who looked older than us walked toward the court and stared at us with his hand in his dip; the other fellow approached the building, apparently knowing the three-digit door code, and went in. I had left my room open because no one was on the campus. After a minute or two, the visitor came away from the building, and they both left. When I returned to my room, my wallet was gone. We had nonstop fights with the guys from the local housing projects throughout my four years in college. Our noblesse oblige, which had us volunteering for local tutorial programs, didn't stop us from surcharging them more than registered students to attend our parties. Would the guy have pulled out a gun if we moved out toward him or the building door? Was he bluffing and signaling he thought we were punks, afraid to try him? It never occurred to me to contact either a campus safety officer or the local police. I just thought, I suppose, better next time to lock the door.

This same view about my own obligation for my personal security has guided me since the time I started taking the bus to grade school. It is a paranoid view. On an early Saturday summer evening when I was old enough to walk down to the store alone, two raw-looking teenagers waylaid me on my return. They had tracked me in the store and followed me out, striking up a friendly conversation and asking where I lived. After walking together for a block they turned ugly and demanded the dollar in my shorts, threatening to "serve" me. I had been completely unaware of their kind. I was five houses away from home, not more than one hundred feet, and the distance had never seemed so far, the doors had never seemed more securely closed in place. Before going inside I cried it all out on the bench on our porch, deeply ashamed to have been violated, and also feeling like more heroic and intelligent behavior was required on my part. I didn't get past the coin box that time.

Since it is daytime, I scurry along to use the credit union during the momentary wait for the shuttle. While down the street at the commercial bank, a man holstering a rubber-handle .357 stands on the street in front of the doors during business hours, no threats are on the horizon this side of Thirty-Third Street. I am not in the habit of going to any ATM at night, and but a handful of gas stations after dark. Money in my wallet improves my sense of well-being, but whenever I withdraw cash, I habitually calculate the size and weight class of the men who might plausibly observe my transaction. Just before I am about to pass the boy on the bench, he rises abruptly and disappears, the exact behavior to arouse my suspicion. He's dressed in a yellow hoodie and his jeans have yellow stripes, like a cavalryman.

A portly white woman smokes in front of the entrance to a cookie shop, and a Chinese woman of the same physique, accompanied by two of her countrymen deep in conversation, passes her. While Asians constitute about 6 percent of the state population, nearly 40 percent of the school's student body is Asian. I presume they are parents and I briefly marvel at the economic revolution advancing the Asian woman into a social class above that of this white woman manning the cookie counter. Is it the same evolution that has me living in the house where my church mother's father worked when she was a child? And yet, even if my surmising is correct, the white woman has a way of life that is attractive to her and is not connected to the same system of sacrifice, material striving, and generational advance adopted by the Asian woman or me. Before the Marlboro woman would funnel her family's fortune into sending a child to Hopkins, she would shelter a boat along the Chesapeake Bay or stable a mare in Carroll County.

American whites and Asians, the globe's chief consumers, coupled fleetingly on a sidewalk, capture the explicit fault line of the nature of the contemporary world. It bothers me that the police force initiative on the campus is emotionally tethered to the oddly American dynamic of mass school shootings, outrage that I associate with white male economic panic, manifesting itself first in sexual anxiety about being unable to secure desired mates. White men's conviction that they were losing has been the animus that fueled much of American history. The day before, I had been astounded by a right-wing radio pundit, not even the most popular in his class, whose homilies rang out with severity. The man, who has a markedly irritating nasal twang, one that would nearly disbar him from masculinity in my own ethnic group, shouted to his audience that he "had been poor!," but even when so, knew that he was blessed to be living in the planet's most advanced society. How did he know that? Because he had a freezer and a television. I had never heard the basis of supremacy distilled so primally, the achievement of the Western world to its beneficiaries reduced to ice cubes and sitcoms. But there it was. It occurs to me that a fresh-caught fish on a spit over a fire and the warmth of a companion is a better deal, but obviously I am a primitive. And perhaps that's why I prefer the book in my lap on the bus.

As I stepped beyond the shelter of a high rise to regain the bus stop, I paused, bracing for the wind. Even with my pockets flush, the older I get the more elusive is warmth. I dither over the wisdom of having moved north eight hundred miles during the last third of my life. Will I have the courage to find a warm climate before I die, or will I pit my waning strength against the ice and the seasons at the end? In the same way that it is feasible to secure a cabin by a lake, or an upper room in Paris, I could manage a house in Bouaké, where I lived before—what is holding me back? Then the yellow cavalryman appears in my two o'clock. I have to admit a new feebleness. I had missed his return. He closes the distance and begins a conversation I am startled to have.

He calls out in a flat, toneless, unaccented way, "Excuse me, sir, but are you a student here?" On that afternoon I am fifty-one years old. I can't possibly imagine that he believes I am a student. I had, however, spent some effort on my own appearance that morning, trimming my beard. Plucking and snipping the gray, shaving down the sparse areas, adding the scented oil. As a self-trained barber in college and graduate school, I obsessively notice the details of facial hair. I am also encumbered with the notion that I resemble a piebald horse, so I trim the beard every seventy-two hours, a hobby going back decades. After thirty-five years, my hirsute festival of compromise has something of a crescent shape, save a cavity where it doesn't connect on the left side of my face. The denuded area looks like an arrowhead, with the tip pointing toward my earlobe. Two "Indian Arrowes" and a fifth of whatever gold they found "from time to time," was King Charles's request to Cecil Calvert in the original land patent for Maryland.

My grandmother Christine Mitchell always took pictures with her "good" side, a predisposition on her part that was then impossible to understand. But now I do. While my mustache had come along by the time I was seventeen, it was only about ten years ago that the right side of the beard connected from ear to chin. At this pace, one of the timeless attributes of male gender will be fully mine near the time I retire. Of course, considering the various concessions to beauty and one's concept of gender that must be borne, this one is light. Regardless, the best part of the hairstyle is the blend at the top of the ear where the hair begins. The goal is to incline by infinitesimally perceptible blended degrees the completely shaven portion to a rather raw and untamed lamb chop of hair by the bottom of the jaw and chin. I have days when the clipper blades seem rigged against me, out of line and skewing the cut with little mealy dots. But today I was careful with the clippers and finished up with my shears.

Still, I don't look like a student unless you think that to be black here you need to have been through some kind of war. Multiple surveys say that being a professor is a cushy job. Maybe it's only the black people I know who seem to be dying on the job in their fifties and sixties. Why does the young man want me near his age? What sort of information can he plausibly be after? Is he mad, like the other black boy I have seen in his age range who sometimes jumps aboard the shuttle?

He continues, "Can you tell me about what this environment is like?" Is it an honest question or the beginning of some sort of grifter ploy? Is someone looking for him and he needs an alibi? Did he really want to know what was taking place behind the doors of this college where I was teaching? The day before I had six black and one Latino undergraduates in an introductory course go through a training so that they could venture into nearby barbershops and hair salons and conduct recorded interviews for an assigned podcast. I wanted them to know and share with their peers what the environment "outside" was like. They were to solicit public opinion on whether or not the university should be permitted to field its own police force. The students overwhelmingly chose to interview the salaried employees or proprietors of the shops rather than breaking the social distance and talking to the "real" citizens of the city. The students wanted the seat beside the busdriver.

This begs a question. Do everyday black Baltimoreans who are nonemployees ever find themselves on the Homewood campus? A university campus is, in its official, nine-to-five warrens, an unusual haven affording protections of language and personal space that might be paid for in blood or land elsewhere. Nonetheless, when I invite a group of local poets to campus— honored guests in their sixties and seventies to whom I am giving honoraria—they counsel their family members to refrain from taking pictures or making any kind of digital record. They are anticipating reprimand for possible violation of some unusual protocol or code from the era when the school aggressively excluded black students.

"Well, I am actually a professor here and you have asked a complex question," I respond blearily, still mystified. The boy resembles my long-ago friend from elementary school, a guy who went on to join the Nation of Islam. Where, I wonder, were the boys from that original 1973 class of Mrs. Jackson's, when they used to wheel in the stainless steel cart with aromatic hot lunches in lidded styrofoam boxes? Andre the rascal and Ben, who had a conically shaped head and who I had to fight, all of us sharing a surname. Erick, who wore heavy glasses, and baritone-voiced Kevin, the twins Troyd and Lloyd, and Jesse, who later let me borrow his digital watch. Christopher Hopkins, who "went off" from the ridicule. Gary, who imitated Daffy Duck first-rate. Derrick and Maurice, whose mother held an unregulated post by the middle doorway. Antonio and Terence, whose older brother competed in the Akron Soapbox Derby. Lost boys of long ago.

I had never been approached by a young brother on the street asking a question about this university, or, for that matter, any university. The boy with the close-cut fade resembled my elementary school classmate for another reason; he looked young and innocent, unscarred by the blocks just beyond the campus. Those of us who are parents of black boys can feel this scarification rather keenly, the pressures that incline so heavily to eliminate their innocence, to make their purity and gentleness and fumbling into a value not worth having.

I was thinking about some of this as I talked to him. The boy had street wariness and seemed like he caught on quick. He bore the same light acne as my own son, with only a bit more facial hair. I notice his teeth are soft, but in a straight line. A metal clasp is hooked on to his back pocket, which tells me that he has a three-inch knife. I don't begrudge him the utility weapon; I keep mine in the car. It is an even bet throughout the city that if you see a young man wearing a fanny pack you should assume he is armed. The black writers I have composed lengthy monographs about all carried knives for personal protection in the 1930s, 1940s, and 1950s, when personal firearms were uncommon. With hundreds of millions of guns circulating throughout America, the infrequent appearance of the pistol is no longer true. I regularly have the feeling that in this country I should keep a gun in the car and my knife on me. Counting on police is foolish; mobs have been known to breach even the US Capitol. When I wear my construction clothes, usually a couple of times a month, I always have a knife or a box cutter in my pocket. Usually when I am bitterly insulted or threatened with harm I am wearing shorts and sandals.

I hear myself talking to him and it is embarrassing. "Well, this is an exclusive, really elite place, like others in New York, Philadelphia, Boston, and Chicago," I reply. I point up the hill to the main campus, "They call it the bubble." The boy smiles and nods. It seems to me partly like the beginning of a hustle, and partly like someone who has already had life experience with the forces that can inflate a bubble or burst a bubble. The distance between Hopkins and the average city school student from developed Baltimore is quite a bit farther than the distance of a person living in underdeveloped West Africa today going to secondary school, which they would of course be paying for. A sizable portion of the gulf is attributable to attitude and expectation. In Baltimore, in a given year, some sixty graduates of the entire public school system will produce the standardized test scores and grades that could make them competitive for admission at Hopkins; most of those top scorers will be white. That's out of about eight thousand high school seniors, the massive attrition loss between ninth and eleventh grade notwithstanding.

Systemic racism is the obvious culprit here, which includes our foundation in slavery, a regulatory barbarism and genocide. Slavery simply did not end but continued by other mechanisms: vagrancy laws, black codes, poll taxes, grandfather clauses, rape, and lynching. Segregated doesn't only mean apart, and it doesn't only mean inferior. It means a rigid system that imparts divergent mortality rates. It is a strong series of gradations in housing, hospitals, schools, and inaccess to skilled jobs and seniority that is always represented as failure of effort on the part of the unskilled. None of it is new and it is maddening to have to repeat that before the slave regime had ended, financial instruments and government regulations, and new territories of crime and punishment had coalesced to secure perpetual bondage. The problem is that the remedy has always to be sought in the courts, and the onus is on the person wronged to show the overwhelming evidence against the wrongdoer. When President Obama told the Morehouse graduating class "nobody cares" about their hard luck story, he was cautioning the young black men away from redress they were unlikely to obtain from the US attorney general. But in a hyperlitigious society like the United States, the black part of it is largely bereft of competent, affordable legal representation or a speedy court system, civil or criminal anyway. Four point six percent of 1,160,000 American attorneys are black, and many of them have attended law schools where the bar exam passage rate is below 75 percent. The capacity for legal redress is not exactly steady.

Assured that the Leviathan of government can offer no remedy, sensible actors are wont to take the enforcement of justice into their own hands. Most Baltimoreans think the high proportion of people shot dead has something to do with illegal narcotics, or what used to be thought of as illegal narcotics. In any given year since 1968, around 277 black males are annually killed by violence. But in years like 2010 and 2020, that number of dead is drawn from a total population of barely 130,000. We are talking about 1 in every 433 black male citizens facing violent death in a year. During the Vietnam War, in which nine million served, 58,000 died, or 1 in 155. The war took place over ten years. Baltimore has played host to a killing field for fifty years, and we might anticipate the number of the black dead looking like 13,850. That is like one in eleven. The presumption and the statistics have been unchanged since black male unemployment reached a catastrophic nadir during the early Reagan years. Since the murder victims are typically unemployed and have been arrested before, the real group of victims and villains is even smaller than the subset of the population that they represent. Violent death over the decades might be confined to a group of about 35,000. That places the real city murder rate in

the neighborhood at two out of every five. My mortician friend
Marcus told me that a man thanked him for repairing his deceased brother's flesh so that the cadaver "looked like his self"
for the wake and funeral. "When I leave this earth I want you
to take care of me," the bereaved continued. When Marcus reminded the man of his youth and probable longevity, he distress-
ingly replied, "I pray so but I don't know. It might be sooner than
what we would all think." Funny, as teenagers our conversations
used to flit over the same topic. There is an eighteenth-century
lilt to the cadence of the young man's lament.

While the narcotics markets are extraordinary vehicles of
commercial exchange and their abusers the defining temperature
of the public health climate in the city, the economic relationships across drugs, black and white, rich and poor, are rarely explored. In 2013, a graduate from one of the departments I teach
in published a lyrically dense, nationally reviewed chronicle of
his heroin addiction while a student and his familiarity with the
city's drug subculture, in a sense the giant engine for the violent narcotics exchanges. Although the memoir did not set out to
do this, the narrative reveals the basic economic flow from the
comparatively affluent white zone down to the black street corner. This unregulated sale of narcotics today features as many in-
dustrially produced synthetic remedies like fentanyl and Xanax
as it does ancient staples derived from plant life, like heroin and
cocaine. In another way, the book shows the unyielding preoccupation that the comparatively affluent have with getting high
and enjoying themselves while remaining oblivious to the socio-
economic ruin their pleasures are derived from.

No person living in Baltimore and obliged to pay a water or
electric bill thinks the police are charging enough of the gun-
men with murder. The police detectives tasked with investigat-
ing city homicides include cynical, overworked bureaucrats and
political animals as well as some righteous defenders of the
citizenry. Their attitude is one of attrition. They believe that the

wizened public is partly to blame for refusing to adhere devot-
edly to their requests for information, even from people who
have suffered debilitating wounds. The detectives reason that,
faced with manpower shortages and equipment failures, they
should persist in squeezing their networks, the criminal infor-
mants inside and outside prison. Eventually, most of the murders will be exposed by people attempting to save themselves
from prison time. Besides, beyond the occasional child or employed woman who is inadvertently slain, the dead are among
the most marginal, if not, indeed, the most despised of the city.
It was probably before the end of the nineteenth century that the
saying "Nigger, I got you in my pocket" shifted from the threat of
being sold from the cornfields of Maryland to the cotton fields of
Mississippi to the willingness to produce a concealed cartridge-
shooting handgun and end a life.

There can be an obvious structure to daily incivilities. The
sharp declension on the street from the well fed to the skinny
youngsters to the veterans chasing drugs rips the social bonds.
Prompted by the police and Hollywood, gangs arise with bloody
initiations and the tattoos that render in plain sight the dire narrative of violent trauma and retribution. In *The Corner*, an influential docudrama directed by Baltimore actor Charles Dutton
and written by journalist David Simon and former police detective Ed Burns, the real-life character whom major portions of the
miniseries depicted speaks for himself in a brief cameo at the conclusion. Attempting to explain the difference between the film and
his own grasp of his life, DeAndre McCullough tries to define
the culture on the street at the end of the 1980s. The twenty-five-
year-old says, "You couldn't even buy a friend." He is alluding
to the disintegration of a social world when a generation of children entered the narcotics exchange markets as the "rock" cocaine helped to balloon the hard-core addict population in the
city from three to thirty thousand in a decade.

McCullough came of age at the decline of the ethos of "word

is bond" or a person's word is his bond, as well as the end of the Afrocentric movement. With so many people to choose from for career-making arrests and prosecutions, the police benefited from tips by rivals who wanted to decrease competition. As the perils of longer and longer prison terms and the sentencing of juveniles as adults became what is called today "mass incarceration," the kinship bonds of neighborhood, primary school, and extrafamilial social cliques became increasingly fragile. The older players on the streets responded at the beginning of the new millennium with slogans of "Stop Snitching" on T-shirts and even a documentary by the same name, mourning the disappearance of loyalty to kin in favor of collaboration with the police. The ambiguous mercury of fidelity is what makes us both tribal and capable of the faith to battle against odds.

Arguably the question about how many more state-authorized police and large prisons are necessary to address the measurable criminality of black men is the most begged in American history. A term like "black crime" is a tautology, when the premise "black" already asserts the conclusion "crime." "Black crime" is an American redundancy, like "Native savagery" or "white purity." "From the late 1890s through the first four decades of the twentieth century, black criminality would become one of the most commonly cited and longest-lasting justifications for black inequality and mortality in the modern urban world," insists Harvard professor Khalil Gibran Muhammad. Sixty years and more can be added to his twentieth-century assessment. A century and a half is an impossibly long time to carry the burden of being a social pariah. But contemporary society is profoundly shaped by language rules that foster "blindness" when it comes to racial determinations. The codes are excellent at revealing sloppy language gaffes of explicit fools. In fact, we live now in a world where a person's innate antiblack animus is on display if they use a term like "black crime." The preferred term in our own moment is to invoke a disembodied specter that haunts the moors, the rising tide of abstract, disembodied "gun violence."

I was weaned during the epoch of "black-on-black" violence, a term I always understood to have been generated by caring black commentators, but which was also difficult to parse out from the channels that circulated it in a broader Reagan-era vanquishing of the Soul-era slogan "Black Is Beautiful." Replacing the one with the other was like the dream of a Ku Klux Klansman. The current discussion of "violence" without the black tag but used only to describe homicide and near homicide in black neighborhoods, which are, by definition again, working class or working poor, seems like one with a silent referent. Because is it really possible for Baltimore, as a city, to have a "violence" problem? Are people inside the city's limits prone to settle disagreements and disputes outside courts of law by recourse to threats and willingness to cause bodily harm? Does the Baltimore City Health Department field reports of more children spanked in the city as a form of family discipline? Are cases of domestic and spousal abuse here more prevalent and more vicious? Does the school system report more disciplinary removals from its senior high schools for fighting? In the city population, do the criminologists measure a higher proportion of males between sixteen and twenty-five than in previous decades? Possibly all of these questions can be answered in the affirmative. But the standard statistic that is called forth unendingly is the city's homicide rate. If fewer than 300 people lose their lives within the city limits during the year, it is a victory, and the deadly beast has been chained. But if 301 persons perish, committed evildoers from the land of Nod they may be and even within ten feet of the county line, then Camelot has fallen, and the arc of justice is bending toward something hot and smelling of sulfur.

I remember the lesson of the public town hall at Coppin and the debacle of "What are you going to do?" Maybe that was what enabled me to see the situation with the boy in the hoodie for what it really was. "Where do you go to school?" I ask the child. He says he is enrolled at the REACH! Partnership School, one of the city's newly created academies to offer technology-readiness classes. In my era he would have attended Dunbar, Eastern, or Lake Clifton, but twenty-five years ago the city addressed a failing social order's scholastic underperformance by dismantling the large high schools. The public schools are one-third the size they were when I was a teenager, and they are all that stands between a lot of black middle-class Baltimore county taxpaying educators and poverty. We are, in a way, a school system specializing in special education. There is, of course, a 120-person-capacity juvenile justice residential facility, spacious with only about 50 resident boys.

Since it is 1:45 p.m. on a school day, I ask him why he is at his ease. He confesses to some sort of minor indiscretion, the sort I was lucky to have avoided throughout school and from my two-parent home, and he is now home-schooled. I ask him about his possible field of interests, and he says internet technology, one of the academy choices at REACH!, along with other fields like law and, the favorite target of Jamaica Kincaid, hospitality and tourism. He modifies his response swiftly, telling me, "I know that's what everybody says nowadays." I tell him that is where growth and jobs are. But his choices are up to him.

I wanted to tell the him about my project named after Billie Holiday, and the partnership with high school students we were supposed to be getting underway at Frederick Douglass Senior High. But in February, two days before our long-delayed meeting with the principal, an aide was shot in the school foyer by a student's disgruntled relative, whom the armed adult felt had been improperly dishonored. The firearm as the surcease of self-protection, which is honor, is always credited as bringing about the end of feudalism. The portable, weathertight gun in the American system and in the Western tradition is as basic to democracy as free speech and practice of religion, the foundation of Western education. "THEOW and ESNE art thou no longer," Cedric said to his liege Gurth in Walter Scott's *Ivanhoe*, lifting off the yoke of bondage and endowing him with land in recognition of his fealty. Maybe there is an outcome with our murder and killing that is more momentous than we can envision. I wish I didn't have nightmares about being shot and stabbed, mercifully fewer of them now than when I was younger. Maybe I am just soft. Muhfucka, come back here.

There was a time when I felt so at home, so delighted in having conversations on the street, when I was convinced like Walter Rodney, not in the value of the academic training, but in the value of the grounding. In the June days following the Los Angeles Rebellion of 1992, I happened to be in Nickerson Gardens and I felt like a person being given small treasures to build with some Crips on the corner there, a place that was as geographically foreign from what I knew growing up as it is possible to be in the United States. It was where I first heard the young men use the term "love" in the same sort of complex way Claude Brown began to use the term "baby" in the 1940s.

Today I can feel alienated from the block where I was born. The young set spray-paints "P[ark] H[eights] G[angster] C[rips]" on the metal covering shielding the barbershop where my father took me to sit in Odell's chair when I was a boy. The graffiti artists are deadly serious about a rap song they heard or a Hollywood film they saw. It raises no outcry when men and women of all ages are found dead on the street or in cars, along my old routes Belle, Calloway, Ayrdale, or Cold Spring Lane. Now I feel like I am losing my connection, and that the subculture to which I once belonged is gone and I am old. The freedom fighter Rodney, was assassinated at thirty-nine, the age I was when my son Mitchell was born. For so many years I had thought of myself as belonging to a comfortless daring intellectual band, black and in touch with the revolutionary vanguard. But now I want burial insurance and the means to pay college tuition, and my romance is for more regular luxuries and tranquil hedonism. When I consider my life and possibilities this way, I think I have exchanged my youthful dream of black liberation for my house with my sons in Homeland.

The boy in yellow-striped jeans came into awareness of his membership in the American nation state with an African American as president. I would guess that my own convolutions and adjustments wouldn't just yet make any sense to him. But I badly want to get closer to reality and to acknowledge the risk and maturity he has taken in initiating our conversation. So I say to him, "When I was your age I started to make decisions that I am dealing with at this moment." I tell him this with a world of fists flying, guns, motor vehicle accidents, drugs, and unprotected sex flashing before my eyes. I know this is terrible, the prejudging that I am doing, the affinity I am drawing out with the young man in a territory where I should enjoin him to a project of distinguishing difference. I feel like I should unveil an anecdote that would inspire, not banally relate. I feel like I am asking him if he has seen *The Wire*. And why should I invoke for him the most powerful underdog associations available to me, rather than connecting him to other ways I might see myself: the scholarship, hard work, and endurance, the best ethical choices, the religious, marital, and parental fidelity, the sacrifice? Karl Marx thought that economizing on your capital through "self-denial, the denial of life and of all human needs" was another folly. In essence this: He has addressed me in standard English. Why am I turning the conversation toward the vernacular? Am I uncomfortable in a philosophical sense with vernacular language because it represents something impure, a distinguishing benchmark of black American culture, a willingness to mix and make use of a taint? Or is the vernacular actually necessary to contain the contradiction of what I really want to say, that he should strive without assimilating, and amass experience without accumulating things?

I find it a sharp edge to dance upon. The boy's question reminds me of going with David over to the house of his girlfriend, who then called up a girl she knew with a reputation. The policemen casually threatening to kill us. Running a gee. Cutting school to shoot guns in Leakin Park. The watches and clothes from the Benetton store at Security Mall, and freezing at the sight of the boy loading the pistol for us at the school. The boys trying to kill us that night and them wrecking my father's car; jumping through the windshields and Rod's brother being stabbed and fighting down at the harbor. The death lists in the yearbook and teenage pregnancy and the girls whose boyfriends protected their honor with weapons and the girls who protected their own honor. Even something lewd on this same campus, before it wanted a police force. All of it well before we started getting high. Then, all of the clique battles out in front of Odell's and in the alleys behind the club. Chasing niggas with bats. Donald bleeding to death on Lanvale Street and the police holding off the stretcher, asking about drugs.

The boy asks me, "Sir, I don't mean to be rude, but could you say exactly what some of those choices were?" I don't want to spell out any of it, but I am feeling abandoned by ideology, Afrocentrism, Negritude, Garveyism, radical marronage, futile rebellion. Maybe I am more powerfully feeling bereft of faith in an eschatological view of the end of time. The Pennsylvania Avenue Royal Theater glory days of my dad's generation were the anchor of the romantic past upon which to invent the better future, but it seems irresponsible to invoke those mystery lands. I tell him some of it, but I feel torn, in the same way I do when I hear people try to ground their authenticity or their connection to the poor by using bushels of profanity. Because when people told it to me, they were pretty sure that their honesty was enough to change my behavior. But I think telling it now, where everything is always recorded and lodged and replayed, is more like justifying and valorizing missteps. What's more, my recapitulation is inaccurate—the years between sixteen and twenty are running seamlessly in my memory now, but the distinctions are as valuable to him as they were to me then.

I can see the boy's charm and vulnerability. I think he can make it. He's young, curious, he hasn't made a choice yet that he can't take back. Maybe he should go to Wyoming or Vermont or Paraguay? I emphasize that leaving the city for college three hundred miles away was good for me. I can't bring myself to tell him that you have to be able to handle being called "nigger." Some people can't deal with that alone. I tell him that I was the only person to make it through college in four years that I knew from my block, and I mention the high schools my homeboys attended. He's heard of them, the same way that even the urchins of Cedonia will have heard of faraway Poplar Grove and Bloomingdale. The street corners are still cheered by the DJs in the local songs. I say to him, "You have to be independent from your friends, you always have to be thinking in terms of foresight and hindsight at once." I'm not sure about that, but he takes it in and nods his head.

And then I think all I am doing is digging into him about responsibility and dignity and implying that it is his fault if he fails, just like Obama would say, except that people like Obama are too calculating to spend much time talking to a boy on the street. Fatherly advice has its limitations. I know plenty of boys who grew up with their father in the house and the main thing they wanted was to live someplace else. Certainly with my own teenagers it can seem like the nonstop muttering of dissent and pulling away. Purpose so great.

The square nose of the bus comes into view, and I ask my young friend if he is going to ride. He says, "No." I shake his hand, tell him who I am and say I would be glad to hear from him if he wants to send an email. He tells me his name is Darius. King of Persia.

What growth there was consisted of rank weeds and the trees
were mulberries and locusts and sycamores—trees that partook
also of the foul dessication which surrounded the houses; trees
whose very burgeoning seemed to be the sad and stubborn remnant of September, as if even spring had passed them by, leaving
them to feed upon the rich and unmistakable smell of negroes in
which they grew.

  —William Faulkner, *The Sound and the Fury* (1929)

Is this the Region, this the Soil, the Clime,

. . . .

Receive thy new Possessor: One who brings
A mind not to be chang'd by Place or Time.
The mind is its own place . . .

  —John Milton, *Paradise Los*t (1667)

Roland Park-Guilford-Homeland offer woodland . . . elbow
room . . . and architectural distinction; more spacious quarters,
a place where your children can dig and riot.

  —Guy O. Hollyday, The Roland Park Company (1930)

Ordinary Time:
The Gentle Brushing Fescue

After the children were born I revived the intriguing family name songs and word games I had learned as a child. I wanted to induce in my brood the same curiosity I had about our bloodline. My father groomed us with a family name jingle that was popular during the second Eisenhower campaign. Whenever there was enough wet snow in the alley at No. 58 to take out the old Flexible Flyer, he would sing the jingle to my sister and me along with the choral music he had learned in college, Ivor Tchervanow and Richard Kountz's "The Sleigh." To my mind, his caroling was an ornament inseparable from the heraldry he had begun to devise for our family, half installation art, half portraiture. He was amused by a twin mammy salt and pepper shaker made of green plastic that found its way to our kitchen table, then the shelf over the sink, then the rail heading down to the finished basement. He fashioned two or three poster-size Nubian paintings of mother and child: a black and white canvas hung atop the mantle of our faux fireplace; one painted on an orange piece of plywood covered the window of the garage. These crests were mysterious to me, but an indelible part of us.

I resumed the campy noir legacy when I bought my first house. I wanted to christen our new place in honor of Nanny or Cudjo, or call Negro Hill or African Hill, not quite having the requisite hubris for Jackson Hall or Jackson Moor. Remembering a placard I had seen in St. Augustine, I settled on Seminole Hill. But I couldn't single-handedly infuse the children's memories with the term and it took more than a little for me to dredge up that name myself. In the same way that African flight to St. Augustine and the etymology of Seminole are brushed over spots of the Southeast's black story, none of my children today recall baptizing our house. Really, they showed only faint interest in the fantasies of heraldry; it was not at all like the "brow of a soft and gentle eminence" from the patriarchal romance stories. I console myself by flying from the porch the same Maryland colonial flag I saw at Wye Church, the kind of ensign that Mathias de Sousa, a black colonist aboard the *Ark* in 1633, might have seen billowing in the wind.

Lacking in the wonders of lore, I target more practical Elysian pasture. After three years of treading water alongside the shoals of motley turf, I am determined to swim to land and gain the eminence of healthy grass. My front lot is split into two plots, forty feet deep, twenty feet wide, separated by the original flagstone walkway. The northern plot gets a fair amount of spotty sun, but the southern bed only registers strong shade. The sunlight hitting there through the trees lands like the dots of brown inside the black rosette on the leopard's white fur. Shoring up the degraded soil by the southeastern edge, which someone far less conscientious than I used full-sun sod to cover, and which has worn away until only the plastic netting used to transport it remains, is a prime goal. The showpiece of any house, the front is one third of my manslot, the oxgang or bovate of the middle class, the quarter of the quarter acre that can be dressed by an adult in a day. The conjunction between an appropriate share of land for service made to the nation and the practice of divination and random award is reflected in the word "lot." For years the property record didn't even list a street address, just Roland Park Company, Plat of Homeland, Block 7, Lot 2.

Although it only takes an alert twenty minutes to mow the grass, I can no longer perform the season-to-season transformational yard work in a single day, even a long one. My body is too outraged. The job begins with pruning the trees from a ladder, trimming all the shrubs and decorative green cover, pulling all the weeds, then collecting the trimmings and leaf debris onto a tarp. The heaviest task is lining the entire yard perimeter and tree bowls with a shovel and removing the soil. The finish work involves trimmer edging, raking, mowing, sweeping, and finally mulching. And now, as a person more intelligent than I was before, I have to accept a new master: the weather. The same week that the night air regularly stays above freezing and the tree buds start to sprout, the ground will have to be scored if I want grass to bathe in strong sunlight and have a chance to thrive.

Guilt about possibly missing these few sunny weeks without leaf cover drives me off my bunk and onto the land. I made the first pass over the grounds in early January, a circumstance that was as incredible as the fact that my Atlanta boy would have a "spring break" that started in February. That January day only required the work of the Trash Gang, clearing a little rubbish and then spreading granules to repel the moss. I used a machine. A neighbor had abandoned a wheeled broadcast spreader and, Fred Sanford that I am, I acquired it, finally even apportioning the limber its own hook on a garage rafter. At the end of February the hosta shoots had been aboveground for two weeks. It would be a gamble either way: plant grass early to reap sunlight and risk its germination, or wait until the cold weather was over and lose the sunlight to the tree canopy. A hard preparation for spring in the dead middle of winter seems to a city man like myself the very end of the seasons. The enslaved-farming farming tribes of Jones and Jacksons and Hundleys and Wallers, and Mitchells and Baskervilles I belong to probably considered the coy weather in a different way.

That January pass insisted that I dethatch, or scrape off the dead layer of grass and live layer of moss with my garden rake. Before exhaustion set in, I had tried about a fifth of my lot. As a kind of minor reward to myself, I planted seed on the eastern lip of the south side by the sidewalk. With my twin hollow-tine manual aerator, I put a few hundred plugs in the sod, the difficulty relative to the amount of moisture in the soil. Using my boot to penetrate the earth with metal tines is far more satisfying than raking and enables me to peacefully aerate the soil without destroying fragile grass around the plug. There is an ungentle gas-powered machine available from the big-box stores that does the same job. But the 270-pound aerator that burrows turning the corners, catches on roots, and liquefies any shallow grass was designed for the flattest of treeless suburban yards. Three years ago, when I did bring the leaden engine to bear, I added topsoil to my yard and now there is a rich black loam underneath the moss in place of the unforgiving clay with its striated bands of starchy mortar, the remnant undoubtedly from some sewage project snaking through the yard. But after booting in the plugs I run out of steam and stow the rakes and shovels in the wheelbarrow for another day.

In the second week of March, with rain in the forecast and new buds visible on the stems of the beech and oak trees that will soon cast a shadow across the fledgling grass of the yard, another day is today. In spite of knowing that time is running out to prepare the land, I can't step foot in the yard before the afternoon. A review session with a student, a long coffee with a prospective colleague, reading *Waverley* and getting *Ivanhoe* from the library, the panic associated with the globally circulating, deadly virus that leads to my institution closing the following day, and my gasping, flailing decision to reroute my retirement away from stock indexes to at least some holdings in bonds and real estate, put me dressed and in the front yard at 2:30 p.m. A typical day in America.

Donning olive-drab dungaree vestments signals my readiness for a day of property veneration. My ancient mentor, the kidnapped orphan Venture Smith, called them "just what clothes were comfortable for common days." At Christmas dinner at my mother's, her uncle reminded us that "when we lived in the country, we wore overalls." Comfortable clothes for common work hid some of our family's more uncommon pretensions. My great-grandfather Joseph Macklin named his last female child Lavinia, from a Roman model, Latinus's daughter, Aeneas's bride, and mother of Iulus. While it seems impossible that this man was perusing Virgil alongside the farm catalogs, Uncle Harold did say to me recently that his father did not fit in with his own family or with local whites. Everyone between Bracey and South Hill thought he was getting beyond himself. Reading the *Aeneid* would certainly do that. Like my burgess's life in Homeland.

From the garage I retrieve the wheelbarrow, still stocked with tools, seed, and fertilizer. Some neighbors suppose I am a Latin American yard worker, a misidentification that mainly says to me I am achieving a professional result. Like other experiences in life that are exciting visually in ways that they only approach tactilely, the saddest thing about having a house you admire is that it is your neighbor's house you will see during your moments of lingering comfort or extended ease. Since I park in my garage, I only enter my own front door when I have forgotten something and the car is idling across the street while I dash in from the rain. Looking out the window, I see the neighbors' stone giants of five or six gables, gambrel roofs, bay windows, pyramid chimneys, and curved pediment dormers. We were all built within a year or two of each other. Their early owners saw my plain, six-room, three-gable house going up. And yet I take a deliberate daily pleasure and walk out of my front door and turn around and look at the yard and the house. Sometimes I walk across the street to gain further perspective on my modest stone barn, the haven of the unfrilled traditional middle class.

After dreaming over the situation, I conclude that I have about three days of chores for a person using hand tools. Taking a flat-edge shovel and edging the perimeter into sharply lined divisions between the turf and the bedded mulch with the shrubs is the toil that has the most impact. This digging, driving the blade at a ninety-degree angle straight down to reveal a flush edge, requires ranging the perimeter as well as two circular beds of pachysandra surrounding the trees in the yard. The pachysandra is a diamond-shaped, ragged-edge, spreading vine with a white spring blossom. One bed encompasses the birch tree; the other surrounds a miniature Japanese maple, dead now for the second year. Of course, it should be replaced, but in its slender mourning, as the trunk ribbons slowly into splinters, it conveys an end-of-life, furled grandeur. In addition, there are, flanking the opening to my walk, two quarter circles of mulch wanting to be licked with an edge. The beech tree lies in one, matched on the other side of the flagstone pavement by a bed of hostas. Both beds are raised a foot or more above the sidewalk. The difficulty with a lot of the edging around the tree lines is that tenacious roots have come up with the frosts. But if the edging is done crisply, it affords a sheer, luxurious look. What I have learned over the years is that to make the edging powerful and dramatic, the shovel lining also requires collecting the earth and removing it. The job is painstaking and precise.

In terms of rootwork, I am in fair territory with the southern side, but dethatching and tilling have not been done to the north plot. The rented tiller died there two years ago, in the battle with the oak tree roots. Since trees are duplicated under the earth by a root network somewhat mirroring the branches visible aboveground, I am only slightly fearful about removing roots from the leaning oak tower, with its bicep and forearm menacing the neighbor's living room. But just the thought of this hard, un-requited labor puts my lumbar number five on spasm alert. The raking needed for dethatching is not too bad, and scoring the yard 250 times or so with the aerator is the equivalent of only a minor leg press, like walking upstairs two at a time. Seeding, in fact, is more demanding, more like something from the cotton-picking regimen. To guarantee the seed is getting into the hole requires bending down to the ground and letting a half handful trickle out from your fist.

With the aerobic rake, I am indecisive and peripatetic, made more so by the Belgian ale I can't finish but needed during the retirement fund transaction. For the rest of my life undoubtedly, I will remain bewildered by the shellacking I took in the stock market in 2001, when Silicon Valley and the internet were the next sure thing. I had a very small book advance and wanted to do something conservative with it to be able, eventually, to buy a house, the little ranch piggy that went to market during the Great Recession. My lesson from the misadventure, which evis-cerated a third of the principal, was to run when storm clouds appeared. My March anxiety turned fully into a comedic vision of my thirty-year-old son shaking his head in disbelief when I tell him I have only enough in retirement to get through the first winter out of the classroom.

I toss the rake aside and vengefully deliver preliminary blows with a freshly sharpened hatchet. A day at the roots will take it all, and I aim licks at the aboveground portions of the leathery tubers that obstruct the line between turf and mulch. At first, I think there are roughly half a dozen but, closer to ground, that number quadruples. My pattern from the walk-way is an edge line, then the turf, another edge line, mulch, and then some shrubbery before the masonry division walls with the neighbors. On the northern plot, beyond the mulch is a blue rug

creeping juniper that rises to knee level, intermixed with ivy, before meeting a low brick wall separating me from the neighbor,
whose front door is on a street perpendicular to Albion Road.
(I note with more satisfaction that a low stone wall, in need of
a little mortar, separates me from my neighbor to the south.) I
bite into the dry roots with the ax, spraying a few chips, but,
like a child striker, never lingering in the grooves, fleeting from
one tentacle to the next as if I were anointing a magic blade. It
is too much intractable work to commit to one place. As I move
the blade nearer the sidewalk, I begin to lather, and I decide to
make a furious stand against one of these infernalities. I send
the wedge home, angling forty-five degrees left then forty-five
degrees right until there is a new dimension of sound, the blade
through fibrous resistance and home, the iron into the sod. Just
as I raise a blister where the ax handle has a curlicue fence to
prevent it from slipping, I remember gloves. I go to the garage,
take the gloves, and, brigands be damned, leave up the gate, and
return to continue cleaving through a few more of the roots,
wondering how it will help as I try to worm them to the surface,
usually with a twist and a back-troubling pull. A few children
have been released from the public school and they walk by in
their khaki and navy. I pause so as to eliminate the infinitesimal
possibility of accident.

Impressed by my array of tools, I return merrily to rake.
Some parts of the lawn are flaxen and desiccated, with a fescue that dies out, and without too much visible moss. Some of
the grass is sparsely green, looking more like rye or Bermuda
than fescue, our zone's Gemini grass, carrying us from snow to
Sahara. Then, looking closely, I see the tenacious green scabs of
moss peppering the ground, in some places forming what looks
like an impermeable crust. Wherever it congeals, you can be
sure that a tree root courses underneath and is working to create pus where there had been surface life. As I rake, I try to run
the tines completely parallel to the horizon of the ground, leav-

ing as much healthy grass in place as possible. I come to realize that the aluminum soft-tine leaf rake is better suited to the task than the steel garden rake, that is, if I am willing to bend it to the point of destroying it. Since I have three such rakes, I have little problem with the sacrifice. I move the rake with the speed and force of a person swiftly beating eggs, and it scores the moss into particles, probably better to spread their message like an evangelist at an all-day revival.

And the idea of eviscerating, a possibility beyond which there can be nothing further, is enough to begin another mental process, and I remember the pruning shears. Another neighbor discarded Black and Decker lopping shears and also fiberglass shrub trimmers; I understood him to have moved in the direction of electric equipment and to be declining the work of his hands. I nearly leapt into his trash, my desire was so great, though I stilled myself until night, with my bandana firmly in place to do it. I return to the garage, pleased to have discarded the neighborhood common sense of meticulously closing the doors against thieves.

I am now in full kit for my battle against the root. With the lopping shears I begin to snip through the most vulnerable surface tendons of the trees webbing over the front lawn, starting near the shrub bed. Using the spar end of a pick, I trough out the topsoil to unearth the throaty lengths, the width of a pickle. The rhizomes coursing out perpendicularly like veins make the removal a mean adventure for my lower back. I cleave at them with my pick, (whose thin alloy chisel is sadly bent from a previous minor skirmish) and lop them off before pulling up the ropy lifeblood to the wood. Various lengths of pickle- and carrot-size bark affront the ground, the scraps from a process as frustrating as pulling the comb through knotted hair.

A two-year-old and an older man wheel past as I am getting the pieces up that will constitute a complete barrow full of root lengths. The grandfather looks just like the man I heard speaking Russian into a telephone while walking by a minute earlier.

The boy glides on the two-wheeled balance bike, the new vogue to get them early onto the pedaled bicycle proper. He has a gently rounded forehead and mouth, softly curled black hair and dark eyes; he reminds me immediately of pictures of myself a little older, and all my tribe from the slums of Bahia to the pitches of the Sky Blues. I think that he will live his life as a nonblack person and be disinclined to hear different. I ask him if he wants to plant some grass and make a flower, but he is not yet ready for strangers. I wonder from which side of his family all this soul comes from. Avum regeneravit Aethiopem.

The child wheels past and, furlough over, I return to the earth obstacles. To close the jaws of the lopper around the pickle requires the force needed to carry all of the week's groceries from the floor to the counter. Some of the limbs are overthick and insist upon the hatchet to make a course for the curved lopper blade. Always there is needed an additional insisting vigor. Squatting and digging, wrenching, twisting, and pulling, I fill the barrow with this ancient, ribbed sponge, giving myself to this annual task of taking a plane to knots. Finally, there are just the spiderwebs of the roots, coursing throughout the now heavily turned rich black earth. I sow the blue fescue seeds into a slight furrow, washing them back over with earth, and repeat the process again, a half step closer to the house, and then a third time, thinking that the most arid span has been revealed and reseeded.

The hand aerator goes easily into the soil and I work the bare spots, moving back toward the house. Using a wide-board snow shovel as a brake, I rake and shovel into the barrow the dead grass, moss, and thatch, trying to shake out the earth, then aerate, then add seeds, then rake soil over the seeded ground. At twenty feet, I realize that with so much thatch to collect, I could gather it with the lawnmower at its lowest setting. I return to the happily open door of the garage to obtain the machine, priming it on the gravel-and-dirt pathway back to the front, and double pass the remaining portions of the lawn. By the time I fill the mower bag with thatch, I notice the time. My son is ready for pickup from school.

The squawks, trills, whip-poor-wills and hoots of the aviary family remind me the next morning to prepare the scarecrow, or the eaters of seed will plunder my errand. I use Mitchell's Hulk costume for its base and put him in a blue Gore-Tex jacket with one of his Bushido swords as arms, and arrows for legs. I sit the scarecrow in the busted wicker chair that my mother had as a child. I had speed-patched its bottom with pineboard waste and the chair had been spoiling in the attic, where surely it would make a couple, if I had it, with Grandma Macklin's rocker.

The birch tree blossoms have brought out a delicate pink, willowing and arrayed like gigantic bunched snowflakes against the gray overcast March skies. It is the first week of the novel coronavirus, and high schools have been closed, leaving my baseball-desolate freshman at home. The presence of another human being marching to the refrigerator and pantry, tossing books and computer gear over the table, showering to a symphony of tinny rap tunes, and chortling like the sheriff from *The Dukes of Hazzard*, unnerves me. But if my idea of serenity inside my house during the work day has difficulty accommodating my own flesh and blood, the world outside my door blares acoustic chaos. My mind and ear are beset by the platoons of landscapers from companies like New World and Maxalea that festoon upon the local gardens and preen the grounds. It sounds as if a dirtbike race has begun in the living room. From the groups with logo uniforms to the two-man crews without even matching sweatshirts, the landscapers mercilessly deploy high-pitched whining 2cc engine leaf blowers, spewing the remains of grasses, leaves, petals, and twigs either up against the house or out into the street. The striving outfits bearing ethnic names like to break the day at 7:45 a.m., shaving off minutes from the Homeland Association's regulation, which sets the outdoor work start time at 8:00. They dutifully blare throughout the day, winding down after suppertime. Rather than a peaceful enclave, choice Homeland is actually a neighborhood of bruising unquiet during three of four seasons, as often a sawmill as a reflecting pond. When the whine of the blowers ceases, the rumbling hum of the HVAC units begin, drowning out the choir of birds. The noise all presumably goes unnoticed by my neighbors, whose working lives can be so order-driven as to eliminate everything beyond the sound of their own voices, their unending pitch to the world for calculated recognition. Although barely nine houses are visible from any window of my home, by May the din is steady and constant.

The yardwork is done mainly by Latino men on the margins of citizenship, bossed by a white manager from a telephone. The migrants have a reputation for honesty, hard work, and being inexpensive. Though it seems obvious to me that landscaping during the pandemic is risky, the exterior yardwork continues as it always has. In the months that come, across the nation, Latinos will account for about twice as many deaths and hospitalizations of those under sixty-five compared to blacks and whites.

From time to time, the higher class of workers, the masons, carpenters, and plumbers, arrive in trucks with small Confederate flags and "TRUMP: Best President Ever" bumper stickers. From time to time, I am piqued, and leave messages for the homeowners, trying to shame them about the professed attitude of their employees, which wouldn't be tolerated in their own workplaces. But despite the irritations, there is an obvious truth: The lots they tend are the best in the city. A standard was set and it is maintained at a high cost.

Erected in 1929, the corner dwelling, on a street named for the first English bishop of Canterbury, has four men at work all day. Two of them constantly blow the leaves that had seemed hidden to the sloppy eye. They resolve their efforts among the pachysandra beds and then come with twenty yards of mulch and three wheelbarrows, capaciously laving the beds and the edged-out lands in brown fiber. I watch them and then circle the block, marveling at their techniques, their using small spatula-like spade weeders for the fine details.

The accomplishment of the neighbor's workforce inspires me. I reconvene with my youth and bid him to edge the southern-most plot, which, last year, I simply ignored. In the course of four seasons, a kind of freshet has been created, running off topsoil down to the sewer at the bottom of the dip in the yard toward the sidewalk. Nathaniel edges and brings it up to the mark by the yew shrubs. I take the hedge trimmer and out-line the pachysandra beds, then sculpt the yews, and shape up the ivy, work on the roots and aerate more of the soil. After fif-teen feet of making the edge between the grass and mulch bed of pine chips that bends into a tertium quid between abandoned fallow land and ivy, the wheel barrow is full of fresh dirt. I be-lieve that this new manure should be spread over the adjoining hearth which typically suffers the run off and where we have just reseeded.

When we have filled an entire wheelbarrow, I direct Nathaniel to the backyard to get a shovel's worth of sand to mix in. For several minutes he pounds the barrow, cutting the sand and clay together, which we spread over the freshly seeded hillside. Balancing the heavy wheelbarrow, sifting the clay with the sand, cutting it in from the sides, is ancient work. My son weathers the first load without comment, but balks by the time that the third barrow lilts heavily with dirt. The edging by then has taken on a wedge shape and fully resembles a trench, and I realize that fill-ing it with mulch will not address our erosion calamity. The next thing I know, I am coercing my unwilling boy into the car and to the home improvement store for pond stones.

I would actually love to put down pebbles, the ultimate ac-
coutrement of high Gunston Hall style, a pebble corn driveway,
but I have ever been at the mercy of too many leaves to indulge
that rapture long. At Lowe's I send my son to find new leather
gloves while I analyze the choices, and he comes back having
matched the color but not the size and is sent off again. For pond
stones, the merchant is unbelievably flush. Tempering our quarrel, I ask my strong boy how many of the bags does he think
we will need? Ten or twenty? I settle on fifteen. I brush the seasonal refuse off likely plastic sacks of stone, half a cubit foot and
weighing about fifty pounds, then position them onto an eight-
foot cart. I like to lay them out slowly in precise rows of three.
Nathaniel keeps bellying the bags, and I try to show him how
to lift using the thighs and biceps. He doesn't want to listen to
his old man.

Avoiding the touchpad and the air trail of the friendly clerk,
I pay for the bags and instruct my son to get the disposable plastic liner to cover the bed of our station wagon. He grumbles and
goes forth, and I try to rib him in a good-natured, bad-natured
way. I am mixing sugar with my salt, but it sounds mainly like
obligation and penance. I can't dislodge the memory of contests
with my own father, his long silences, and my strong desire to
prove to him that I was his equal. We drive home wordlessly, so
I appreciate Nathaniel's avidity to unload when we arrive. He
chucks the bags down and we start to fill up the trench, which
he enjoys, playing out his new strength. I can't figure if I should
cover the stone with mulch or pine bark or leave it bare. I ask
Nathaniel if I seem like the person too poor to afford landscaping and garden services or someone who just enjoys tilling
his own field.

My pond stone gulley won't distinguish the lawn; I need
ground cover. The next day we fetch the first load of bagged
mulch. The premium variety, advertised as never losing its
color, costs about fifty cents more than the store brand, pine

bark mininuggets, which I have preferred in years past. I decide to splurge. We create a grid and wedge twenty-three bags of mulch into the compact station wagon, with room to spare for two more. As a reward, I stop at Burger King and buy us sandwiches and milkshakes.

At home I carefully guide my son to unload the bags: "One at each of the circles, three at the quarter circles, and then start from the bottom and work your way up alongside the pond stone." It becomes plain that we won't have enough and must apportion the precious mulch sparingly. With my box cutter I slice open a bag and see that even with just a thin cover, the quarter circles at the front, the beech tree, and the hosta bed, respectively, will both easily consume five full bags. We won't have enough left to begin the wings, and should instead resupport the yew bushes at the face of the house. My son brings out the rake and we spread the mulch together and he asks alert questions, just like the day he was reading the Bible at church. I am grateful. Then I wonder if I am less encouraging a skill than eliciting servitude.

Maybe neither. When we get another twenty-two bags the next afternoon, he is surly. "I think this is just like slavery," he tells me, this child who has never been spanked with a brush, slapped in the mouth, or cursed. Like most of the people I know, I was spanked often as a toddler, to the point that my disobedience was regulated early. Naturally, I had the same feeling about slavery as a teenager when compelled to labor, which in my household was never linked to pay. Nonetheless, I always enjoyed yard tasks, painting, and carpentry, labor that brought favor on our appearance, work that seemed to prime our increase. Edward Anderson, our next-door neighbor opposite Mr. Washington, complimented a carpenter building our porch in the way a boy will savor. "I have never seen a man drive a nail better," Mr. Eddie, a cigar smoker and afternoon nipper, said admiringly from across the fence. The saying from my relatives was always if there was a job that needed to be done, you only had to "Get a man." By the time I entered high school, my father and I joked about being peremptorily excluded from the category, which required building trade skills and working knowledge of tools.

The first tool I ever borrowed was from Mr. Otis Washington, who lived next door. A tall, dark-skinned man with a shaved head, he was a grandfather to me. Mr. Washington and I used to sit side by side on our porches on Saturday afternoons and listen to the Orioles game on the radio. In the summertime he wore old gray khaki suits and house shoes. As he sipped his ice water while Eddie Murray stared down another hapless pitcher, Mr. Washington would talk about the world a little. My grandmother in a rare moment of sport once referred to him as a "patent leather black man," by which I presumed that she meant a gold toothpick and Stacy Adams shoes. He did drive a Lincoln and dote on his petite wife, who had straight hair like a Native American. Mr. Washington had retired from the steel mill, and he kept his own yard immaculate. To do so, he applied a manual rotary edger, which gave a professional line to the grass, showing a lovely layer of dirt between the cement sidewalk and the healthy, wide-blade fescue on his yard, tiered like a piece of succulent coffee cake. I had only been able to slope down the sides of our front yard where the grass met the sidewalk using the hand trimmers. We didn't fertilize and we had weeds taking over the gaps in the concrete. Somehow banking on our baseball friendship, I asked him one summer afternoon if I could use his edger and he allowed me the privilege. He did so without hesitation, or even any safeguards, which certainly would not have been the way of my other neighbors.

I learned that, even with Mr. Washington's edging machine, it was difficult to make a smooth edge line on the hard, unforgiving turf. I was also surprised by the amount of dirt with healthy grass spilling onto the walkway. To properly maneuver the spring-loaded blade to slice through the dry sod took a lot of

boy power. Within a couple of years, the inventors and marke-
teers came out with the weed trimmer, and people stopped edging their grass by hand.

I don't think I ever got enough joy out from the task to work
on the slender grass rectangle between the sidewalk and the
street, where passersby, especially children, threw candy and
food wrappers, popsicle sticks, and older people dropped tis-
sues, napkins, newspaper coupons, chicken boxes, and cigarette
butts. A liquor store, at first owned by black people striving to
join the middle class, opened three blocks away near the car
wash at Cold Spring Lane. By the time the thirsty traffic reached
our house—men drinking beer and shorties, quarter pints, and
flask-sized glass bottles of liquor in brown paper bags—they
had drunk the contents and discarded the empties into the gutter. It wasn't daily, but it wasn't unusual. At one time it had been
customary to throw any sort of trash, but especially cigarette
and cigar butts, into the gutter, which was swept weekly or so by
the city. The city also maintained metal waste cans at the curb's
edge of a public bus stop. These amenities ended, but the habit
of discard continued. A broken liquor bottle stands between the
rampart of the middle class and the ditchy yard of the poor.

The English who remade themselves into the New World
bourgeoisie found Virginia and Maryland completely unforgiving places to launch habitable models of increase. "Here . . .
we are obliged to do everything with one's own servants and
thise Negros," grumbled the frustrated colonial-era builder of
a nice home, John Carlyle. Putting up a house in the 1750s that
continues to inspire us today required "constant attendance &
care, so much trouble that if I had suspected it woud [have] been
what I have met with I believe I shoud [have] made shift with a
very small house!" In my head, this Negro knows that he can't
afford to die in this house. The day I stop working, which may
coincide with the day that I stop folding the property tax into the
escrow account with the mortgage and insurance, will force me

to see it for the millstone it is. The day I stop making my own improvements and resorting to the mercies of the market, I will want to have "made shift with a very small house!"

My son has not yet put in a twelve-hour day working with his hands, which is funny, because ironically the intensity of the lawn competitions of today far outweigh what was known during the predial days of the rounds by the colored yardman with his rake and broom and a push mower. Mainly it is the age of the trees. Homeland was an oddly clear-cut place when my street was laid out in the fall of 1924. The pictures preserving that season are remarkable. For the black workers who did the heavy labor of chopping trees, digging foundations and drainage ditches, and lining out the roads, 1924 was not different from the laboring methods of 1524, or, indeed, of just 24. They were Iron Age men working with axes, saws, plows, wagons, and mules. But the white middle class can be seen in early tractors, cement mixers, and automobiles, every technological advantage. Seeing the black men in the pictures, including one man who was a giant, doesn't simply strike me as evidence of unfairness. I don't want to naively believe that common hands could have built the houses without the architects and foremen. But the utter disappearance of the significance of what they did accomplish, somewhere between them clearing the land in 1924 and Mr. Washington lending me the hand edger in 1979, unnerves me. Mr. Washington started his long life of heavy labor in the early 1920s, as did my mother's father. My father's father started in the 1910s. I am not sure why I wouldn't have dreamed that black men just like them carved the foundations for Homeland. I wondered why I never thought about any of the foundations that I knew of that they did carve.

Originally, at the top of the hill overlooking the convent was a thickly mortared stone house, and farther north, near where David Maulden Perine's "Homeland" villa was pulled down, were four Georgian Revival homes. Whether brick or stone, the houses took Buckland's design of George Mason's Gunston Hall as their model. By the 1930s at Witherspoon Road, they styled manor houses in the "Williamsburg tradition." The oldest is the truest to colonial simplicity and symmetry, its brick walls laid in courses of overlapping stretcher bond, its dentelated cornice heavy and simple. The other houses are Flemish bond, stretcher then header courses, interpretations guided by the Great Gatsby era of American confidence. One has a curved facade with cement-cast door and window frames and casement windows.

A handful of architects for the Roland Park Company were responsible for the Georgian, Tudor, and Colonial Beaux Arts interpretations built in the early and mid-1920s. As the houses went up, one of the men, Edward L. Palmer Jr., was criticized for making Roland Park "monotonous," a charge that annoyed him. He defended himself, proclaiming that the neighborhood, like its residents, was "progressive and varied." Variety in Homeland and Roland Park basically meant that Celts and Anglo-Saxons and some Franks might live readily together. By the 1930s, when they were advertising the neighborhood in *Gardens, Houses and People*, they justified the "Restrictions" protecting the homogeneity of Homeland by noting, "Every ship must have its crew and captain, every court its jury and its judge." The logic of the justification was as inviolable as the conclusion was obvious. "In the neighborhood around your house, decisions must be made—what may be done and what may not—the size and type of other houses—their architectural design—the position of their kitchen windows and garage doors—the colors of their paint—even their type of occupancy."

For a few generations, Homeland's occupancy restrictions maintained the racial exclusivity of the neighborhood. The salesmen were regularly in a quandary about transactions with Jewish Americans. John Mowbray was prepared to extend the benefit of diversity to fully assimilated American Jews, the kind of people he believed "[have] now joined some Christian faith." Observant

Jews were treated differently. Professional advance within the Roland Park Company probably was connected to the expert ability to ferret out ethnic difference. "I told him not to sell [to] Diehl," an executive informed Mowbray about a less than racially scrupulous salesman. "He was very apologetic and said he had no idea that Mrs. Diehl was Jewish." The company officers did not conceive of blanket anti-semitism. They acknowledged individuals, but balked at anything beyond a couple. The Walter husband and wife, "very prominent in the social life of Baltimore," might not have raised flags alone, but they "do have a number of Jewish friends who visit them, and for this reason were excluded from the District."

Baltimore had then and has now a large population of Conservative, Orthodox, and Hasidic Jews, who preceded African Americans in the neighborhoods of West and Northwest Baltimore. In the rowhouse I grew up in, mezuzah scrolls lay underneath slender metal pouches diagonally nailed to the doorjambs. We just painted over them as curiosities until the day my sister brought home a thin man in a black suit wearing a fedora who identified the doorpost Hebrew verses. The Roland Park Company did not want to be seen as flagrantly opposing Jewish people, but they successfully discouraged anything that might indicate tribal fellowship. A Czech man named Novack was nearly turned down in 1935 because he had "a few Jewish friends"; it became necessary to rely on the testimony of a neighbor, who reassured the corporation that he did "not think there are many of them." In the 1930s, the Roland Park Company did not want Homeland to become known as a neighborhood hosting Hebrew gatherings. The rejection of Baltimore's Jews persisted until after the Second World War, but without any synagogues nearby and ringed by a Catholic cathedral, two other Catholic churches, two Catholic colleges, a Methodist church, and an Episcopal church, Homeland never became a place of invitation for Jewish residents.

There were no interoffice memos about black Americans. We were simply forbidden. As early as 1926, the Roland Park Company distributed a pamphlet highlighting the "Restrictions." The prohibitions against African Americans appeared early in the document, in Subdivision II, under the heading "Nuisances." Until 2018, the language on all of the Homeland Deeds read, after the exposition against accumulations of outdoor feces, that

> At no time shall the land included in said tract or any part thereof, or any building erected thereon, be occupied by any negro or person of negro extraction. This prohibition, however, is not intended to include the occupancy by a negro domestic servant or other person, while employed in or about the premises by the owner or occupant of any land included in said tract.

During that era, when the federal government made some surveys, they found that about one-third of Americans were willing to live in integrated neighborhoods; today, slightly fewer than 30 percent think it is permissible to discriminate in the sale of a house. It has taken a century to shift the attitude of a third of the population on a crucial issue possibly because the history is so poorly known. I have found one "maid walk," a path half the width of a sidewalk that cuts through the blocks and allows a little unobtrusive egress for servants. This path extends from the cul-de-sac at Paddington and snakes across Tunbridge into an alley that disgorges at Homeland Avenue, a modest street where there might have been a bus stop or simply the preferred exit out of the neighborhood to the Wyndhurst train stop. The Civic Leaguers would have been keen to maintain order with crisp instructions to their help. I would never have recognized the significance of the path, but a white colleague who had married into wealth pointed one out to me when I taught in Atlanta. The descendants of my relatives who worked in service didn't think of it as a story worth passing down. And, realistically, those slights were minor considering the vast scheme of racial segregation. Discriminatory measures were reinforced by the banks and federal guidelines.

But, as financially conservative as I am, I wonder if my mindset about purchasing a home and my expectations of my neighbors is very different from Bouton's and Palmer's? Every black person I have ever met has always expressed dismay at the property upkeep regimen of their black neighbors. Every single one. That's what Robert E. Lee said. After my father's mother died in Cleveland, we maintained her house so poorly that within ten years the city sent out a bulldozer.

Men like Palmer and Bouton fought a battle whose outlines today are blurry. It is hard to imagine that they were genuinely concerned with keeping blacks out as the houses went up. Few blacks were wealthy enough to live in Homeland during the neighborhood's first thirty years, when black people had no access to the state's best higher education institutions, and belonged to no part of the professional world of banks, real estate, or heavy industry. The wealthiest black man in the city in the 1940s and 1950s was a numbers runner and saloon owner, "Little Willie" Adams. He built a political machine and contented himself with a home near the Hanlon Park reservoir. The Restrictions were really designed to coach white people who hadn't been to England and didn't know the novels of Walter Scott or Jane Austen. The neighborhood deacons sought to align the exteriors with a dream that had died in World War One, an ever-expanding white city of model British garden neighborhoods.

Bouton was the man tasked with retaining the nineteenth century ideals in the cut-rate age. He had the job of reviewing the buildings after approved drawings had come out of the meeting between general contractor and homeowner. He attempted to align the contract with the original garden ideal, putting to work unsparing comments. "The committee would never have approved the wooden bay window except in connection with white brick work," he angrily wrote to a new resident in 1926, furious that a redbrick house with a wood-shingled bay window had slipped through. "The appearance of the house as it stands now is deplorable." Monied or not, some people needed a harness on their desires.

Bouton was attempting through exclusivity to convey tasteful, modest tradition to the newly arrived middle class. As the lots were sold and neighborhood was built up in the 1920s, exhibitions were held, and the Roland Park Company partnered with the Arts Committee of the Women's Civic League to stage model homes that would convey the mantra of Chesterfieldian elegance to the newly arrived. League members were the apogee of cultivated city style. The Civic League women had in their possession ladder back chairs, letters from Charles Carroll, Betsy Patterson's couch, and the property of Jérôme Bonaparte. (Black women even had a parallel organization, the Cooperative Civic League, and the two groups sometimes associated at Frederick Douglass Senior High when Eleanor Roosevelt came to town.) Their housing models represented examples of "artistic home surroundings without spending large sums of money." They were put off by the art experiments that forced viewers to figure out the artist; they spurned "the bizarre tendencies created by the 'modernist' movement in art." Instead, they staged exhibition houses with a few antiques, Queen Anne wing chairs, and Chippendale sofas in muted colors.

Throughout a long career, Bouton's acolyte Palmer tried to maintain the neighborhood's standards of "appearance" and "suitability." In 1946, as the housing crunch hit and people sought to add on to existing structures, Palmer raged that "more damage can be done [to Homeland] by alterations to existing houses" than by building newer, plainer styles, a handful of which made their way onto the few remaining lots. Palmer, who lived in one of the most elaborately designed homes on a bluff on Spring Lake, grew dismayed. "It is all very confusing and disconcerting, and far be it from me for being in a position of 'holding the line,'" he wrote to Mowbray as the veterans returned and the race question kept getting pushed at Maryland's graduate schools, "but it does seem to me that we have something of a line to hold." Writing for *Good Housekeeping*, Helen Koues, a venerator of the old ways, put succinctly her charge to people who might have misunderstood ornament to avoid, "the gables and turrets and gimcracks of the Seventies, Eighties, and Nineties!" She wanted to make sure that the view of the new middle class was everlastingly toward the colonial vigor and simplicity of Williamsburg. "It is the beauty [that is] treasured in the finer houses built in this country from 1750 to 1830. Labor as well as materials was not so costly in those days, and time and thought were given to the embellishment of the structure as well as to sound construction. Let us follow those good precepts. Let us work for beauty of proportions, beauty of design, knowing that the beauty of the Greek orders, which inspired American Colonial, has endured through the centuries." Helen was right: labor wasn't so costly during Perine's days.

The architect for my house was a man named John H. Ahlers, who came on the Roland Park Company team at the very end of the traditional neighborhood's development, in the early 1930s. Ahlers, who died in 1983, also designed the main academic building, Wheeler Hall, of my high school, Loyola Blakefield, founded in 1852. I can remember my shadow day visiting Loyola, and the impression that the massive Gothic stone building set on a promontory at the edge of Charles Street made upon me as a child. The expansive greens and shade trees afforded the two-story L-shaped building an inspirational majesty, and it became an embedded ideal, or was already, in a way that is impossible to tease out. Older than Ahler's building was a brick colonial house on the grounds that had been the home of Elihu Jackson, the governor of Maryland, during the years of the creation of the state flag and its reconciliationist Calvert and Crossland family emblems. My visit to the Jesuit school on the city's outskirt would have been unlikely without the inspired work of two Baltimoreans, the NAACP attorney Thurgood Marshall from Division Street and the NAACP lobbyist Clarence Mitchell, nicknamed the "101st Senator," from Carrollton Avenue, bookend streets of St. James Church. Probably those two men, one connected to the *Brown* decision, the other inseparable from the Fair Housing Act, enabled my opportunity to have attended white schools and to later purchase homes in white neighborhoods. Mitchell, who had to bogart back against Martin Luther King Jr. when King attempted to take credit for the 1965 Civil Rights Act, said to President Johnson in 1968 about the Fair Housing Act, "The reassurances of the worth of your efforts are endless." In my case the luster of school and home was envisioned by the same Roland Park Company man. Thirty years after high school, my reassurances were still being scripted by the 1930s suburban motifs of John Ahlers.

Ahlers sketched plans for my Albion Road house originally for a man from New Jersey named Wikoff, a printer's-ink salesman who bought it at age thirty-nine. Frederick Wikoff and his wife Marion were both high school graduates, and, on his salary of $5,000 per year, he qualified for a Federal Housing Authority loan. He could pay for his house and send his son to college. Wikoff must have been doing well in the 1930s and, at first, he had bigger dreams than Homeland. He had hoped to live in Guilford, a tonier neighborhood, and he had contracted for a house including shrubbery and a two-car garage for $9,138 in June 1934. Somehow the deal collapsed. Salesman Bernard P. Hoge pursued his contract with Wikoff for the rest of the year. Wikoff wanted to move from the far west side of the city, in the Windsor Hills neighborhood, where he lived in a two-story house on Queen Anne Road. My childhood best friend lived on Talbot Road, a block over from Wikoff's first place. Only at the

residences where I received mail have I have spent more time in
the city than I did on Talbot Road in Windsor Hills.

Mr. Hoge kept after Wikoff, and by January 16 he had interested him in Block 7, Lot 2, and sold the quarter acre lot,
probably for $4,500. For $100 Ahlers produced a plan for an un-
pretentious, three-bay-wide, three-bedroom stone house. Quartz-
flecked granite blocks were inserted throughout, and the mortar
colored sandy, faintly modish accents. Mowbray, who had altered
an executed contract, agreed to inspect the lot while the contractor Frederick Wurzbacher completed the eight building stages
for which disbursements would be made: foundations and floor
joists; setting the stone and rafters; layering the slate roof; stud-
ding the interior; rough plumbing and electric wiring; plaster-
ing interior walls and finishing exterior walls; laying hardwood
floors; trimming and painting; exterior grading and making the
walks. While teams could certainly have dug out the foundation that winter of 1935, delivered materials and sized stones,
cement mortar work needs to be done in weather above freezing.
The company's builders had a process to heat the mortar, so that
the work could continue in spite of the temperature. A cheaper
method of using salt to prevent the water from freezing was used
elsewhere, but not in Homeland.

The precautions were probably unnecessary. The winter of
1935 was mild, without heavy snow or ice, and many days that
February were in the middle forties. The interior millwork was
done with white pine, and it included a built-in dining-room corner cupboard with scrollwork trim. Before fall of 1935, the new
house was ready for the family from Windsor Hills.

Until they sold their house in 1966, the Wikoffs presumably had the same relationship with black Americans as other
people in their class, a variety of "seen but not heard" with
only the slightest bit of sight. But we were always here, from
the first days that the trees and the Villa came down and the
roads were cut. Adonia and Horace Dudley worked "in service"

seventy yards away from the Wikoffs, toward the lakes on Saint Dunstan's. My churchmother's father, Elisha Chandler, a graduate of Virginia State University, served the Wikoffs when he wasn't at his full-time job at the US post office. At night Mr. Chandler went home, at first to a house on Ruxton Avenue, and then to Morgan Park. He died in 1960 and he may have been an aspiring writer. That was the world that segregation and American race relations made: talented, high-achieving blacks tidily serving and dying in place.

By April my neighbor's yard is alive with brilliant yellow forsythia blossoms. In the 1940s my grandmother's oldest sister living in Baltimore, Sarah Frances Macklin, was a school bus attendant at the Quaker academy run by his family. Aunt Sarah died of cancer in 1953. Since I didn't meet her and her life is rarely recalled by relatives, I am surprised to find myself thinking about her workday near me in the 1940s and early 1950s. During my court custody hearing and investigation by a guardian ad litem, I had secured a place for Mitchell to attend the Friends School, which I thought would suit his personality. I went to summer camp there right before starting high school, and I remember taking the public bus home.

Movement around the city's neighborhoods reminds me of Frederick Douglass, a genuine rambler when he lived in Baltimore. Frederick Bailey, as he was then known, began to attend Methodist revivals in Strawberry Alley. He attended them on Maryland's Eastern Shore. He kept attending them in Baltimore County. He could easily have been roaming north; in fact, he almost certainly roamed into Baltimore County in the north, because all of the churches he was connected to, like Sharp Street, Bethel, and St. James, had strong ties to Philadelphia, and he wanted to expand his knowledge of all of the northern escape routes. He was the sort of person who would have been suspected of having burned down David Perine's home in 1843;

strapping twenty-year-old Bailey is the best example of the property that the passbook laws were designed to control. African Methodist Episcopal Saint John's Church is about three miles straight up Bellona Avenue from where Taplow Road, one of my cross streets, hits it. It was founded by a man noteworthy in the Bare Hills area named Aquilla Scott. If Bailey made his way twelve miles from Fells Point on a Saturday after a week's worth of caulking, he could have picked up Greenmount not far from the Bethel Church on Fish Street, then gone up the York Road to Bellona, passing through the land Perine had purchased in 1832. Perhaps he had a good, knowing guide, to avoid the toll roads and bridges where they checked passes and curtailed the movement of black people, and he stayed closer to the Stony Run path. I would be inclined to think that Perine's man William Anderson would not have looked favorably on Douglass's taking some apples for his trip up Bellona to St. John's. But, then again, Anderson might have been a churchman, as devoted to the runaways as he was attached to Perine. Or, a third way, he might have been an Obeah man, like Sandy Jenkins from the Eastern Shore.

Douglass, who appreciated neat quarters, would note my house for the mulch beds. I am always excited to complete the mulching, at least out front. But when I am able to return again to the garden store for pine nuggets, I strike a chord of deep unenthusiasm from my filial assistant. A portion of his life is now lived in the kitchen, and he is closing in, hour by hour, on the holy grail of six feet in height and two hundred pounds in weight. We have regular, bilious discussions over what the interruption of the school year might practically mean. To me, it must bode a swept interior and an enviable exterior, renewed obligations to the tabernacle. He is thinking in terms of unending video games, especially the basketball one that connects and updates its software on its own. The game depicts contemporary life so accurately that it features the self-chosen protagonist, who can be attributed any of a dozen skin hues, physiognomies, or hair textures. The doppelgänger digital athlete himself sends text messages and plays video games. Playing a video game of a cartoon figure playing a video game is to me beyond the acme of absurdity; it is the end of absurdity and the ushering in of full control to a world of the biometric signature and nanochip activated by the tetahertz frequency. I have the fears of the people who work the Homeland grounds, a terrible patrimony. I want my son to have the confidence of the people who owned the land, without having to hate himself for it. But really, I just want him to be the kind of person who keeps up his own yard.

So I dispense with the cuddling and the trip for fast food and just order him into the station wagon. The youngster forgos any communication in reprisal. We muddle through, our orchestra playing notes of disharmony. Nonetheless, in under an hour we have loaded twenty-five bags and returned to the house and begun distributing the sacks throughout the garden.

Once eighteen of the bags are down I am so pleased with the look of amplitude that I colonize new land. It is a fallow girdle, an unattended leafy croft, a spear between my landscaping and the three-foot-high stone dividing wall, a soil tributary that separates my plateau from my neighbor, whose two lots take him to the bottom of the slope three hundred feet from where the ponds roughly begin. Nearly two hundred years ago, in Perine's time, there was a large field-size English garden directly behind the house, flanked by two plots that were his kitchen's vegetable patch. According to the 1842 plat map, enslaved William Anderson's family quarters were either in the same yard as the barn and the outbuildings behind the manager's house, or toward the ponds.

To bring in line the feral southside tongue requires raking out the leaves and pruning, pulling up the twigs I have discarded over the years and repairing the garden box, which has become jagged. I am reluctant to put the new dark-brown mulch all out in an area I hadn't previously dignified. So I reclaim the remainder of the ten yards of mulch from last year, a desultory series of mounds in the back. Roots have grown throughout the compacted mulch, requiring me to chop with my shovel and break up the loam before spading it into the wheelbarrow and walking around the front. Since I have freshly replanted the grass on my side of the slip, I walk the barrow through the neighbor's ivy bed, confident that I am keeping up both our properties in a manner that is desirable. I have to scatter the mulch over the wall by hand to distribute it.

Within minutes, sidewalk strollers approve of the territorial reclamation and tell me, "It looks beautiful." I walk across the street and adjudge, sometimes with admiration and sometimes with misery. Whenever people in cars stop to look I think they are either burglars canvassing or government agents spying. After the first day of the school closures, I wind up pacing back and forth at the end of my street, four blocks from my house, for about twenty minutes. Several hours later, the owner of the house I had walked in front of parked in front of my house and took pictures with his telephone, recorded by my son on his telephone. The man works for the government's bureau of cybersecurity and infrastructure, and a friendly real estate agent has made him known to me, but we have never met. He has the most beautiful, heavy, even stone block lintels over the window frames of his house. The lintels on my neighbor's are so heavy and wide they could weigh a thousand pounds each. But when Mowbray and Ahlers built my house during the Depression and the dressed quartz stone began to enter Wurzbacher's building mix, they spanned the window frames with an easily concealed steel slat and filled stones and mortar overtop. It's the sort of detail I was incapable of noticing before living in Homeland. Discarding the megalith blocks over the windows brought to an end one of the most original architectural features of the neighborhood's stone houses.

The next week I am stunned to have to tell my son that school will not reopen until the fall. While he has approximately the same unconcern for academics as his peers, the cancellation of spring athletics is a blow. He was the last athlete selected for the baseball team, an achievement of mark for a person who has played only a single year of the sport at an organized level. The season of practice and repetition of the fundamentals is badly needed. The closure strikes me as so craven, so cowardly, in the same spirit as the newfangled dismissals or delays after a weather report has been issued. Danger no longer has to exist; it need only be imagined. Rejecting the effect on volition of insinuation was a primary obligation of the black children of black parents born in the 1920s and 1930s. I try to instill it today, but the admonition only seems punitive.

My son, who has received his second school-issued computer after swiftly breaking the first, sets up his remote learning station at the end of the dining room table, whose legs had to be reset earlier in the year. Seated at the table we built together, he is to me bumptious, noisy, loving kitsch, and oblivious to all the better angels of my nature. His glance is always one of surveillance and reprimand. He is the cruelest vigilante, making me feel like all I have ever done is watch television and eat cookies. Certainly, it becomes all I want to do. The presence of another human being listening to every cracker and chip that comes out of the pantry, and who can equal their consumption, is a hard reproach. I know that I must forge a new place of study and respite. The weather has broken, so I retreat to the opposite side of the house, to the sunporch.

In the space of an afternoon spent on sunporch lawn furniture, I conclude that the ten dozen stacks of homeless books are also barristers adjudicating my sloth and indifference. They judge me in their randomness, the sentinels consisting of the orphans from old book contests, books purchased only to round out a syllabus, library collections of abolitionist papers, and literary arguments by refugee Palestinian mandarin intellectuals. They crowd my father's college table, which we used for breakfast when I was a very young child until it was replaced with a sturdy slab from Sweden and a long bench. Other books swim perilously along the edge of what had once been my favorite piece of woodworking until the third time I moved it askew a crowded flatbed truck and raked it against an octagonal stop sign. The cicatrix dining room table has a computer and the remnants of Mitchell's Christmas booty, an art easel, paint tubes, brushes, and solvent. After a few hours I start to fling them into order with my mind's eye up against the lone wall, what at one time had simply been the exterior of the house. I see shelves on either side of the stone face hugging the throat of the fireplace. I see them wrapping around to make a complete unit. I see the boards angled at forty-five degrees to capture a complete flanking of the two-foot deep, ten-foot-long outcropping. The visions won't abate. In two days the idea has overwhelmed me like a conversion to a new theology. I will build towers capable of supporting themselves with boards and posts two inches thick, and instead of cleats I will score dadoes to hold the permanent shelves. As happened when I bridled the fireplace with CD cases during my first days on Albion Road, I have found my kabbala and have to circle around.

On Friday I fly to the improvement store for six boards of fir lumber, Gunstock stain, a new titanium drill bit, and three-inch screws. The improvement store is a spiritual place in which visions can be made manifest, in the same way as I had once worshipped in the hobby store, my second love after the blanket. At the far end of the stain aisle, an older black woman wearing a mask is coughing uncontrollably. I need to look through almost the complete run of canisters before I find the lone jug that I am after. To add mystery to this vision, I am totally unfamiliar with the stain. The wood, mainly two-by-eights, is selected with some care, but my idea is to antique the boards, like they came straight out of *Ivanhoe*'s Saxon world of wood, stone, and iron. Getting the loot home is tricky. I open the window to the compact station wagon, imagining that I will direct the lengths outward, but then I send one board all the way up to the windshield on the dash, having placed a floor mat underneath it, to see if the tailgate will close. It does. I put in a longer ten-foot board and then angle two of them out the window, followed by three eight-foot pieces. When I get into the car, I notice that the first board up against the windshield has cracked the glass.

From the pain of previous experience, I measure the height from the floor to the ceiling several times, which seems pretty close to eight feet, an inch and five-sixteenths on the north end and nine-sixteenths on the south end. The unit is designed to fit just above or below the natural differences in the stone outcroppings so that the shelves can fall flush up against the wall. Adding twenty feet of shelf space seems like overkill, so I am completely comfortable with the bottom shelves at eighteen inches apart. The first night, Friday, as I router out the bottom dado, making a second pass through the cut I hear a different, deeper moan, like flesh is being bored out of something that is living but cannot cry. I am unused enough to the tool to stop immediately. The straight router bit has slipped. The spinning metal blade has gouged a deep, irregular trough, half an inch lower than the design and threatening the integrity of the board. At best, the shelves will be imperfect, exactly like all my other furniture.

Gut shot, I am slow to regroup.

It takes a long while before I can bring myself to inspect the gouge and to imagine the repair. First, I take a wrench to tighten down the router bit and then rout out a rectangle so that a patch can marry. I need to plug the seven-and-three-quarters-inch passage with a half-inch strip and line the grain up so that it will connect with only a string of the wood filler showing. But I am wrestling with so much lost purity. It hurts me to face the ruin.

I am unconvinced that the bandage will dispel the wound. I hastily mush random scraps of the planed wood shavings into the abscess I have filled with glue and wood filler. I never go back to the measuring tools; I just chip off pieces by eye. There is a word familiar to Perine or Mark Twain for all of this. I disgustedly sift and maneuver the wet junk and then block and clamp it all in place to settle overnight. I torque down screw clamps using the claw of my hammer. Morning revives me, and I more carefully rout out the excess and patch it cleanly with a little more wood filler. The plugs are crooked but the grains are more or less headed in the right direction. True, the error will be ten inches off the floor and difficult to see, but I feel like that is all I am good for, a patch, triage. I can't figure out whether this is the best or worst image of myself, or just the reality of claiming that term, nigger.

To atone for the ugliness, I work feverishly with the hand plane to further dress the edges of the shelves, hoping to distress and weather the wood as if it has its own story from the nineteenth century. I shave the angles and make violent depressions and sandpaper the boards into something I might associate with a Tuscan farmhouse. However, to save time, I stain the pieces before cutting the lengths, so I don't have to work with ten two-foot shelves in the garage where I might be overcome by the fumes. When Nathaniel starts rolling on some of the stain it looks like thick, cheap, red paint. Since we had gone to work on the front door, I had been intoxicated even by the mere name of the stain. I had recovered an elusive batch imprisoned among the many cans of cherry and American oak, and warded off an elder coughing behind a face mask during the ten minutes it took me to find it. The name Gunstock had mystically drawn me out and made me long for the last time I had caressed one, some twenty years earlier, firing the mercury-tipped rounds until the magazine ejected and the police helicopter circled overhead.

On Monday afternoon I head out to the grocery store with

my industrial mask on to the bemused consternation of the other patrons. I wear the mask to safeguard against the fumes that imperil my nervous system and bring on headaches and runny sores, but now international favor is turning in the direction of protecting nasal pharynges from the deadly virus. I select the best ones for the shelf I imagine I will look at the most, the western shelf near the rear door closest to the love seat. In the darkness and with my face mask in place, I lose track of the direction. Queuing up the shelves into the dadoes and squaring the top and the bottom anchor shelves, gluing, clamping the unit, and driving the screws, I reverse the order. The antiqued edges that I have belabored will butt up against the wall. When I stand them up the next day and after the glue has dried, I can see that the shelves with the most interesting shaving and sanding declensions, my aged farmhouse motif, have been put on the back of the unit and will be invisible.

The problem is light. The two-car, stone-and-slate garage is a handy workspace, a solid protection from the elements if needed, and even features a fairly level cement floor. But the most fundamental luminescent items in it, the timed sixty-watt bulb on the garage door opener and two twin fluorescent lights, are discount. My garage is filled with all sorts of light fixtures that I bought and never attached. Although most of my work takes place during the mean daylight hours, I know that without regular light my shop is deficient. If I wanted to recreate the world anew, I should start there, with a globe of bright luminosity.

But I act and ignore, to the point of forgetting, the serious problem. It is of a piece with my daily school conundrum, my obligation to a social order that I regard as corrupt, and that rewards adjustment to its lie. I know, for example, that American sport utility vehicles, thrust forcefully onto the market after the first Gulf War, are more environmentally destructive than other cars. I also know that their introduction into our economy at such scale coincided with military adventurism and the fossil fuel industry's profiteering. But driving on the road with a population committed to SUVs makes driving in smaller cars hazardous. Your vision is frequently obscured, and, moreover, in the same way that larger people expect smaller people to move out of their way, in the same way that louder people expect quiet people to listen, in the same way that the form precedes the content, the great-size vehicles arrogate the lanes of the road. I believe their popularity, especially as preferred transport vehicles to schools, introduces a circumstance whereby it is perilous to be altruistic. Suffering and injury are a predictable portion for favoring environmentally friendly, reasonably sized vehicles. I use a gas blower for its efficiency and hate myself. I wonder if I am any different from my next-door neighbor, who hires a gardener to blow for four hours on Easter Sunday.

Standing up the heavy and ungainly towers in the sunporch is difficult. At the exact height the right edges scrape the ceiling, preventing me from getting them vertical. I carry them out with Nathaniel and resize them, relying on a design drawn with a carpenter's pencil to find the contact points and then trying to remove slivers from the post edges. I think I will overdo it with the circular saw, so I just start brushing the edges with the sander at sixty grit. The eastern shelf goes in perfectly but, in a fit of pique, when Nathaniel goes back to his schoolwork and I have to carry the shelf back and forth to the garage alone a few times, I put the jumpy saw to the western unit and when the shelf goes up, there is a gap at the ceiling of one-eighth of an inch. The work isn't flush. I stain the shims I use to fit the shelves snug, not wanting the parade of amateurism to blare out all at once, the shims on the west, the bandaged gouge on the east. I wouldn't belabor the sawmill square shelf edges at all.

I throw the formerly homeless books up on the shelves with satisfaction, and then actually spend several hours cataloging to form at least six rough groupings. In the living room there is a shelf for Frederick Douglass and one for Billie Holiday, my hometown research topics since I returned to the city. The new stalls have a space for the Civil War, with the focus on Missouri, where the battles were most cutthroat and the black massacres intense, a cubby for Hollywood cinema, media studies and Westerns, one shelf with contemporary Western imperialism, and one for heavily politicized literary criticism. This clears off my dad's old card table with the turned legs that he stripped from the lime green paint I had known from childhood, down to a washed-out gray. I can see the table now as a real piece of art-work, like the landscape watercolor of his that I have in the living room. I fold one of the leaves and put the faux-wicker lawn chairs around the table and place on it my computer and lamps and a few books.

Within days of anchoring the shelves, I have an attractive work space up and running. I have a whole new vantage on the world of Homeland. After the quarantines and school and work closings begin, but before the death toll escalates in Maryland, I see my neighbors in the flesh. Families walking together down the street, the sound of children's voices at play. A brother and a sister sharing a meal in Adirondack chairs in front of their house, then riding scooters together. A pageant of incredibly fit people jogging past. Two couples of older African American exercisers at a trot, then an Asian duo, and from time to time an African American family who seem to be adventuring. But mainly the neighbors are youthful-looking, fit, white Americans, like the models from a glossy magazine. Wearing trendy fashions in muted or neutral colors, people attended to by health care professionals, speakers of foreign languages, and keepers of regular hours.

From the porch window I spy through a gaping azalea and a holly to the front of our labor. The grass is a shimmery emerald and long enough that it's hard to see the barren spots. The coronavirus death toll in the United States has reached five hundred per day. The frightening global illness seems primed to remind us of the power of the seasons to absorb the airplanes, cars, air conditioners, and insect-killing pesticides. I notice that the grass roots are already holding the soil in place. The batter of sand and clay sod isn't running off as easily as the dirt had before. Adding the barrows of sand and soil to the southern slope has already shown an improvement, a bit of increase. My dream is one day to be rich enough to go completely organic. I push a few more dozen plugs into the soil and fill them with seed.

A deep instinct wants my house to compare favorably to my Albion Road neighbors, the heart surgeons and public health leaders, the neuroscientists, venture capitalists, fund managers, and managing partners, the electrical engineers, architects, and circuit court judges, people whose talent and sought-after skill I admire. I don't want my house to imply tokenism. The restrictive covenant was enforced, though, not because black people's aesthetic choices would have degraded the neighborhood, but because our appearance as homeowners and not servants would have made the neighborhood seem unexclusive. We weren't part of the vision. Like some black people I know, I tend a hedgerow that restricts my conversation with people who have shouldered so few of the burdens I have carried, people whose ordinary comments prickle my skin, people whose reflex is to feign ignorance, discount, or countermand what I know about Maryland, about Homeland. But the pandemic briefly opens a window of mutual vulnerability, and I allow myself to exchange a few pleasantries when I am working in the yard.

As the smell of the stain and the varnish begins to subside, I dress an old memento from a time before Nathaniel was born when I was less fussy. It's a CD case I had patched together from pieces of scrap pine on an afternoon when the electric sander was too handy on the bench. To stain the shelf, which resembles a homemade stool for a toddler, I travel back and forth to the garage a half dozen times. Uncertain of where my project is taking me, I never seem able to assemble all my supplies at once. The stark case has survived five homes—Druid Hills, Hardendorf, McClendon, Henry, and now Albion—voyages in which so much was abandoned, so much forsaken that I had promised to keep sacred before the Lord. I cannibalized an old pair of pants for rags but the piece seems unwilling to take much of the stain, whose color I am forcing myself to accommodate to. But after the second coat dries, and I turn it to its best side, the shelf holder reveals the true good color made by a piece of wood strong enough to contain a fire in iron.

The day after Easter, I am bedridden with a cough that eventually produces blood and my throat constricts enough for me to gag trying to get out phlegm. Did someone cough on a milk carton that I handled at the grocer? It's three weeks after I shared an aisle with the coughing elderly patron at the garden store. I haven't known this sort of paranoia since I took the ciprofloxacin during the wave of unsolved anthrax killings in 2001. My mail had been distributed by the facility where postal workers had died, and I got an infection that week, heading into DC past the smoldering Pentagon. After ten voiceless days, I feel like I am improving, having ingested all of the most sensible of available remedies—oregano oil and ginger and garlic and lemon. It's like I am a meal of fish. Then, after a dinnertime conversation, the ails resume for another six days, a week culminating with the deaths of two friends and nationwide virus fatalities at over two thousand a day. But as my strength seems to return, all I can dream of is working the ground, trimming the fur and making the first tall cut. Maybe it is my time to pass from bronze to iron. With mainly hand gestures I get Nathaniel to man the lawnmower and to try to keep him at his line.

After a week of frustrated messages, an assistant schedules a video conference with my primary care physician. We have met once before, for about seven minutes. I can only pantomime a response during this feat of technological medical advance, which yields an antibiotic and tiny gel for my snare drum cough. The prescriptions eliminate possible illnesses, but they don't resolve my symptoms. I am coughing up a lot of old blood, which looks like pieces of soil suspended in bubbly glass. An itch lodges behind my tonsils, and when I hack to scratch my throat, a six-cough snare rattles out an attack, shutting the pipe closed. All of the blood rushes to my forehead, then drains to my ears and softens my knees and my heart stops. In half a second I get high and pass out. To preserve the purity of the air in the house, I sneak out the back door to cough. During one coughing fit I lose consciousness and awake with my cheek on the stone. I have fallen into the screen door, breaking my glasses and puffing my eye. It ebbs and flows like that for seven weeks. I try to adopt the life of a snail.

By Memorial Day I am hale enough to cut the turf and the meadow is a fluffy lime marvel. I fix a pepper-relish kabob meal, inspired by a Taliban potboiler. Heavily bidden, the university announces a moratorium on its effort to create a police force. The Homeland Association replaces the detachable letter sign with a board of deeply engraved letters in dark olive. In my upper room, when I spin toward my window, I sail over the inviting sward of undulating green.

Acknowledgments

I would like to thank the Creator and my mother and my father.

Illustrations

Notes

1. Advent: Color Storms Rising Almost to a Hurricane

24 **"bright"**: "No. 366 Nat McLin"; Free Persons Registry, Mecklenburg County Courthouse, Boydton, Virginia.

26 **"pestilence"** . . . **"low-income Negroes"** . . . **"gracious"**: Anthony J. Lukas, "Mount Royal Fight Looms on Renewal," *Baltimore Sun*, March 14, 1960, 28.

30 **"integrated, with power"**: Martin Luther King Jr., *Where Do We Go from Here: Chaos or Community?* (Boston: Beacon, 2010), 64.

32 **"This Indenture"**: Baltimore County Circuit Court, Land Records HW, Liber 2, fol. 81.

32 **"tangential"**: Barbara Jeanne Fields, *Slavery and Freedom on the Middle Ground: Maryland during the Nineteenth Century* (New Haven, CT: Yale University Press, 1985), 7.

33 **"Negro houses"**: William B. Marye, "Baltimore City Place Names: Part Four: Stony Run, Its Plantations, Farms, Country Seats and Mills," *Maryland Historical Magazine* 58.4 (December 1963), 369.

38 **"a black girl, a slave"**: "City Court," *Sun*, February 10, 1840, 1.

38 **"servant"** . . . **"laborer"**: David M. Perine, Baltimore County, Maryland, 1860 US Federal Census. p. 204

39 **"nature and tastes"** . . . **"Having left school"**: David Maulden Perine, diary, box 3, file "Biographical Material," Perine Family Papers, Maryland Historical Society.

40 **"vulgarisms which were never heard"**: Roger B. Taney, autobiography (1854), box 9, Perine Family Papers, Maryland Historical Society, 52–53.

40 **"a blot"** . . . **"these unfortunate beings"** . . . **"created equal"**: *Proceedings of the Bench and Bar of Baltimore, upon the Occasion of the Death of the Hon. Roger B. Taney, Chief Justice of the Supreme Court of the United States* (Baltimore: Printed by J. Murphy, 1864). John B. Simon, *Lincoln and Chief Justice Taney: Slavery, Secession, and the President's War Powers* (New York: Simon and Schuster, 2006), 11.

41 **"often thought of the pleasant days"** . . . **"enjoying the fresh country air"**: Roger B. Taney to David M. Perine, August 6, 1863, box 2, folder "1863 July–November Correspondence," Perine Family Papers, Maryland Center for History and Culture.

41 **"scheme for turning the world"** . . . **"the poor vulgar upstart"**: Albert Bledsoe to David M. Perine, August 9, 1866, box 2, folder "1866 August-December Correspondence," Perine Family Papers, Maryland Center for History and Culture.

41 **"a good deal of Southern sympathy"**: Peter Wilson Hairston, diary, November 14, 1863, Louis Round Wilson Special Collections, University of North Carolina, Chapel Hill.

42 **"intellectual and moral debasement"**: Albert Bledsoe, *An Essay on Liberty and Slavery* (Philadelphia, 1856), 54.

43 **"If eloquence and pen fail"**: "Richard T. Greener," *Chicago Tribune*, October 16, 1883, 1.

43 **"devote [his] talent and [his] learning"**: Daniel C. Gilman to W. E. B. Du Bois, April 1894, Daniel Coit Gilman Papers, Special Collections, Sheridan Library, Johns Hopkins University.

43 **"sectional, sectarian, or political purpose"**: "American Philological Association," *Baltimore Sun*, July 11, 1877, 1.

43 **"the privileges of social position"** . . . **"material guarantees"** . . . **"the present or future profits"**: Basil Gildersleeve, "Sambo and the Ass," *Richmond Examiner*, April 5, 1864.

44 **"experts in the science of language"**: "American Philological Association," *Baltimore Sun*, July 12, 1877, 1.

44 **"It is true the Northern people"**: Richard T. Greener, "The Emigration of the Colored Citizen," *Social Science*, 1894, 27.

44 **"talented old colored man"**: "Richard T. Greener to Speak," *Baltimore Sun*, January 25, 1907, 14.

2. Christmas: Long Quarter at River Bend

50 **"responsible civic action"**: Lawrence Jackson, *Ralph Ellison: Emergence of Genius* (New York: Wiley, 2002), 415.

51 **"secluded, dark"**: Frederick Douglass, *My Bondage and My Freedom* (1855; repr., New York: Penguin, 2003), 49.

52 **"live over in memory"**: Frederick Douglass, *The Life and Times of Frederick Douglass* (1892; repr., New York: Macmillan, 1962), 445.

53 **"execrable commerce"**: Thomas Jefferson, "Declaration of Independence," draft, Merrill D. Peterson, ed., *The Portable Thomas Jefferson* (New York: Penguin Classics, 1977), 238.

54 **"efforts to speak and act"**: William S. McFeely, *Frederick Douglass* (New York: W. W. Norton, 1991), 97.

54 **"in terms of great admiration"**: Oswald Tilghman, *History of Talbot County, Maryland*, vol. 1 (1915) (Baltimore: Regional Publishing, 1967), 208.

54 **"no refuge could save the hireling"**: www.britannica.com/topic /The-Star-Spangled-Banner.

55 **"The despot's heel"**: James P. Randall, "Maryland, My Maryland, A Patriotic Song," music by A Lady of Baltimore (Augusta, GA: Blackmar,1862).

55 **"Beguiled by the siren slavery"**: Tilghman, *History of Talbot County Maryland*, 1:196.

56 **"The millere sholde noght stelen"**: Geoffrey Chaucer, The Reeves Tale, prologue, *The Canterbury Tales*, lines 4010–11.

58 **"very fine looking"** . . . **"about as white"**: Douglass, *My Bondage and My Freedom*, 86.

62 **"A 'buddy' drinks bilge water"**: Chester Himes, *If He Hollers Let Him Go* (New York: Doubleday, 1945), 51.

68 **"one of the finest sites"**: Hulbert Footner, *Rivers of the Eastern Shore* (New York: J. J. Little and Ives, 1944), 295.

68 **"His chaste house keeps its purity"**: Virgil, *Georgics*, book 2, lines 524–26 (Boston: Ginn, 1900).

71 **"do as much hard work"**: Douglass, *My Bondage and My Freedom*, 191.

71 **"slaveholding priestcraft"**: Douglass, *My Bondage and My Freedom*, 201.

71 **"The plan of escape"**: Douglass, *My Bondage and My Freedom*, 208.

71 **"simply a country"** . . . **"really did not, at that time"**: Douglass, *My Bondage and My Freedom*, 206.

73 **"instigator"**: Douglass, *My Bondage and My Freedom*, 204.

73 **"several acquaintances"** . . . **"quite tall and black"**: "$100 Reward," *Easton Gazette*, September 1, 1827, 2.

73 **"beads in one of his ears"** . . . **"the hole in the other"** . . . **"white and red striped"**: "25 Dollars Reward," *Cambridge Chronicle*, June 30, 1827, 4.

73 **"direct from Guinea"**: Douglass, *My Bondage and My Freedom*, 69.

75 **"hearty for his age"** . . . **"worth but little"**: "1825 March 25: A List of slaves on Wye House Estate now living," folder "Edward Lloyd V Inventory," Lloyd Papers, Maryland Historical Society.

76 **"remarkably buoyant"**: Douglass, *My Bondage and My Freedom*, 203.

77 **"I like this country very well"**: Thomas Brown to J. H. B. Latrobe, n.d. (ca. summer 1836), "Extract of a Letter from Mr. Thomas Brown, one of the Colonists at Cape Palmas, to J. H. B. Latrobe, Esq.," *Maryland Colonization Journal*, n.d. (ca. November 1836), 31, digitized, Maryland State Archives. See also Jacob Gibson to Messrs Latrobe and McKenney, August 31, 1835, *Maryland Colonization Journal* 1.3 (January 1836), 1.

77 **"a very tall, dilapidated"**: Douglass, *My Bondage and My Freedom*, 51.

77 **"a long, brick"**: Douglass, *My Bondage and My Freedom*, 52.

77 **"really understood the old man's mutterings"**: Douglass, *My Bondage and My Freedom*, 62.

78 **"all in all"**: Douglass, *My Bondage and My Freedom*, 56.

78 **"a tribe of them Africans"**: Shepard Krech, *Praise the Bridge That Carries You Over: The Life of Joseph L. Sutton* (Cambridge, MA: Schenkman, 1981), 2.

78 **"there is not to be found"**: Douglass, *My Bondage and My Freedom*, 54.

80 **"long legged yellow devil"**: Douglass, *My Bondage and My Freedom*, 215.

81 **"devoted all her energies"**: Rosetta Douglass Sprague, *Anna Murray Douglass: My Mother as I Recall Her* (1900), 8.

81 **"genuine African"** . . . **"had inherited some"**: Douglass, *My Bondage and My Freedom*, 174.

82 **"both of us"**: Douglass, *The Life and Times of Frederick Douglass*, 443.

82 **"pardon for 'speaking'"**: Douglass, *The Life and Times of Frederick Douglass*, 446.

82 **"agreeably"** . . . **"to find that time"** . . . **"in all its appointments"** . . . **"very little was missing"**: Douglass, *The Life and Times of Frederick Douglass*, 446–447.

83 **"Lord of a barren heritage"**: Walter Scott, *Lady of the Lake* (1810), line 592.

84 **"dull, slovenly"** . . . **"never enjoyed"**: Douglass, *My Bondage and My Freedom*, 136.

86 **"fiery curse"**: Virgil, *Georgics*, book 3, line 566.

86 **"grand possibilities"**: Douglass, *The Life and Times of Frederick Douglass*, 450.

3. Epiphany: Sunday Boys

91 **"The colored congregation"** . . . **"unfortunate in Point of utterances"**: William White to James Kemp, March 25, 1824, Kemp Papers, Episcopal Cathedral of Maryland Archives.

93 **"I would not open windows"**: Queen Elizabeth I, oral tradition.

95 **"To make us love our country"**: Edmund Burke, "Reflections on the Revolution in France" (1797), paragraph 130.

97 **"poor and rich"** . . . **"Take away right derived"**: Augustine of Hippo, *Tractate VI*, sec. 25; *The Works of Aurelius Augustine: A New Translation*, vol. 10, *Lectures or Tractates on the Gospel according to St. John*, ed. Rev. Marcus Dodd, trans. Rev. John Gibb (Edinburgh, 1873), 91.

101 **"that 'Homeland' may be retained"**: David Maulden Perine, July 1879, scrapbook, Perine Family Papers, Maryland Historical Society.

109 **"for the use of colored people"**: "Local Matters," *Baltimore Sun*, January 13, 1869, 1.

111 **"the sons of Africa or of Ham"**: David Walker, "Article Two: Our Wretchedness in Consequence of Ignorance," *Appeal in Four Articles to the Colored Citizens of the World* (1830), 22.

111 **"the ancient Egyptians"** . . . **"were black and had woolly hair"**: Henry Highland Garnet, *The Past and the Present Condition, and the Destiny, of the Colored Race* (1848), 7.

112 **"counted by all"** . . . **"the Jews are a colored people"**: William Apess, *Experience of Five Christian Indians, of the Pequod Tribe* (1833).

113 **"living in the United States of America to-day"**: Willard Hunter, *Jesus Christ Had Negro Blood in His Veins* (1904), 16.

114 **"reproduction of the Ascension"** . . . **"the space back"**: "Church to Spend $9,000," *Baltimore Sun*, May 19, 1911, 5.

114 **"That's mighty black of you"**: Larry S. Gibson, *Young Thurgood: The Making of a Supreme Court Justice* (Amherst, NY: Prometheus, 2012), 42.

115 **"One of the events"**: "Ascension Church Grows," *Baltimore Sun*, February 23, 1907, 9.

115 **"slashed"** . . . **"an ear bitten off"**: H. L. Mencken, *Happy Days*, *The Days Trilogy*, exp. ed., ed. Marion Elizabeth Rodgers (New York: Library of America, 2014), 99.

116 **"When he applied himself"**: Mencken, *Happy Days*, 100.

116 **"separate blocks"**: Garrett Power, "Apartheid Baltimore Style: The Residential Segregation Ordinances of 1910–1913," *Maryland Law Review* 42.2 (1983), 289.

117 **"Lafayette Square Section Now Believed"**: "Four Churches Sign Segregation Pact," *Baltimore Sun*, April 23, 1924, 3.

118 **"Memoria, windows and mosaic reredos"**: "Prince of Peace to Enlarge Edifice," *Baltimore Sun*, February 9, 1931, 5.

119 **"Slavery is the price I paid for civilization"**: Zora Neale Hurston, "How It Feels To Be Colored Me," *Pittsburgh Courier*, May 12, 1928, A1.

4. Lent: Appraisement of Negroes at the Folly, or Dinner

140 **"thriving black community"**: Sheryll Cashin, *The Failures of Integration: How Race and Class Are Undermining the American Dream*, quoted in Brian Patrick Larkin, "Forty-Year 'First Step': The Fair Housing Act as an Incomplete Tool for Suburban Integration," *Columbia Law Review*, November 2007, 1639.

144 **"wait twenty years"**: Louis Menand, "Integration by Parts," *New Yorker*, January 20, 2020.

148 **The boutiques are owned by . . . Philip**: Maryland Real Property Search, "York Road."

149 **Deontay McKnight dies . . . TV**: In Govans, men shot dead in the street are 41, 48, 50, 54, and even 60, Baltimore Homicide Map, *Baltimore Sun*, 2016–20.

156 **"in the quiet circle"**: Walter Scott, *Waverley* (1814; repr., New York: Penguin Classics, 1985), 370.

156 **"High and perilous enterprise" . . . "celebrated ancestor"**: Scott, *Waverley*, 370.

158 **"Gitchi gitchi ya ya da da!"**: Labelle, "Lady Marmalade," *Nightbirds* (1974), written by Bob Crewe and Kenny Nolan.

5. Eostre in Lafayette Square

180 **"the No. 1 Banjorine Player" . . . "he had something extra"**: Duke Ellington, *Music Is My Mistress* (Garden City, NJ: Doubleday, 1973), 53.

193 **Greg Butler had been a basketball star**: Justin Fenton, "Man Who Punctured Fire Hose during Baltimore Riot Gets 3 Years Probation," *Baltimore Sun*, November 4, 2016, 2.

193 **"criminals and thugs"**: Barack Obama, April 28, 2015, www.cnn.com/2015/04/28/politics/obama-baltimore-violent-protests/index.html.

193 **"rat and rodent infested mess" . . . "no human being"**: Wilborn P. Nobles III, "Trump Calls Baltimore 'Disgusting . . . Rodent Infested Mess,' Rips Rep. Elijah Cummings over Border Criticism," *Baltimore Sun*, July 27, 2019, www.baltimoresun.com/politics/bs-md-pol-cummings-trump-20190727-chty2yovtvfzfcjkeaui7wm5zi-story.html.

194 **708 abandoned houses in the seventy-four square blocks**: See Colin Campbell, "A Change in the Culture 5 Years After Freddie Gray's Death," *Baltimore Sun*, April 22, 2020, 1. The housing data comes from the Baltimore City Department of Housing and Community Development interactive map, baltimoredhcd.maps.arcgis.com/apps/webappviewer /index.html?id=4f12adf6e5b1475b838f8bf284da1e67.

195 **rioters "space" . . . gather without fear of arrest**: Jon Greenberg, "In Context: What Baltimore's Mayor Said about Space for Rioters," *Politifact*, April 28, 2015, www.politifact.com/article/2015/apr/28/context -baltimores-mayor-space-rioters.

203 **"keep up with their studies"**: "Hopkins Needs $50,000," *Baltimore Sun*, May 10, 1917, 6.

203 **"When tested by the requirements"**: Paul Popenoe and Roswell Hill Johnson, *Applied Eugenics* (New York: Macmillan, 1918), 292.

203 **"Why was the Johns Hopkins Colored Orphan Asylum"**: George F. Bragg Jr., "Will Johns Hopkins Trustees Speak Out?," *Afro-American*, November 22, 1930, 6.

204 **"the one factor in American life"**: Dr. Nima P. Garfield, "Physician Would Keep Colored People from Every Southern Hospital—Flays Johns Hopkins," *Afro-American*, April 13, 1923, 9.

221 **"tax shelter for the endowment"**: François Furstenberg, "When University Leaders Fail," *Chronicle of Higher Education*, May 19, 2020.

222 **"a rupture in the normal order" . . . "the possibility of possibilities"**: Alain Badiou, *The Communist Hypothesis*, quoted in Aijaz Ahmad, "Three 'Returns' to Marx: Derrida, Zizek, Badiou," *Social Scientist*, July–August 2012, 56.

6. White Sunday: "An Invasion of African Negroes"

228 **"the beauty that is being taken out of our cities"**: Donald J. Trump (@realDonaldTrump), August 17, 2017.

235 **"the city is moving"**: "School Order Called White-Flight Spur," *Baltimore Sun*, June 9, 1973, A15.

236 **"assist teachers to develop"** . . . **"White teachers must feel"** . . . **"be understood and appreciated"**: Alvin P. Sanoff, "Funds Sought to Promote Integration," *Baltimore Sun*, January 4, 1969, B20.

237 **"to get rid of"** . . . **"'I have always observed'"**: Robert E. Lee, *Recollections and Letters of General Robert E. Lee by His Son Captain Robert E. Lee* (New York: Doubleday, Page, 1904), 168.

237 **"the most intellectual"**: Carleton Jones, "View from Bolton Hill: The Posh New Life in the Old Gin Belt," *Baltimore Sun*, January 28, 1979, K1.

245 **"special response unit"** . . . **"highly trained former police officers"**: Johns Hopkins University president Ronald Daniels, email to Homewood students, faculty, and staff, Campus Security Memorandum, October 23, 2017.

248 **"strange liberators"**: Martin Luther King Jr., "A Time to Break Silence," *A Testament of Hope: The Essential Writings and Speeches* (San Francisco: HarperOne, 2003), 235.

252 **"good green corn"**: Ralph Ellison, *Invisible Man* (New York: Vintage, 1990), 581.

257 **"from time to time"**: Richard Henry Spencer, "The Provincial Flag of Maryland," *Maryland Historical Magazine* 9.3 (1914), 219.

263 **"You couldn't even buy a friend"**: DeAndre McCullough, interviewed by Charles Dutton, *The Corner*, Home Box Office (2000), directed by Charles Dutton, story by David Simon and David Mills.

264 **"From the late 1890s"**: Khalil Gibran Muhammad, *The Condemnation of Blackness: Race, Crime, and the Making of Modern Urban America* (Cambridge, MA: Harvard University Press, 2011), 20–21.

267 **"THEOW and ESNE"**: Walter Scott, *Ivanhoe*, ed. Andrew Lang (1819; Boston: Estes and Lauriat, 1893), Book 2, 136–37.

268 **"self-denial, the denial"**: Karl Marx, *Economic and Philosophical Manuscripts*, quoted in Michael Hardt and Antonio Negri, *Assembly* (New York: Oxford University Press, 2017), 103.

7. Ordinary Time: The Gentle Brushing Fescue

274 **"brow of a soft"**: Scott, *Ivanhoe*, 2:319.

277 **"just what clothes"**: Venture Smith, *A Narrative of the Life and Adventures of Venture, a Native of Africa* (New London, 1798), 25.

277 **"Here, where we are obliged" . . . "require constant attendance"**: John Carlyle, November 1752, quoted in Mills Lane, *Architecture of the Old South: Virginia* (New York: Abbeville Press, 1989), 62.

291 **"monotonous," . . . "progressive and varied"**: Edward L. Palmer Jr., "Mr. Palmer Corrects a Misquotation," *Baltimore Sun*, November 23, 1920, 8.

291 **"Every ship must have" . . . "In the neighborhood"**: "'Restrictions' You Heads of Families," *Gardens, Houses and People* (May 1939), n.p., Roland Park Company Papers, box 277, Scrapbook, Sheridan Library Special Collections, Johns Hopkins University.

291 **he believed "[have] now joined"**: B. P. Hoge to John M. Mowbray, December 26, 1935, Roland Park Company Papers, box 247, folder 27, Sheridan Library Special Collections, Johns Hopkins University.

292 **"I told him not" . . . "He was very apologetic" . . . "very prominent" . . . "do have a number"**: B. P. Hoge to John M. Mowbray, December 9, 1935, Roland Park Company Papers, box 247, folder 2, Sheridan Library Special Collections, Johns Hopkins University.

292 **"a few Jewish friends"**: B. P. Hoge to John M. Mowbray, December 26, 1935, Roland Park Company Papers, box 247, folder 27, Sheridan Library Special Collections, Johns Hopkins University.

293 **"At no time shall the land"**: "Deed and Agreement between the Roland Park Homeland Company and The Roland Park Company Containing Restrictions, Conditions, Charges, Etc. Relating to Homeland," 6, Roland Park Company Papers, box 274, folder 2, Sheridan Library Special Collections, Johns Hopkins University.

294 **"The committee would never"**: Edward H. Bouton to Mr. Sutherland, Sales Office, September 3, 1926, Roland Park Company Papers, box 241, folder 38, Sheridan Library Special Collections, Johns Hopkins University.

295 **"artistic home surroundings"** . . . **"the bizarre tendencies"**: "Exhibition House 104 Witherspoon (1927)," Roland Park Company Papers, box 242, folder 26, Sheridan Library Special Collections, Johns Hopkins University.

295 **"more damage can be done"** ... **"It is all very confusing"**: Edward L. Palmer Jr. to Bernard Hoge and Roland Park Company, April 8, 1946, Roland Park Company Papers, box 236, folder 53, Sheridan Library Special Collections, Johns Hopkins University.

296 **"the gables and turrets"** ... **"It is the beauty"**: Helen Koues, "The Enduring Value of Good Architecture" *Gardens, Houses and People*, September 1937, 27, Roland Park Company Papers, box 274, folder 23, Sheridan Library Special Collections, Johns Hopkins University.

297 **"The reassurances of the worth"**: Clarence Mitchell to Lyndon Baines Johnson, December 20, 1972, quoted in Denton L. Watson, *Lion in the Lobby: Clarence Mitchell, Jr.s Struggle for the Passage of Civil Rights Laws* (New York: Morrow, 1990), 724.

297 **had contracted for a house**: In December, the plan for the Guilford house, including shrubbery and a two-car garage, still specified $9,138: John Mowbray to Bernard Hoge, December 22, 1934, Roland Park Company Papers, box 248, folder 4, Sheridan Library Special Collections, Johns Hopkins University.

Lawrence Jackson is the author of *Hold It Real Still: Clint Eastwood, Race, and the Cinema of the American West* (Johns Hopkins, 2022), *Chester B. Himes: A Biography* (W. W. Norton, 2017), *The Indignant Generation: A Narrative History of African American Writers and Critics* (Princeton, 2010), *My Father's Name: A Black Virginia Family after the Civil War* (Chicago, 2012) and *Ralph Ellison: Emergence of Genius, 1913–1952* (Wiley, 2002). *Harper's Magazine* and *Best American Essays* have published his criticism and nonfiction. Professor Jackson earned a PhD in English and American literature at Stanford University, and has held fellowships from the Guggenheim Foundation, the National Humanities Center, and the William J. Fulbright program. He began his teaching career at Howard University in 1997, and he is now Bloomberg Distinguished Professor of English and History at Johns Hopkins University, where he directs the Billie Holiday Center for Liberation Arts.

The text of *Shelter* is set in Times LT Std.
Book design by Rachel Holscher.
Composition by Bookmobile Design & Digital
Publisher Services, Minneapolis, Minnesota.
Manufactured by McNaughton & Gunn on acid-free,
100 percent postconsumer wastepaper.

TO SOSS

AUG 1 0 2022